MW00574357

JOURNEYS TO THE EDGE

Best Regards,

Randy Peeters

JOURNEYS TO THE EDGE

Where will your vision take you?

RANDALL PEETERS, PH.D.

SASTRUGI PRESS

Copyright © 2014 by Randall Peeters

All rights reserved. No part of this book may be reproduced or transmitted in any form or by any means, electronic or mechanical, including photocopying, recording, or by any information storage and retrieval system without the written permission of the author, except where permitted by law.

Sastrugi Press / Published by arrangement with the author

Sastrugi Press: 2907 Iris Avenue, San Diego, CA 92173, United States
www.sastrugipress.com

Journeys to the Edge: Where will your vision take you?

The author has made every effort to accurately recreate conversations, events, and locales from his memories of them. To maintain anonymity, some names and details such as places of residence, physical characteristics, and occupations have been changed. The activities described in this book are inherently dangerous. The publisher does not have any control over and does not assume any responsibility for author or third-party websites or their content.

Any person participating in the activities described in this work is personally responsible for learning the proper techniques and using good judgement. You are responsible for your own actions and decisions. The information contained in this work is subjective and based solely on opinions. No book can advise you to the hazards or anticipate the limitations of any reader. Participation in the described activities can result in severe injury or death. Neither the publisher nor the author assumes any liability for anyone participating in the activities described in this work.

Library of Congress Control Number: 2014942992
Peeters, Randall
Journeys to the Edge - 1st U.S. ed.
Summary: Randall Peeters was the eighth person in the world to complete the "Adventure Grand Slam" by climbing the highest mountain on each continent (known as the "Seven Summits") and reaching both the North and South Poles.
ISBN-13: 978-0-9960206-1-9
ISBN-10: 0-9960206-1-6

910.4
Printed in the United States of America

10 9 8 7 6 5 4 3 2 1

Dedication

To Jesus Christ, my Lord and my Savior and to Doris, my wife, my lover and my best friend. Without them my journey will never be complete.

This book was also written in memory of my fallen friends who are always on my mind.

Contents

FOREWORD

Randy Peeters is the kind of person many of us wish we could be like. He's well educated, had a successful career in what he likes to refer to as "rocket science," and has been happily married long enough to be contemplating his Golden Wedding Anniversary.

Randy would be the first to say the success in his life had nothing to do with wishing and certainly wasn't because of any special "gifts" he possessed. In fact, the incredible story of this man, who has seen life from both the top of the world and through the bars of a jail cell, will reveal how typical he actually is in his book *Journeys to the Edge*.

Few would consider anyone who has climbed the tallest peaks on all seven continents, surfed gigantic waves, BASE (acronym for Building, Antenna, Span, Earth) jumped from Yosemite's Half Dome and kayaked through the Grand Canyon as typical. Yet Randy's no-nonsense and simple approach on how to get the most out of life is now helping others to do the same.

Still, Randy isn't just about an adventure-filled life with a devil-may-care attitude. In fact, he would be the first to say some of his most rewarding achievements are his devotion to Jesus Christ and the love of his family. He readily admits his life has been far from perfect. As for risk, in spite of his adventures, he says he is a risk manager and not a risk taker.

Randy owes all he is today to one simple vision he developed at an early age. He summed it up in his own personal vision statement, "When it's over – no regrets." He admits he has to work at his vision every day, because his life hasn't been without some regrets.

In spite of some setbacks, he uses his vision techniques to mitigate those regrets and grades himself to help stay on course. His life's guiding light has steered him to a point where he can now share, what he has both discovered and accomplished, with those who also desire the most out of life.

This book demonstrates by example why CEOs from around the world invite him to speak and instruct on the basics of a successful career and a rewarding lifestyle. And you, too, can learn from Randy Peeters how to experience a life with no regrets.

Journeys to the Edge is first and foremost an autobiographical sketch of an ordinary man doing extraordinary things. It is not written chronologically, but rather interspersed with a collection of embedded elements based on extreme sports. To aid in reading, these extreme sports segments have been formatted categorically by the sport or activity Randy has followed to fulfill his vision of "no regrets." In this sense it resembles an anthology.

It takes the reader beyond the satisfaction of a quest and into the realm of living life to the fullest by setting and achieving goals in pursuit of a personal vision.

The reader can follow Randy's amazing footsteps taking it one page at a time, or one chapter at a time. Either way, this book will both entertain and inspire everyone who reads it to climb the mountain that exists within each of us.

Jim Linsdau, The Foresthill Messenger, Owner

ACKNOWLEDGEMENTS

Writing a book turned out to be a much bigger undertaking then I ever imagined. The process took over eight years to finish and, without the help of others, it would have never been completed.

First I want to thank my editor, Jim Linsdau. Through his diligent effort, my rambling text was crafted into a book.

I was also fortunate to have a dedicated and tenacious beta reader. Her personal vision involves sharing her talents in an anonymous way and she is certainly doing that. Through her, I hashed out things that did not make sense and corrected many grammatical and structural issues.

I also wish to thank Linda Wright and Tim Linsdau who were critique partners. They not only helped me fix grammatical problems, but also checked for readability and story flow.

I want to thank my sons, Shawn and Todd, for a final reading and being sounding boards before publication.

Finally, to Doris, my wife of 49 years, thank you. Without your loving support and encouragement of this book, I would never have completed *Journeys to the Edge*.

INTRODUCTION

It's early afternoon and I am sitting in the Yosemite National Park Jail awaiting arraignment for BASE Jumping Half Dome and all I can think about is how I could have avoided capture in the first place ... Fast forward ten years – Base Camp, Mount Everest. After learning my climbing partner had fallen to his death on the Lhotse Face, I was devastated and didn't know what to do. My options were to either descend to a lower altitude until my frostbite healed and then finish the climb, or give up and go home.

This book may not be for everyone, but it is for anyone who wants more out of life and is willing to take that journey. It isn't necessary to BASE jump Half Dome or climb Mount Everest to have a terrific life – but it is necessary to know what you want and how to get there.

This book is not only about what I have done, but it also explores my character and how certain elements in my life allowed me to accomplish great things. This is a book that analyzes how a man of average upbringing can achieve high levels of competency in a variety of life's challenges.

These pages offer wisdom to enrich your life and describe in exciting narrative why there is value in taking *Journeys to the Edge*.

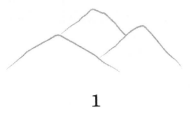

1

OUT OF THE BLOCKS

Growing up

In 1962, a classmate of mine entered the room wearing a long fur coat that concealed a large dart made with a nail stuck in the end of a three foot long dowel adorned with cardboard fins. The class was rowdy that day, with students throwing erasers and chalk while our teacher did algebra problems on the blackboard. Right before the bell rang, he stood up, threw the dart and planted it into a corkboard a few feet from the teacher's head. Almost as if he didn't notice, our teacher finished working on the problem and then calmly removed the dart.
He then turned to the class and said, "My kids will love this."

I was raised in the San Bernardino Valley area of Southern California. The city where I spent my teenage years, Rialto, had been a sleepy, little orange-growing town since its beginnings in 1887, but in the early 1950s, the orange groves were being replaced by subdivisions and other developments.

During the 1950s and 1960s there was a delightful mix of lush groves and friendly new neighborhoods. It was an idyllic place - beautiful, virtually crime-free, wholesome and prosperous. The blight of crime and poverty that would eventually strike the Inland Empire of San Bernardino County was still off in the future.

My father was a policeman and my mother worked as a civil service clerk typist. I was the second of three children and we were a typical, middle-class family. I developed a keen interest in astronomy and owned two telescopes while still in high school. At 16, I was also a general-class amateur radio operator.

I participated in Little League baseball, went out for track in junior high and played freshman basketball. I became proficient in those sports, but nothing exceptional. I also joined the Cub Scouts, then the Boy Scouts and later joined an Explorer Post. Eventually my interests turned to sports other than what was offered in school.

While in high school I did become the drum major of the band, which I did for two years. One incident taught me valuable life lessons.

It was during a regional marching band festival in which I managed to lead our band into a wall. Our instructor refused to speak to me during the entire bus ride home.

I learned I was capable of making big mistakes and more importantly, that one must not be so myopic in focus that you lose sight of the surroundings. Later in life these lessons would be life saving.

Although I was in the accelerated math program and did above average work academically, I wasn't an outstanding student. In fact, after band rehearsals we often played car tag while ejecting massive flames from our vehicles' exhaust systems. Being typical teenagers, we often looked for trouble and frequently found it.

Two things stand out for me concerning my senior year in high school. One, our senior class president and the one voted "most likely to succeed," would later be convicted of a string of bank robberies and end up spending time in jail. The second was my own personal accomplishment: I met Doris Berry, who would later become my wife, lover and best friend.

It was also in high school that I sustained an injury which plagues me to this day. I was involved in an accident in my dad's 1949 GMC pickup and caved in the truck's dashboard with my knees. Because of this and subsequent injuries, I now wear a knee brace.

In the summer of 1960, I built a surfboard. In spite of the shark scares reported that year along the California coast, I was anxious to give my new board a try. I vividly recall my "first shark sighting" near the Oceanside Pier.

I was so frightened that I actually paddled right off the front of my surfboard trying to escape. I suffered a concussion when the surfboard hit me in the head while being pummeled in a big wave.

What I had "escaped" from was a pod of dolphins swimming in the area.

Shortly thereafter I converted my surfboard into a sailboard, complete with pontoons. Next, I managed to nearly kill myself on it while sailing on

Lake Arrowhead.

What first attracted me to climbing was an Explorer Scout rock scrambling trip. The experience so terrified me that I enrolled in a Sierra Club mountaineering course offering rope and ice-axe techniques. After that, I thrived on rock scrambling. It was also about this time I first dreamed of climbing Mount Everest and even shared this vision with some of my classmates.

I also enjoyed car camping, which my father introduced me to. We visited many parks across the United States and Canada, including Yellowstone, Yosemite and Death Valley. Closer to home we frequently vacationed at both the beach and the mountains.

I took my younger brother on a ten speed bicycle trip from Tuolumne Meadows, in Yosemite, to Fresno. While on that trip we cycled more than 150 miles and hiked up Half Dome. As I dangled my legs over the edge of Half Dome's 1,800 foot face, it forever captured my imagination.

I paid for these ventures by doing a variety of jobs. I mowed lawns, worked in a bee farming business and sold shoes. This taught me to never be ashamed of my work, or the uniform I wore to do the job. Through my outings, I gained an appreciation for wilderness activities and through astronomy and amateur radio I cultivated an interest in science.

College

> It was 10 p.m., while dressed only in a diaper fashioned from a towel, I was carried toward the women's dormitory on the shoulders of a mob. I put up a fuss, but knew it was my fault for getting caught sneaking into a dorm stag party. In spite of a strict rule against being there after hours, I was deposited in the lobby of the women's residence hall. In the early 1960s that was a real no-no, punishable by expulsion from the school.
>
> The next day I was brought into the dean's office and detained. While there, I did some fast talking to keep from being expelled. It wasn't easy, but I got the job done.

I graduated from high school somewhere in the middle of my class and knew the one thing I wanted to do in life was marry Doris. I wasn't so sure about a career, but leaned toward something in science.

While still a teenager, Sputnik was launched and space-related topics interested me. I chose to go to California State Polytechnic University in Southern California (Cal Poly Pomona) to study aerospace engineering. Pomona was also close to San Bernardino, where Doris would be attending junior college.

On my first try, I failed the math entrance exam at Cal Poly. I made it the second time and also convinced my guidance counselor to let me enter the engineering track math courses as a freshman. Marrying Doris remained my number one goal so I frequently took 19 or more units per quarter to graduate as quickly as I could.

Unfortunately, I had developed poor study habits in high school and wasn't ready for the frustrations of college. I recall breaking down and crying the first weekend I came home because I was so confused with my homework assignments. I felt it was more work than I could do in a lifetime.

Before long though, I learned how to dramatically improve my grades and dedicated myself to earning a degree in engineering. In my second year, success went to my head and I annoyed my fellow students in aerospace engineering. Some of them wrote me a rather pointed letter telling me to either straighten up or leave the program. Initially, the letter shocked me, but I decided to take it as constructive criticism – it turned out to be a blessing in disguise.

I made some immediate and lasting changes in my behavior and eventually that painful experience became a significant learning tool. I was later named "Outstanding Sophomore" by the department, received other awards and, in time, received a scholarship. I owe a debt of thanks to those students who took the initiative to set me straight.

My first two years of college included spending my spare time chasing Doris, recovering from mononucleosis, grading papers for the faculty and working to help pay for my education.

One summer I landed a job as an engineering student-trainee for the California Division of Highways. It paid well and the work was so easy it was almost as if I were retired. I even considered hiring on permanently once I graduated.

During that summer, I became interested in sailing and built a Sailfish sailboard from a kit. I also managed to crew a few races on a Thistle centerboard sailboat that year.

My relationship with Doris turned rocky due to complications involving her parents. After several unsuccessful breakups, during my junior year, I made the awesome commitment to ask her to marry me. Thankfully, she said yes. It was scary being married so young, but it turned out to be a fortuitous decision and I have never looked back. To make ends meet, I worked as an engineering aide to help supplement Doris' salary from her job at the telephone company.

I was employed by Edcliff Instruments, founded by Ed and Cliff. I was one of 40 employees manufacturing accelerometers, when one day it was announced half the workforce had to be let go. Fortunately, I wasn't one of those laid off.

In the meantime, our family had grown to three. Doris had negotiated the purchase of a Miniature Poodle named Whiz, who was a joy we shared for the next 14 years.

I put on hold most of my outdoor activities. However, I did manage some winter snow ascents of two local mountains by climbing San Gorgonio from the south and climbing the North Ridge of San Antonio. I also took up body surfing and attempted the notorious Wedge at Newport Beach.

As my interest grew in body surfing, I took Doris on a camping trip to South Carlsbad State Beach in 1966. The trip was so enjoyable we would repeat it many times over the next 45 plus years.

Learning to apply myself in college opened doors I couldn't have imagined while in high school. Being invited to join honor societies and serving them as an officer proved beneficial and after graduating with honors I received 11 job offers. I decided to go with the Boeing Company in Seattle, WA.

My goals back then were simple: earn my degree in science (aerospace engineering) and land a job that paid at least $9,000 a year (which I exceeded). My extended goals of becoming a world-class climber and maintaining a solid, traditional family were then works in progress.

I also learned in college that I could accomplish virtually anything if I applied myself. Graduating with honors from Cal Poly after meandering through high school was a life lesson for me. Earning a degree in a major as demanding as aerospace engineering convinced me ordinary people could accomplish remarkable things.

The Northwest: Boeing

Early one morning, my friend Curt and I were high up on the south side of Mount Adams in Southern Washington when we spotted an incredible lightning storm being driven toward us by strong winds. I freaked out, but Curt was from the Midwest and assured me there was nothing to be afraid of. I took his word for it, but I think Curt's attitude changed when the winds near the summit became so strong that deposits of pumice formed under his contact lenses.

Leaving Southern California for Washington filled me with anticipation. I had accepted a job with the Super Sonic Transport Structural Dynamics Group at Boeing's Developmental Center near Seattle, WA. After four grueling years at Cal Poly, I spent only two days driving up the coastal highway to reach Seattle. Although my tenure at Boeing would only last 15 months,

I forged many strong friendships which have lasted a lifetime.

I met Bob Baker at Boeing. Bob was an accomplished climber who bagged the first ascent of Logan's Independence Ridge in the Yukon in 1962. He was the second to go up Moose's Tooth and Avalanche Spire in the state of Alaska. After a couple of weeks at Boeing, Bob took me up Mount Rainer via the Emmons Glacier Route – that's where I got hooked.

I fell in love with glacier climbing and, along with some of my friends, joined the Seattle Mountaineers. After enrolling in the beginner and later the intermediate climbing courses, we spent that first summer climbing in the Northwest, which was perhaps the most enjoyable climbing season of my life. The weather was fantastic and we bagged a new summit almost every weekend – Mount Adams, Mount St. Helens, Mount Olympus and Glacier Peak.

I've been known to be a little eccentric, but I think this is common among climbers. Consider the time Dick Burwell and I climbed the north side of the unassuming McClellan's Butte just outside of Seattle. It was a long day of trudging through deep snow slopes, but our trek to the top and back was a success. When we reached the car, Dick revealed he had been climbing with a broken ankle set in a plaster cast. The cast was totally soaked through and had turned to mush.

As Dick so aptly demonstrated, injury is something you live with when you journey to the edge.

During our first year in the Northwest, I enrolled at the University of Washington to earn a master of science degree in aeronautics and astronautics. For recreation, Doris and I took up downhill skiing. Before the ski season started, we bought a couple of Recreational Equipment International (REI) starter packages and decided to climb up the lower slopes of Mount Rainier to give the sport a try. That led us to take beginner lessons at Ski Acers in Snoqualmie Pass. There we learned to stem-Christie and use the rope tow. After that, we skied several times a week. Just down the highway was Hyak, where the weekday evening lift fee was only $1.50.

One night, while returning to our car, I had my skis over my shoulder as we entered the parking lot. I slipped on some ice, jettisoned my skis into the air and fell flat on my back. The skis came down and struck me in the head cutting me right above the eye. From there, it was off to the emergency room to get stitched up.

The next week, we returned for more skiing in the cold, rainy and snowy conditions typical of the Northwest. When we entered the lodge for lunch our clothes were soaked and one of the patrons pointed out I had a tear in my ski pants. Upon further inspection, I discovered I also had a three inch gash in my shin – back to the emergency room.

My doctor's visit was fortuitous since the stitches were removed from above my eye while sewing up the cut in my leg. By season's end we had mastered parallel skiing and were able to negotiate most of the runs at Washington's Crystal Mountain, Stevens Pass and Alpental ski areas.

The following summer, I completed the last climb of the "Six Majors"[1] in the Northwest in spite of the inclement weather. I managed to ascend Mount Baker, Little Tahoma, Rainier (Disappointment Cleaver) and Mount Hood. I also started to learn technical rock climbing techniques and picked up 12 units in my pursuit of a master's degree.

Another lesson learned was how to achieve balance between family, work, school and play. I discovered it was necessary to constantly reassess priorities in order to do a good job at whatever I did.

The University of Washington

I experienced my first serious scare climbing an alpine route on Mount Garfield, just outside Seattle. After finishing an easy class 5 open book, I started up a ten foot vertical section of hard snow. As I neared the top, my ice axe dislodged and I fell backward down the face. I barreled out of control toward a huge boiler plate slab – and certain death. Dave Anderson, my climbing partner, was below me with eyes as big as silver dollars. I had placed no protection and our anchor was dubious at best.

Forty feet below, I slammed headfirst into a chock stone and managed to wrap my right arm around it. That stopped me; I was injured, but alive. I quickly recovered and with that episode out of the way Dave and I continued our climb. Ours was only the 13th ascent of Mount Garfield since it was first climbed in 1940.

During our second summer in the Northwest, Seattle's economy was hard hit by the cancellation of Boeing's supersonic transport contract. Boeing suffered massive layoffs and I faced the possibility of a transfer to Saint Louis, MO. Shawn, our firstborn, joined the family and I had entered graduate school full time. Back then, Seattle was a one horse town and the horse was sick. A billboard had been posted in Seattle that read, "Will the last person out of Seattle please turn off the lights?"

While working on my master's I took another journey to the edge. In my first full-time quarter after leaving Boeing, I took Solid Mechanics under Professor Reid Parmerter. My score of 11 out of 100 on the midterm exam was proof that I had no clue what I was doing.

I sought Professor Parmerter's help and found him to be incredibly responsive. He gave me his course notes for the undergraduate program and told me I would have to work hard to pull out a passing grade. I did as he suggested and on the final exam scored the highest of anyone in the class.

In recognition of my effort, Parmerter gave me an A and suggested I pursue a doctorate in engineering. There was one problem: in my other six courses I had all B's which wouldn't be good enough to qualify for the PhD program. Still, Parmerter said if I worked as hard as I did in his class I could make it. He also told me he was looking for a graduate student to guide through the process and thought I would be an acceptable candidate.

With only six courses remaining in the master's program I would have to ace every one of them. I wasn't optimistic. I loved to ski and knew the sport was taking too big a toll on my study time. I also knew the professor of Applied Mathematics was stingy with grades and that was a subject I still had to take. I was right. This professor gave only one A, an A-minus and the rest went downhill from there. Fortunately, I earned the A-minus. Additionally, I scored A's in my other five subjects and was accepted into the PhD program.

Having quit my job at Boeing, I worked as a teaching assistant and a research assistant to help make ends meet. Doris hired on with the telephone company, but the job wasn't full-time. It helped that I was able to obtain a few student loans and received several partial fellowships. Also of great assistance was the lifelong friendship I developed with Reid Parmerter. Not only was he bright and intuitive, but he had an unbelievable understanding of engineering. He was also a pretty fine skier.

He had mastered powder skiing and shared that knowledge with me, plus he taught me how to tree ski. I became a pseudo ski bum making forays to places such as Sun Valley, ID and Whistler Mountain, British Columbia. I loved skiing and thoroughly enjoyed being in the mountains during winter. After hooking up with some of Reid's Cal Tech buddies on a ski junket to Bend, Oregon, he wrote the following poem:

For Randy, By Reid Parmerter
There was that day at Bend
Skiing through the trees
Snow swirling round our faces
Reaching well above the knees.

The woods led to a clearing
Which we skied along the rim
Cutting close to trees for powder
This is Heaven said your grin.

So each turn we cut them closer
You were sure that I would fall
You didn't think that little branch
Would bother you at all!

I doubled up with laughter
To see you lying there.
The little branch won after all
And stopped you in mid air.

Is there anything like powder
And the cold snow in your face
Is there any greater pleasure
Than a friend who skies your pace?

When not able to ski, I spent time sailing in Washington. I had the opportunity to crew with Skipper John Monk on his Thunderbird, a one-design class, 26 foot sailboat. John held a master's of science in aeronautical engineering from MIT and was once ranked fourth in the world in Thunderbird class sailboat racing. Racing was not only fun, but I learned about the practical application of airfoils by observing John. He was extremely aggressive and his tactics were edgy.

After gaining the number one position in both the ocean and lake series, we entered the final race to qualify for the world championships to be held later in Victoria, British Columbia. We only needed to finish among the top three to qualify. As we rounded the windward mark ahead of the others, John decided to split a pair of boats tacking for the same mark. I had deployed the spinnaker and was trimming the sheet from the foredeck when I turned to look towards the cockpit. What I saw was John and another crew member diving headfirst into the cabin.

Suddenly, debris was flying everywhere as I looked up to see our rigging come whipping down. We had hooked masts with one of the other boats above the gooseneck which had placed tremendous tension on our mast. We immediately docked and used our salvageable rigging to repair the other boat. That dropped us out of the world championships.

However, we all ended up in Victoria crewing for other boats. The one I was on finished fifth in the championships. During my time sailing, I also experienced multiday and night racing and saw pods of killer whales as they breached. We even managed to freeze half to death while training in the dead of winter. Still, I enjoyed the company, the thrill of the race and the free food was plentiful.

While participating in a crevasse rescue training program on Mount Rainier, I met a young climber named Al Albright. After he learned I was interested in building my own kayak he introduced me to some other young men belonging to a local Explorer Post. The post was associated with a Catholic Church in Seattle which owned a mold for making fiberglass kayaks. They sold me the kit for $25.

I built the kayak and made several trips on some class 3 rivers in the area. After nearly killing a couple of people, I realized there was more to kayaking than merely paddling a small boat. In spite of that, I was asked to act as temporary post advisor after the church's priest was transferred. I reluctantly agreed and spent the next three years in that temporary position. With the post, Boeing and the university I made some friends and met some climbing partners who would forever shape my life.

In 1968, Doris and I traded in our 1965 MGB for a Volkswagen bus, complete with a peace sticker in the rear window. It was a camper unit, which made it terrific for travel; however, it proved a liability where safety and policemen were concerned. I once received a speeding ticket while on a ski trip to Crystal Mountain. I was speeding one mile per hour over the posted limit. It seemed whenever we traveled in that vehicle it turned into an adventure.

Joe Beasley, a friend of mine at Boeing, invited me to spend a ski weekend with him and his wife at their cabin in Sun Valley, ID. Joe hoped to be laid off at Boeing and receive a severance package so he could attend law school in Florida. He thought taking this trip to Sun Valley without informing Boeing would do it. Unfortunately for Joe, his unique computer skills were too valuable to the company and his tactic did not work.

We took along a few of the kids from the Explorer Post thinking the outing would be a treat for them. However, after a 20 minute stop for road construction our young passengers decided it would be fun to flip off the road crew and yell obscenities at them as we drove by. We didn't expect those workers to pile into a truck and chase us for the next ten miles. I don't know how I managed to get that VW bus to pass a mobile home/truck combination, but it did and we escaped our pursuers – luckily.

When we reached Sun Valley, we decided to sneak into the ski area, but Joe and I were apprehended. Although we received a chewing-out, afterward we simply went to another entrance and purchased a dependant lift pass for $3.

Still, the adventure in the VW bus wasn't over. After a ski trip to Stevens Pass, I was pulled over for a faulty tail light. As the officer wrote out his ticket, our group from the Explorer Post used the condensation in the back window to trace a fist with the middle finger extended. Fortunately the policeman did not notice this clever artwork.

Skiing also took its toll in injuries. I tore the medial meniscus cartilage in my right knee, which I believe was partially due to the lingering damage caused by my driving accident when in high school. Fortunately, the surgeon who repaired my knee was also the orthopedic surgeon for UW's football team and the operation appeared to be a complete success.

But not every doctor's visit turned out so well, at least not in the case of Doug Williscroft's accident. Doug, a member of the Explorer Post, and I were skiing the back bowls of Whistler while on a post trip to Canada. During a fall, he put the tip of his ski through his cheekbone and into his sinus cavity. We drove an hour to Squamish Chief, British Columbia, where Doug was immediately examined in the emergency room. After confirming Doug would be OK, the doctor said he needed to go home for dinner but would be back later – much later.

After several hours passed Doris insisted someone call the doctor at home. It seems Doug's attending physician had enjoyed a couple after-dinner drinks and totally forgot to come back. The doctor returned to the hospital to perform the necessary surgery and whatever he was drinking didn't diminish his skills in the least. That was confirmed when Doug later sought out a plastic surgeon in Seattle, who said he could not have done a better job himself.

Winter mountaineering progressed with climbs of the regular and Forsyth Glacier routes of Mount St. Helens, the Liberty Ridge and Kautz Ice Fall routes of Mount Rainer and others. I drew particular satisfaction from the Forsyth Glacier climb with Gordon Oates. It was an aesthetic route on a beautiful mountain.

One of the scariest climbs was our attempt of Liberty Ridge. As we moved across the upper Carbon Glacier, we took note of many pockmarks in the ice. Because the visibility was so poor, we were only able to reach the base of the ridge where we set up camp.

As I sat quietly in my two man micro tent, I was startled to attention when Nelson Walker called out. I peered out of the tent to see an avalanche that had started high atop Liberty Cap Glacier roaring directly toward us. I was horrified knowing there was little we could do – when something completely unexpected happened. The entire avalanche disappeared into a crevasse a few hundred feet from our campsite. This experience explained why we saw so many pockmarks in the glacier. They had been created by previous avalanches.

On another attempt of Liberty Ridge, I partnered with a Frenchman named Robert Lefine. I met him at Castle Rock, where he impressed me by downing a quart of beer while belaying – apparently something he always did. Our climb was difficult. We encountered hard ice under a few feet of snow during the ascent from our camp behind the gendarme on Liberty Ridge. Small avalanches from above continually bombarded us.

So severe were the conditions, we decided to abandon our climb and retrace our steps. We would have to climb down steep, hard ice while traversing above the notorious Willis Wall located on Rainer's north side. I was roped to Robert and grew concerned when I realized he might not know how to self-arrest. If either one of us had fallen we would have been dragged off the ridge plunging together to our deaths. Fortunately, neither of us fell.

As the routes we attempted became more technical, alpine climbing became quite pure to me. I was gaining the ability to scramble to the top regardless of terrain – rock, glacier, or ice. One classic climb was on the fine, steep route of Rainer's Fuhrer's Finger.

Before the climb, a ranger warned us of rock falls, but we didn't heed his warning because of his rather arrogant attitude. We made our High Camp at the bottom of Fuhrer's Finger where we noticed numerous boulders implanted in the lip of a gaping bergschrund. Undaunted, Al Albright, Peter Flewelling and I set out at midnight to proceed up the 1,000 foot, ice-chocked couloir that rose at a 45 degree angle. Reiner Decher, our fourth climbing partner, remained in camp.

As we made our way from the summit back down the couloir, a basket-ball-sized rock hit Al in the leg causing a green-limb fracture. As Al cart wheeled through the air, he managed to quickly self-arrest – a testament to his skills. We then edged over to the side of the couloir to discuss the situation. We made the decision to descend from there to high camp even though Al had a broken leg. It was only minutes later when a boulder the size of a Volkswagen broke loose and hurtled toward our new position. Broken leg and all, Al ran down that icy slope with Peter and me right behind.

We made it to High Camp and decided to glissade our way down the glacier to the car. When we arrived, Al's leg was so swollen it filled the leg of his oversized wool pants. We agreed the guy with the highest IQ in our group had to be Reiner.

Rock climbing consumed me and in the summers I made treks to Grand Teton, WY, Squamish Chief, BC and Yosemite Valley, CA. We wore old-style climbing boots doctored with epoxy cement making them much like a Vibram-soled mini-boot. For protection, we used soft iron pitons and static gold line nylon ropes and frequently tied in with a bowline knot on a coil. We employed dynamic belays to reduce the load on both the protection and the climber.

Over time we progressed to dynamic perlon ropes, static belays, harnesses, Royal Robin's rock boots and Chouinard chromalloy pitons. We found it challenged our style when chocks and clean climbing became popular in Yosemite. We made our chocks during lunch breaks in UW's physics machine shop and used them in conjunction with our usual pitons.

During this time manufacturers were coming out with hexes, stoppers, lo balls, tri cams and other such passive devices for protection. Within ten years spring-loaded camming devices appeared, followed by specialized pieces such as hybrid aliens. The sport was evolving, even specialized rock shoes with sticky-rubber soles. Climbing would never be the same again.

I remember Yvon Chouinard giving a presentation in Seattle on how engineering had impacted mountaineering. He said, "You can rig a hammock with a single piton, but if you want to sleep at night you use 40!"

Those words of wisdom stuck with me and over the next 35 years I always rigged my portaledge with at least three pieces of protection.

No matter how careful and safety conscious one is, danger always exists. Once, while leading a climb up Sloan Peak, a one ton boulder rolled over one of our members and came close to pinning him against a rock. We checked his vital signs and determined he was stable enough to begin a self-evacuation to the small, hippy outpost of Monte Cristo, WA. A doctor there gave him a quick evaluation and said to take him to UW's medical center. There they determined he was bruised, but not seriously injured.

On another occasion, while climbing up the Roosevelt Glacier on the North Face of Mount Baker, fellow climbers and I nearly met our Waterloos. As we approached the top of a 45 degree ice pitch, our rope leader had gone around a corner on the front points of his crampons belayed by the second on a small ledge chopped in the ice face. Incredibly, we hadn't put a single piece of protection into the system. As I approached the belayer's ledge it broke. The belayer threw the rope into the air and came crashing down on top of me. I immediately went to a self-arrest position and, with the belayer still on my back, we continued to slide toward the lip of the huge vertical face below. We finally came to a halt with my feet hanging over the edge.

From above, the leader took up the slack and we slowly got to our feet. We climbed back up to the original station and put in an ice screw. After finishing the pitch my knees turned to rubber and I collapsed into the snow.

On a trip to Squamish Chief in Canada with Bob Odom, we climbed a few pitches of University Wall, but gave up and set our sights on Grand Wall the next day. Grand Wall was a Grade V rock route and we had more success the following day. From our vantage point high on the rock, we saw a tow truck near our car and feared our vehicle would be towed away. Fortunately, the tow truck left and our car remained where we left it.

When we reached the top of a fantastic pillar, I belayed Bob as he went ahead. Once he topped out the pitch, I prepared to follow and unclipped a 50 pound haul bag tied to Bob's harness to help save some time. After taking off one glove to remove anchors and sort gear, I suddenly caught sight of the haul bag free-flying into space.

I immediately grabbed the haul line to keep Bob from being pulled from his anchors and sending both of us plummeting to our deaths. Unfortunately, I had to grab the rope with my ungloved hand which resulted in a severe rope burn on the inside of my knuckles. In spite of the injury, I managed to make my way up to Bob where we tore up a shirt to bandage my hand. That did the trick, so I rotated into the lead to scale the next pitch. Because it took us until midnight to reach the summit, we had to descend in the dark.

Upon reaching our car we discovered it had been broken into and some of our gear was missing. We figured the guilty party was the driver of the tow truck we had seen earlier, which was probably from the nearby rough and tumble town of Squamish. After discussing the situation, we decided discretion would be the better part of valor and we made no effort to look for the culprit.

We did many things as a family during our time in Washington. Going to the UW football games to cheer on the Huskies and making trips to the zoo were frequent diversions. We would also go out to breakfast on occasion and we played in the snow with the kids. We car camped and generally enjoyed being outdoors.

Our one sad and tragic incident came while we hiked in Canada's Glacier National Park. Doris was seven months into her second pregnancy when trouble developed. A week after our scramble in Glacier, her water broke. After being released from the hospital in Canada we made a frantic trip back to Seattle, but we were unable to save the baby.

I also managed to embarrass myself during our Grand Canyon trip. While there, I decided to traverse the canyon from the North Rim to the South Rim, but didn't start the 23½ mile trek until two o'clock in the afternoon. The temperature kept increasing as I hustled to reach the canyon floor. Finally, it was so hot I stripped to my boxer shorts hoping I wouldn't meet up with anybody. What I didn't know was that the Phantom Ranch Resort was located at the bottom of the canyon, where I proceeded to parade past all their guests wearing only my underwear.

After that, I stopped by the river to rest and told myself I wasn't moving until I saw a raft come by. Not two minutes later, a big commercial baloney boat came into view and ended my R & R. Dark was setting in so, I hiked to the bottom of the South Rim where I camped for the night.

I estimate I made more than 100 treks up alpine routes or rock climbs in Washington and another 25 more in other areas of the Northwest. I managed to avoid many more close calls, but did experience a couple interruptions.

During my climb of Exum Ridge on the Grand Teton, Doris developed problems in her third pregnancy. After summiting, I received the news and rushed home as soon possible. Everything turned out fine and Todd was born February 1971.

The second incident involved two of the boys from the Explorer Post during a trip to Yosemite. The police in Medford, OR picked them up for possession of marijuana.

Having my family and pastimes helped me make it through the PhD program. Much to my dismay, the faculty had decided doctorate exams and dissertation defense should be made more difficult. And if that wasn't bad enough, I compounded the problem by doing some things I should have avoided.

We had an Irish Setter named Dink. I would take Dink to school with me and keep him tethered to an old extension cord he had chewed up. When in the laboratory I would tie him to an old apparatus the department chairman had long ago abandoned. I did this to keep Dink from destroying my dissertation project that I kept on an optical bench. As fate would have it, the chairman brought to the lab two colleagues from Japan to show off the facility and introduce them to me. Unfortunately, my appearance was disheveled by two years of hair growth and Dink kept chewing on the chairman's socks. None of this went over well.

A second falling out occurred when the Graduate Student and Professional Student Senate was denied space in the building where my lab was located. They protested on the grounds I used the place as a dog kennel. I thought it odd that grad student representatives would attack me when they should have been acting on my behalf. Again, it was another thing that didn't go over well and this time with the facility director.

However, Dink did gain the distinction of becoming the only dog to actually log graduate-level course work. He was also a chick magnet and the favorite walking companion of my bachelor friend Ross Morrison. Ross and I also taught Dink to bird hunt and took him on several hunting trips in pursuit of pheasant and chucker.

Another faux pas occurred when I decided to sell our VW bus. I thought it was no longer safe enough for my family to ride in, so I traded it in for a Chevrolet station wagon. The trouble came because the car was new and the faculty members didn't think it was appropriate for a graduate student to drive a new car.

These issues made it easy to become despondent at times. The dissertation was tough and, with the faculty beefing up the standards to obtain a

PhD, I wasn't confident I would make it. I felt guilty because Doris had to work and we had to pay babysitters to watch the boys. I also felt the weight of letting down both my family and the professional community should I fail to earn my doctorate. Ironically, it turned out to be their support that helped me through it all.

Exercise has always been a part of my life. I used to walk 12 miles round trip from UW's campus to downtown Seattle to meet with Doris so we could talk. Not only was the conversation beneficial, but those walks helped clear my mind enough to solve some difficult problems. I later combined the walks with weight training and running to help stay in shape, which is something I've continued to this day. And climbing continued to be a catharsis for me. It flushed my mind and provided me a complete escape from the rigors of daily life.

This chapter would not be complete if I didn't include my side trip into the world of marijuana. I had no problem with the first time or two, but within a week I smoked it virtually every day. I continued using it for the next six years and cannot deny I became dependent on it. For me, pot was psychologically addictive and my attempts to control it, or quit, did not work.

It led to some rather scary moments, such as the time some companions and I were imbibing in our home, which was a converted train depot. I responded to a knock at the door and opened it to find two police officers standing there. Fortunately, I managed to detain them while my friends exited the place like rats leaving a sinking ship.

Marijuana did one positive thing for me. Although it had a firm grip on me, to some extent it opened my mind to the concept of a higher power.

In spite of it all, I eventually received my PhD and opened another chapter in our lives. I will always be grateful to have Reid as an adviser and friend, for the academically sound committee we chose and for his skills in steering me through a difficult time in my life. I successfully defended my dissertation in December 1972 and landed a job as a materials engineer at the Air Force Rocket Propulsion Laboratory, Edwards Air Force Base, CA.

If I had to describe myself, I would say I'm about average, but highly successful in numerous interrelated aspects of life. As an ordinary man able to envision excellence, I started out with nothing and ended up with everything. I found I could juggle family, career and spiritual responsibilities while living life on the edge. It isn't pride, but about being blessed with a full life and taking nothing for granted.

I learned to dream big at the University of Washington; that nothing was impossible. With a vision, virtually anyone can achieve amazing results. Help others and good things will come your way. My vision: When it's over – no regrets.

Hopefully this will give some insight as to who I am and how I've managed to accomplish the things I have. It isn't necessary to BASE jump Half Dome or climb Mount Everest to have a terrific life – but it is necessary to know what you want and how to get it. This is the story of how one man with an average upbringing could achieve great things, his way. Hopefully these pages will offer some ways to enrich your life as we proceed on this journey to the edge.

Randy and Doris Berry
December 1962

The Peeters Family 1951
Louis, Suzanne, Randy, Joan, and Steve

John Monk racing Thunderbirds
Puget Sound, WA

Liberty Ridge
Mount Rainier,
WA

Reid Parmerter tree
skiing,
Mammoth Moun-
tain, CA

Bob Baker and
Doug Williscroft
Northwest Arête of
Mount Sir Donald
Selkirk Range, BC,
Canada

Randy leading Angle Crack
Castle Rock
Tumwater Canyon, WA

Doris and Shawn Camping
in Snow Creek Canyon

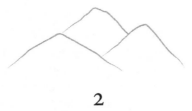

2

PSEUDO SKI BUMMING

As Reid and I stood there while sheriff's deputies trained shotguns on our heads, I realized I was terrified to the point I could not even breathe. The next thing I heard was, "Go inside and stay there."

From inside the Dog Trailer, we watched an ongoing tragedy unfold. A box girl from the local Safeway had been accidentally shot by one of the deputies and died right in front of us.

Although we were quite affected by this terrible incident, we moved to another location for the night and the next day enjoyed some fantastic powder skiing.

As mentioned in Out of the Blocks, downhill skiing in the Northwest virtually consumed me during the winter months, even though I was working and attending school. After moving to Tehachapi, CA in 1973, I was more determined than ever to take the sport to even higher levels. By this time we had two boys and my initial goal was to have the entire family take part in the sport.

Doris was already an accomplished skier, so teaching the boys was relatively easy and they quickly picked it up. There is something about kids at that age (four and six) that surpasses expectations when it comes to sports like skiing – bottom line – they were fearless!

I took every opportunity to ski and on one Air Force Rocket Propulsion Laboratory business trip to Utah, I met up with Reid and Chuck John.

Chuck's Initiation

Chuck had borrowed his dad's truck and camper unit and met us in the Snowbird parking lot. Soon after settling in for the night, a big snowstorm blew in and created optimum powder conditions. Chuck was not a powder skier, so in the morning as we smoked a joint, I explained that Reid and I would not ski with him that day. He pleaded that we let him go along and if he held us up in any way we could ski off without him. Reluctantly, I agreed.

After exiting the aerial tram, we headed straight for Little Cloud with its long, steep, powder-covered slopes. In preparation for the day, Chuck tightened down his bindings as far as possible so they would not release.

After a flawless steep run, Reid and I turned around in time to see a human snowball approaching the bottom of the slope. The snowball was Chuck and the moment he reached us we skied off to the next steep, powder section – a classic run named Peruvian Circ.

As we looked over the edge we saw several small avalanches had peeled off below the rim. We picked a line and blasted down the slope enjoying another exciting run. After resting and looking back at our tracks and the run, once again we skied off as Chuck approached.

We did this all day and Chuck essentially was never able to rest between runs, other than during chairlift rides. At the end of the day, his eyes were actually recessed into his eye sockets. He entered the camper, collapsed into bed and fell into a deep sleep.

The next day, we moved over to Alta for some tree skiing in whiteout conditions created by another big storm. To his credit, after two days of this, Chuck developed into a proficient powder skier.

Higher Levels of Downhill

Skiing in Southern California was a little problematic since there were no nearby ski areas. Undaunted by distance, we made numerous trips to Mammoth Mountain in a 13 foot long Serro Scotty we had dubbed as the Dog Trailer.

On one trip with Reid, we arrived in the Chair 2 parking lot in late afternoon and decided to make camp. Later that evening, we were asked to leave since a storm was approaching and the area would have to be plowed. The area operator suggested we go to the Safeway lot in town and spend the night there.

We arrived at the Safeway lot at 8:30 that evening and looked for a place to whiz before turning in for the night. After walking across the parking lot, I decided I would use a baggie and later dump the contents in a snow bank.

Reid continued his search to see if he could find a better solution.

After returning to the trailer and using the baggie, I opened the door to see Reid walking back across the icy parking lot. At that moment, several sheriff patrol cars sped into the parking lot and immediately trained shotguns at the heads of both Reid and me. The unmistakable ka-chung followed, along with the command, "Freeze!" Being stoned at the time, I was too terrified to even breathe.

I could not imagine this was a bust for possession of pot and casual camping in Safeway's lot. So, I stood in the doorway, arms raised, unable to breathe and holding a baggie full of urine until I heard the order to "Go inside and stay there." At the same time, the officer aiming at Reid yelled, "Get out of here, now!"

I slowly set down the baggie and closed the door. Reid attempted to comply by running away. Without traction, he began to slip and slide on the ice looking like something from a "Road Runner" cartoon. Eventually, he made his way back to the trailer from where we watched the ongoing tragedy unfold.

During a robbery taking place inside the store, a bag girl had been taken hostage by a gunman. Seeing the sheriff department arrive in force, the gunman bound and gagged the hostage and left her in the restroom, while he climbed into the attic to hide. Upon entering the building, sheriff personnel accidentally shot the girl, who later died right in front of our trailer.

It seemed too surreal to be true. Although we were quite affected by this terrible incident, we moved to another location for the night and the next day enjoyed some fantastic powder skiing.

On one run, Reid managed to hang up in a tree suspended over the edge of a cliff. We often skied outside the marked boundaries of ski areas and considered such signs as "Danger Cliff" or "Avalanche Danger" as little more than the designations of other ski runs.

Another classic trip involved Chuck John, Doug Williscroft and a couple of Chuck's friends. We met up in Mojave and drove up Highway 395 in our station wagon with the Dog Trailer in tow. Chuck surprised me by asking if I would mount his bindings for him after we arrived. I could not believe he would show for a trip without having his gear ready, but I reluctantly agreed to do it.

Being stoned, as usual, we entered the town of Mammoth and stopped at a ski shop. I asked a salesman if I could use an electrical outlet, to which he said OK. So I grabbed my toolbox and set up shop right in the middle of the sales floor. I drilled the skis and mounted the bindings. After that scene, we proceeded to the main parking lot to spend the night.

Toward the middle of the next day, after smoking a prodigious amount of weed, Chuck complained that his binding kept releasing. He said he tightened the binding to its highest setting, but it continued to release, especially when he went over jumps and was airborne. I took a look at his bindings and couldn't contain my laughter. I had mounted one of his toe pieces sideways. I corrected the mounting and after that it worked perfectly.

How Chuck managed to ski half a day with that binding self-centering sideways was beyond me. After dinner we did the usual. We snuck into a spa at one of the nearby resorts and then drew straws to see who would have to sleep in the back of the station wagon for the night. After drawing the short straw, Chuck presented us with another classic the next morning. He failed to take proper care of his Levis which were wet from skiing and they had frozen into a crumpled ball. Seeing him attempting to put on those frozen Levis the next morning was entertaining. Doug eventually gave Chuck a pair of his pants to wear.

Other trips to Mammoth with Doris and the kids were great fun as well. Both boys learned to ski at an early age and it was fun watching them rapidly progress. To further our enjoyment, I went to one of the local resorts near where we were camped and offered to pay for the use of their hot tub. Not wanting to set a poor example for our young sons, I thought it best to ask.

The clerk leaned over the desk and quietly said, "I can't allow you to do that – just sneak in." So we did!

Off to Los Alamos – The Land of Perfect Powder

When we moved to the mountain community of Los Alamos, NM, our ski education accelerated. Los Alamos had a small, local ski hill 15 minutes away on Pajarito Mountain. It had one chairlift and one T-bar with a vertical drop of 1,100 feet. For $214, we purchased season passes for the entire family. The town had a ski swap annually, so we outfitted all four of us with equipment and clothing for next to nothing. This was convenient since the boys kept outgrowing everything. We enrolled them in a junior racing program and their skills improved rapidly.

Pajarito only opened three days a week so during good snow seasons there was often plenty of untracked powder to ski. I worked flex time at the Los Alamos National Laboratory and would leave work at 8:30 in the morning on Wednesdays when the ski hill was open. I could make a dozen or so powder runs and be back to work by noon to finish out the work day. By Saturday, when they reopened, there would be new powder to ski.

One winter, Chuck John was hitchhiking his way back to Southern California after skiing in Canada. He stopped to see us in Los Alamos with his skis in tow, so we took off to do some powder at Pajarito.

On one run, Chuck took a bad spill and was slow getting up. I was surprised to see him lean on his ski poles for a time since I knew Chuck was tough as nails. Afterward, we skied down the slope and lined up at the chairlift.

A young lady standing behind us tapped Chuck on the shoulder and said, "Sir, you're bleeding."

It turned out Chuck had a big slice in his ear and had bled all over his parka. After weighing the situation, we decided not to waste an excellent powder day and kept on skiing.

By the time Shawn turned eight, he was skiing powder with the best of us. Reid, Doug and I would take him skiing on our trips to some of the country's finest ski resorts. At Snowmass in Colorado, Shawn tried racing Doug back to the lift and seriously injured his foot after hitting a metal pole. After a trip to the hospital it was diagnosed as a massive sprain. During another trip to Colorado's Steamboat Springs, Doug was nearly knocked unconscious when he slammed into an aspen tree.

We always took the Dog Trailer and camped in parking lots where we could sneak into the spas of close-by resorts. While Shawn and I were soaking ourselves one afternoon in Vail, a television crew came by and wanted to interview us on how to ski cheap. We wisely declined, not wanting to jeopardize our game plan.

Other destinations included Sierra Blanca, Taos, Purgatory and Aspen. Reid enjoyed our trip to Sierra Blanca and loved hearing the locals tell us that "If God had wanted Texans to ski he would have made bullshit white."

Moving East in Search of Perfect Ice

Career moves took us next to Upstate New York in the summer of 1980 and boy was that an eye-opener.

We frequently went skiing as a family and the surface conditions in the East were quite different than anything we had previously experienced. When ski reports said icy, it was unbelievable. On one trip, I actually saw the ground through eight inches of ice!

We took racing lessons to learn how to handle the conditions and once we had mastered the vertical ice at our local area, we branched out with Dog Trailer trips to other resorts. Camping in the parking lots and enduring the incredibly cold skiing conditions of the Northeast, we all became much better skiers.

The boys and I visited many of the New England ski resorts. Doris had begun to lose interest in the sport and didn't care much for the cold. The humidity mixed with the cold in Eastern States can penetrate right to the bone.

Still, Shawn, Todd and I continued to haul the Dog Trailer from parking lot to parking lot to ski in tortuous winter conditions at many different resorts.[2]

While living in New York, we were introduced to ski touring. Our home was located in a rural area and we frequently put on our skis and toured for miles without ever seeing another person or crossing a road. We had remarkable neighbors who permitted us to ski on their property which opened endless opportunities for us to explore. Wildlife was abundant, offering hours of enjoyment on family tours. Many times, I would return from work, put on my skis and tour for an hour or so enjoying the solitude of that frozen wilderness.

One day, 82 year old neighbor Ralph Baker decided he would go skiing with me. Considering he had suffered a broken hip the previous summer, I did my best to discourage him but he would have none of it. So, I skied over to his house where he was waiting for me in his front yard. He had a pair of eight feet long 1917 wood skies with leather straps holding them to his feet. I did not think this a wise idea.

Fortunately, after going ten feet one leather strap on his ski broke and he decided to give up on the tour. It turned out, he last used those skis while he and his wife, Dorothy, were on their honeymoon some 60 plus years before. Years later, they gave those skis to Doris and me and they hang on the wall in our home to this day.

After moving to Northern California in the fall of 1982, Doris' interest in skiing was rekindled. The boys were excellent skiers, so we traveled throughout Northern California visiting different ski areas. We especially enjoyed skiing the Tahoe Basin with its incredible views and often encountered powder conditions with great tree-skiing.[3]

Dangers Near the Edge – California Style

Chuck John and I were tree-skiing powder at Kirkwood on Rabbit Run. While partially airborne in my attempt to reach the speed of light, I realized there was a huge pine tree directly in front of me that I was not going to miss. Instinctively, I lowered my right shoulder and collided with a tree trunk measuring five feet in diameter. Following impact, with my feet above my head, I dropped head-first into the bottom of the tree well which was eight feet below my initial point of contact.

Chuck came over, looked down at me and asked if I was all right.

"I don't think so," I replied with a breathless grunt. However, I righted myself and climbed out of the tree well.

We finished the run and then hiked up to the double-diamond[4] chutes located atop the Wagon Wheel bowl. It took one run for me to realize I had better quit before I killed myself. I felt this incident sort of evened the score between us concerning Chuck's first powder day at Snowbird many years before.

Having worked with the Boy Scouts, I started an Explorer Post and we took several ski trips over the years. On one trip to Homewood, I gave my troops a valuable pointer regarding the proper technique to use when skiing on an icy surface. It involved completely unbuckling one's boots while skiing making it necessary to keep one's weight perfectly positioned over the skis.

After following my instructions, one youth, Dave Harlan, took off down the slope. Halfway through his run, he stepped out of his boot and both the boot and ski continued on without him. What a sight to see him madly hopping along after it.

During one Super Bowl in which the San Francisco 49ers were playing, Shawn and I hit the slopes at Sugar Bowl. Perfect conditions greeted us, 18 inches of powder, sunny skies and no crowds. We were able to ski right up to the chairlift and catch a chair without a moment's wait. We made 25 fantastic runs and still made it home in time to see the second half of the game.

During one trip to Kirkwood I would prefer to forget, I attempted a jump and botched the landing so badly I ended up in the hospital. As I fell, I buried my arm in the snow up to my elbow while my body cartwheeled and dislocated my shoulder. Fortunately, I had Todd with me and sent him for help. Within ten minutes, a ski patrol snowmobile showed up with my rescuer and his girlfriend on board. I asked him to put my shoulder back right then and there but no matter how much I begged he wouldn't do it. He said it would be best to wait until someone at the medical clinic could do it. With that, he departed saying he had to drop off his girlfriend before returning to pick me up.

Forty-five minutes later, I was in the Kirkwood medical clinic being pumped full of valium and morphine while two guys tried in vain to put my shoulder back in place. I was then transported by ambulance to the hospital at South Lake Tahoe. I had a severe dislocation and required two courses of general anesthesia to put the shoulder back into place. I wasn't released from the hospital until the next morning.

I was still groggy and had only one good arm, so I had to have 11 year old Todd help me drive home. I started chiropractic treatment where I received "electrocution therapy" (electrical muscle stimulation) and in the process met Denny Swenson. It turned out Denny was not only a chiropractor, but a Christian and a good skier. We became close friends and spent many days on the slopes together.

In over 50 years of skiing powder, I often entered the closed areas or those locations considered out of bounds. I did that because that's often where the best snow was. However, such excursions weren't without consequences.

One day while Shawn and I were skiing Sugar Bowl, we crisscrossed the boundary to find uncut deep powder. I was wearing my Walkman listening to loud music and didn't notice the four ski patrolers as they shouted at me from behind a tree. Unaware I had been spotted, I jumped the taped marker and blasted downhill through trees at breakneck speed. When I reached the bottom of the slope, I turned to focus my attention on Shawn's arrival, but he was nowhere to be seen.

Suddenly, Shawn skied into view escorted by the ski patrol. One of the patrolmen immediately called his station to request the sheriff meet us at the base area where I was to be arrested. Unfortunately for the patrolman, the only way out of where we were was down a steep chute that he wasn't able to negotiate. I helped him to the bottom where he was embarrassed enough to listen to my request that I not be cited or arrested. He then took me to meet the ski patrol supervisor. I pled my case.

I told him I had assessed the avalanche danger of the area and found it to be stable. He agreed with me, but said others who followed my example might not be capable of making that assessment. Still, to the sheriff's dismay, he did let me go following a stern warning.

Alpine Out - Telemark In

In 1992, after 25 years of alpine skiing, I became bored with it and decided to take up telemark-skiing.[5] Having done a fair amount of ski-mountaineering by that time, I was proficient at traveling in the backcountry. The advent of stiff plastic boots and improved skis with three-pin bindings made telemark-skiing a revolution in off-piste skiing.

I signed up for a two day course in telemark-skiing where I learned a basic tele-turn. With the new equipment, I discovered I could parallel ski by slightly shifting my weight back on my skis. I called this "free-heel skiing" since it was neither alpine nor telemark. With this technique, I could ski in and out of incredible terrain with little or no effort and that opened tremendous opportunities for out-of-bounds skiing. I started searching ski areas for long, double-diamond type runs in restricted areas among the trees.

The only drawback I found to "free-heel" was that a fall in powder snow could prove to be catastrophic. With the heels free, putting weight on the tips to prevent a fall, as can be done with alpine bindings, wasn't possible and that meant falls would take place over a much greater distance. The thought of that possibility was unnerving when making a steep powder run through trees, especially with the increased prevalence of deep, wide tracks being made by snowboarders.

In the 90s, Heavenly Valley was one of my sponsors. I was doing a radio show and bartered commercial time for ski passes. While skiing there, I discovered an "underground" or "outlaw" set of runs which existed outside the ski area boundary.[6] I tackled these runs both solo and with Denny and other friends. We used the chairlifts to travel to the top of the mountain and then would head off into the trees out-of-bounds for some uncut powder runs. These were double-diamond slopes dropping thousands of vertical feet and coming out on the highways below the resort. From there, we would hitchhike back to the chairlifts and do it all over again.

Rating the powder from one to ten, I soloed down several of these runs on a ten plus day. At the end of the fifth run, I spotted a parked car with ski racks on top and asked if I could catch a ride back to Heavenly. "I think so," said the driver, who identified himself as Dan Osmond. "I'll ask the guys who hired me if it is OK."

It turned out Osmond had been hired by a group of guys doing the same thing I was doing. They had split up his asking price and were enjoying the equivalent of helicopter skiing for a fraction of the cost. They took me into their group and I had no problem keeping up with them, even though they used alpine skis.

After finishing two more runs with these guys, the group informed me I had completed the "triple crown," i.e., all the out of bounds runs in a single day. In all, I logged more than 20,000 vertical feet in perfect powder that day.

I took other Heavenly trips in the company of the "Crud Doctor" and "Coyote." They tabbed me as the "Tele Tornado." We ended up making "outlaw" out-of-bounds runs with ski instructors, area operators and even ski patrol.

The best run descended from the top of Heavenly 3,500 vertical feet down to near the town of Gardnerville. It was a fine steep run complete with trees, glades and included 1,500 vertical feet of double-diamond, followed by diamond and intermediate terrain.

"This is better than sex," Coyote said after one run, "I've never had a 45 minute orgasm."

I had always enjoyed the winter wilderness and free-heel skiing drew me even closer to the rugged terrain of the Sierra. I did a trans-Sierra in the spring of 1990 along with Bill Briggs and Graham Connors. We made the Mammoth Mountain to Yosemite Valley traverse skiing all but five miles of the 55 mile route. We reached Yosemite Valley in three and a half days.

No Problem!

Not all trips were of the ten plus variety. In January 1994, Harlan Reese, a work friend, Chuck John and I decided to go from Kirkwood near Carson Pass along Highway 88 to Echo Summit along Highway 50. It was typically a one day trip but we decided to do an overnighter. There had been a ski race the week before along the route we planned to take and we figured it would be clearly marked. The winning times had taken a few hours, so we weren't expecting any problems – our first mistake.

I should have gotten a clue when Chuck showed up carrying a suitcase with concealed shoulder straps he used to wear it like a backpack. Undeterred, we started out early the next morning forging our way into the white wilderness. The progress was slow and the snow started falling: three to six inches of heavy stuff in just a couple of hours.

Handheld GPS units were yet to be invented, so by nightfall we had no idea where we were. The trail markers had been buried by the fresh snow which created whiteout conditions. Our map, compass and altimeter were of little use to us and we were scared, so we set up camp.

That night, the snowfall was so heavy our tent collapsed. Harlan and I would have slept through, but Chuck woke us up to let us know we could suffocate. However, after knocking the snow off the tent, we made it through the night.

The next day, we moved along the ridge and periodically worked our way down through the cliff bands to find the Highway 50 corridor. Having no luck, we would return to the ridge and travel in a northwest direction.

After spending another anxious night, we eventually found our way to the Echo Summit Snow Park where our car was parked. What a relief – I started to have visions of what it must have been like for the Donner party having to resort to cannibalism.

The following year, Denny Swenson, some of my friends from work and I traveled from Carson Pass to Ebbetts Pass along Highway 4 near Bear Valley. It proved a tough two days during which we covered 24 miles in light snow showers.

In 1995, Ron Spencer (a work friend), Andy Martwick (who I met skiing) and I tackled the Sierra High Route. This spectacular traverse goes from Symmes Creek near Independence to the Wolverton Ski Area in Sequoia National Park. It was a distance of 51 miles with 34 of it continuously above 11,000 feet and crosses nine passes and saddles. With only one major route finding error, it took us six days to complete.

This time we had GPS, but became convinced we had entered some erroneous way points. We decided to ignore the GPS. It was late in the day and snow was falling as we climbed over a particularly difficult pass. After traveling the wrong route for an hour, we broke through a cornice and had to down climb a difficult rock face.

From there, we skied a half mile into a valley and came to the conclusion things didn't look right. After consulting our map and cross-checking our GPS coordinates we realized we had skied into a real mess. Avalanche danger was everywhere and the snow started coming down even harder. We decided continuing down the valley was not an option.

We set up camp and prayed it would stop snowing. To our dismay, it snowed all night.

The next morning, we had little choice but to traverse some extremely dangerous avalanche terrain to reach our original route. It was scary, but we pulled it off and a few days later arrived where our car was parked. It was an incredibly intense, but beautiful wilderness experience.

In April 1996, Denny, Michael (a friend I met skiing) and I did the 34 mile, two day trip from Echo Summit to Rubicon. In March 97, Denny and I skied from Alpine Meadows to Rubicon and were treated to an incomparable view of comet Hale-Bopp while camping at 8,000 feet. We also completed a traverse from Sugar Bowl to Squaw Valley together.

Over a seven year period, I twice traversed the Sierra Nevada from east to west by two different trans-Sierra routes and covered a distance of more than 70 miles (as the crow flies) following the crest of the Sierra from Highway 4 to Highway 80.

Approaching the Dark Side

In the beginning, I truly hated snowboards. They opened the floodgates for riders with little or no skills to invade the precious powder among the trees and they left deep, wide tracks. I also found it difficult to handle the attitude of these intruders. Although I tried to ignore this revolution as the boys and I continued to ride and ski together, it did create some conflict.

In particular, the terrain for free-heel skiing and snowboarding was often incompatible. Snowboarders could face horrific walkouts from the bottom of deep powder chutes. In the world of snowboarding, it was known as "terrain f ... ked!"

In spite of my initial feelings, in December 1997 I bit the bullet and took up snowboarding. I truly felt I had crossed over to the dark side and the learning curve was pure misery. I took more hard falls in a single day than I did during the previous 30 years of skiing. After my first day of snowboarding, I ended up so sore I could hardly walk for an entire week – I nearly gave up on it then and there. But once I got the hang of it, I enjoyed "surfing" down a mountain of powder. I discovered there was a symbiotic relationship between snowboarding and surfing. As my skills improved on the snowboard, they also improved on the surfboard. Eventually, I worked my way into the trees and enjoyed snowboarding every type of terrain except ice – I found snowboarding on ice to be no fun at all.

A New Millennium

Moving into the new millennium, the family-owned Donner Ski Ranch sponsored me based on my successful climbing expeditions. Reminiscent of the 1950s and 1960s, this small ski resort became my new home for the next eight years. After a storm, the uncut powder would often last for days and I loved the feel of the place. Donner had some great out-of-bounds runs and I took advantage of those gems whenever possible. I thought of Donner as a vertical gymnasium and would shovel snow on powder days before riding to get additional exercise by working at a higher altitude.

One year, they issued me an employee season pass, although I wasn't actually an employee. Still, I felt like a member of the team knowing my efforts were appreciated. The resort also hosted a "Summit with Randy" day and raised $3,900 for my future expeditions.

Having mastered both tele-skis and snowboard, I would do one or the other depending on the conditions and my mood. I took full advantage of both resort skiing and wilderness traveling. Denny and I did tours to Castle Peak that included a technical rock climb in winter conditions among other backcountry experiences. Several times I even went to ski-touring resorts and would cover more than 20 miles a day using skinny skis on groomed trails.

Helicopters – The Ultimate Chairlift

In April 2004, I did my first heli-boarding trip. Randy Katen invited me to join his group at Mike Wiegele's Helicopter Skiing in Blue River BC, Canada. Katen was one of California's best snowboarders at the time and I was apprehensive when I discovered who else would be in our group.

Among them were Don Bostick, sport organizer for the ESPN X-Games and World Cup Skateboarding; Dave Duncan, the announcer for the 2002 Olympics snowboard half-pipe; Jeff Ching, national champion in senior snowboard racing; and Marshal King, an incredible rider from Donner.

We were transported by helicopter into the massive Monashee and Cariboo mountain ranges, where we would be making runs on glaciers. We were first taken to the top of a pinnacle and dropped off.

After exiting the aircraft, it was necessary to stay low and hang onto one's gear as the whirlybird lifted off and blew clouds of snow in all directions. Once I had a clear view of the surrounding terrain, I was truly horrified.

Below was a steep ice face that I wouldn't have climbed without an ice axe and crampons. Now, the only way down was on a snowboard strapped to my feet. I managed to make it down several hundred feet of this steep couloir before I fell and did about 15 cartwheels among rocks that seemed to whiz by at the speed of light. I became rag doll before coming to a stop and was thankful I had on a helmet – ouch!

All together, we rode down 68,000 vertical feet of corn snow and mush during those three days and I have to say my snowboarding skills improved dramatically. It was a great experience, but I missed not spending Easter with my family.

The following year, I did a two day heli-boarding trip into the Ruby Mountains of Northern NV. The light-powder conditions were incredible. I chose to camp out in my car in the parking lot to save money and it was a thoroughly enjoyable trip. Although it wasn't the challenge of Canada, the runs were first class and included the infamous Cum Line.

I also tried cat-boarding in the Sierra. By using a snowcat, we accessed wonderful terrain with virtually no effort. I organized a group and we had a great time, but I wished I had gone with skis instead. The extremely steep entries and long trails out to the cat would have been more straightforward on skis, but I had fun just the same.

In 2009, I found it pays to have a chiropractor for a ski partner. While tele-skiing with Denny, I suffered a hard fall in powder. I got up slowly as things didn't feel right. I made a couple more runs but then quit for the day. Denny asked to take a look at my right shoulder, so we went to the ski patrol room where he discovered I had a partial dislocation. The ski patrol wanted me to go to the hospital, but Denny popped the sucker back in place before anyone could protest.

Randy Katen, Tom McCauley and I did a helicopter trip to Alaska in April of 2010. After flying into Anchorage, we rented a 24 foot RV, stocked it with food and drove to Thompson Pass in the Chugach Range. We camped in the Alaska Back Country parking lot and took the required avalanche training. We then waited to fly until conditions improved.

While waiting, we hiked to the nose of the Worthington Glacier and visited some impressive ice caves. We traveled to Valdez for pizza and a shower and otherwise watched movies in the RV.

After a three day wait, we were given a "window shopping" flight to a steep, long powder run. Snowboarding this run was intimidating and the visibility wasn't good, but at least it quelled our anxiety. However, the snow continued to fall for several more days, dumping another 18 inches and grounding the helicopter. During that time, I met Leo. Leo was a skier and snowmobiler and we made some plans to kill time by making a shuttle run at Thompson Pass.

The snow finally stopped and the helicopter was cleared to go. We ended up in some pretty scary stuff making an extremely steep run with a difficult entry that triggered a huge avalanche. I ended up cartwheeling down that section.

Next was a run with an easier entry but it had some horrible flat sections. I fell a dozen times and had to dig out from under some incredibly deep powder. The conditions were made difficult by three feet of new powder covered by a heavy upper layer of snow.

After moving to a different area, we were treated to two fantastic runs in awesome powder. The first presented an exposed knife ridge with a steep entry which I handled successfully with no falls. The second had a 40 degree entry that I nailed perfectly. These two runs were pure bliss.

The next day proved to be wait-and-see, but I was too stiff and sore to care. I would have preferred the day be canceled rather than sitting around and waiting.

The next morning was our final day. We were greeted with two more inches of snow, continued flurries and poor visibility. Leo and I took his snow machine for a ghost run on Gulley 1. It was fun and actually quite scary going uphill on that machine.

Overall, it was a great time with a total of seven runs in four days of riding down 22,500 vertical feet.[7] The terrain was unbelievably steep.

The trip taught me a valuable lesson – snowboards were definitely not the tool of choice for this type of terrain. The traverses were difficult so I decided then and there I would come back with skis the following year. I learned snowboards are great toys, but skis are the proper tools for the backcountry.

Fat Skis

The next year, I transitioned to Sugar Bowl as my home resort. There, I hired on as an employee so I could shovel snow for an hour or so in the mornings. They wouldn't let me shovel the snow as a volunteer for liability reasons. I told them I would only be able to report for work on days I planned to ski, so they made me part time.

I spent several days shoveling during the months of November and December before receiving a call from the resort on Christmas Eve. They said I wasn't working enough hours and would have to be let go. I said "no problem" and hung up. That's when I fantasized as to what I should have said. "I realize I am 65 and this is probably age discrimination, not to mention that it is Christmas Eve, so could you discuss this with my attorney Finkelstein on Monday and see if we can work out a free lifetime season pass in order to quietly settle this entire matter?"

By the way, Sugar Bowl has fantastic out of bounds terrain – oh well, here we go again!

My new, all-mountain fat skis arrived in January 2011. They proved to be really fun and easy to ride in any conditions. I mounted randonnée bindings so I could unlock the heel when necessary for ski touring. These skis were almost like having a snowboard on each foot, as the total surface of the two skis together was virtually the same as my snowboard.

I think fat skis may have saved the ski industry. The only disadvantage compared to a snowboard was the possibility of one ski tracking away from the other resulting in the splits and a twisting fall. With a history of chronic right knee injuries, I had to avoid this situation.

I worked hard to master my new gear in preparation for my upcoming trip back to Alaska. All was going well until one fateful day in late February.

Back to Alaska…Maybe

I had been skiing Sugar Bowl in two inches of new powder and decided to spend the night in my Rav4 in the resort parking lot. A massive storm had been forecast for the next day and I wanted to be on the slopes early before Cal Trans closed the roads. In fact they did close interstate 80 leading into and out of the Sierra.

After some great powder skiing the next morning, the conditions worsened and the resort closed. I removed my skis and shuffled across the parking lot in my ski boots. With winds beginning to gust up to 75 miles per hour, I slipped on the ice and fell down hard onto a manhole cover. I knew I was hurt, but everyone else had already left except for one employee gathering up parking cones from the lot.

He helped me up and assisted me to my vehicle. I used my ski poles for balance and was in tremendous pain. Once in the Rav4, I took off my ski boots and knew my only option was to slowly drive back down the closed highway to Auburn and the hospital. To make matters worse, the Rav4 had a manual transmission and the road conditions were frightening. There wasn't another vehicle to be seen anywhere as I made a two and a half hour trip down that treacherous stretch of highway. I used my cell phone to contact Doris every ten minutes and let her know my location. I believe the intense concentration required to make that drive was the main reason I managed to endure the pain.

I was in shock and my systolic blood pressure was over 190 mm Hg when I reached the hospital. I was scheduled for surgery the next morning.

My femur was broken near the hip joint and required two large pins and two screws to repair. Fortunately, my prognosis was excellent.

I was discharged the next afternoon and returned to Foresthill and our snow-covered home. I had no choice but to cancel my Alaska trip and turned my attention to a kayak trip down the Grand Canyon coming up in three months. Thanks to having one of the best surgeons in the area and some intense physical therapy, I was able to manage the pain and got off the crutches quicker than expected. We had a tremendous snow season that year and I skied Donner July 2, only four months after the surgery.

The following winter, I again took the snowcat trip, only this time on skis – an excellent decision. We skied what I would call some scary double-diamond plus runs with steep terrain and trees but it proved to be incredible fun.

I eventually made a solo trip back to the Chugach Range in Alaska in March 2012. Since I was by myself I had no one to share expenses with, but I was also free to call all the shots.

I rented a 19 foot RV, stocked it with food and headed for Thompson Pass for an eight day stay. Although it had been a heavy snow year in Alaska, I arrived under perfect conditions. The helicopter flights had been going strong; I made 21 helicopter runs and skied 73,100 vertical feet of incredible powder in four days. To give some idea of the landscape, the runs had names such as Blood Stain, Cold Smoke and Ripping Ridge. They averaged 3,500 vertical feet where falls could be devastating. If triple-diamonds existed, this is where they would be found.

It was much easier on skis than my previous snowboard adventure. I did trigger some sloughs strong enough to sweep me off my feet, which was scary, but overall I had a lot of fun. It was, by far, the steepest terrain I ever tackled. When it comes to skiing in Alaska, they say, "go big or go home." I preferred my own version, "go big and go home alive."

Back Home

I'm planning my next helicopter outing in my own backyard, the Sierra Nevada Mountains of Northern California and snowcat trips have become an annual occurrence.

Being sentimental, I enjoy déjà vu trips to areas I have skied in the past. I take pleasure in returning to Donner Ski Ranch where I watched my grandchildren learn to ski and snowboard. I also enjoy an occasional day of skiing or riding with the boys and their families at other areas.

In 2013, Todd relocated to North Ogden, UT and this is truly powder heaven. We had a great time skiing together at Wolf Mountain, Snowbasin and Powder Mountain in 2014.

It's hard to describe the friendships one forges through sports such as skiing. Jean Paul Duval of France recently reminded me of our trip to the Mount Baker Ski Area in the early 1970s. He didn't know how to ski, but I talked him into it by telling him it was easy. On his first run, he broke one of his skis in two.

Strangely enough, what we both remember most about that trip was a scary spinout we had in my VW bus. It was a continuously dampened series of sinusoidal horizontal side-to-side slides after we hit a patch of black ice in a curve on the Mount Baker highway. Some 40 years later, we remain friends and share many memories together. This is true of hundreds of friendships I formed over the years through sports.

Besides Heavenly Valley, Donner Ski Ranch and Sugar Bowl, I skied 64 different areas in ten different states over the years. Using ski lifts, snow-cats and helicopters, I skied in bounds, out-of-bounds, glaciers, couloirs, through trees and over cliffs. The areas ranged from intermediate to extreme including snowboarding on glaciers in Northern Canada and skiing in Alaska.

I had some all-time favorite powder days in Mammoth with Reid, Sugar Bowl with son Shawn, Bend with Doug and solo outlaw runs at Heavenly. I heli-boarded and skied in numerous mountain ranges throughout the United States and Canada. Although never a ski bum, my excursions included camping in parking lots, being involved in resort operations, as well as skiing and snowboarding on secret "locals only" runs. I often felt like an insider at many of these resorts.

Powder snow is more than a passion, it is an obsession. I have mastered the technique with a variety of equipment on virtually all terrains and in all conditions. And when the conditions are perfect, nothing compares to the feeling of weightlessness while flying down the fall line. It feels as if you are jumping into an endless series of feather pillows. I thoroughly enjoy skiing alone in these conditions. The solitude is pleasant and with no one along to impress, I can absorb the pure essence of the experience.

I rarely ski or ride except on powder days and especially enjoy the experience during a snowstorm. Storms tend to thin the crowds and in the trees visibility is rarely a problem. Whether taking long powder runs or steep powder shots, it is all fantastic.

As for injuries, I have had plenty of them.[8] Was it worth it? You bet.

Doug Williscroft
Mammoth Mountain, CA

Camping in the
Dog Trailer
Vail, CO

Denny Swenson
and Randy snow
camping

Helicopter skiing
near Blue River BC, Canada

Helicopter skiing
Thompson Pass, AK

Helicopter skiing
Chugach Range, AK

Start of the Trans-Sierra High Route

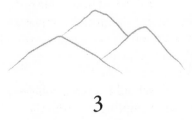

3

FAMILY MAN IN THE TURBULENT 1960S AND 1970S

Tehachapi – The Land of Four Seasons

It felt a little like Peyton Place…Wayne was sleeping with the married daughter of one of the most prominent families in the community and was about to be run of town on a rail…meanwhile her girlfriend was sleeping with the sheriff who was also married…and to top it off, the sheriff had told us he planned to handle our complaint even though the offender was part of his family.

Leaving Seattle was a mixed bag – exciting on one hand with a new job in a different location, but on the other hand I regretted leaving the Northwest, which we had grown to love. I still recall Reid urging me to stay at UW for another year or two so we could ski together. In his words, you will never have more disposable income than you currently have – how true this turned out to be.

As a graduate student, I had teaching and research assistantships, grants and fellowships, which were largely tax-free. Our only real taxable income came from Doris' job at the phone company. When I started as a GS-12 at the rocket lab I was making $15,866 per year. It resulted in less take-home pay than our combined income was as a graduate student.

The late 1960s and early 1970s had been quite turbulent with the Vietnam War raging and protests in full bloom at the university. Reid had advised me that the rocket lab was a good choice since we would then have someone from the "movement" on the inside.

For the record, I was never drafted.

Immediately after high school I entered college, which qualified me for a student deferment thus exempting me from the draft. Then I was given a defense deferment after joining Boeing. And after fathering two children, I was classified IIIA. Although I was opposed to the war, had I been drafted I would have served my country.

We purchased a house under construction in the Golden Hills area near Tehachapi, CA. It measured 1,650 square feet and sat on one half acre. We bought it for $36,500.

Tehachapi was a small, rural town of 4,000 people located in the mountains at an elevation of 4,000 feet and touted as the land of four seasons. The house wasn't completed until 45 days after our arrival, so Doris and the kids stayed with our folks in Rialto, CA and I camped in my office at the lab. At first I used the drafting table as a sleeping platform, but I quickly discovered the women's bathroom had a bed, so at night I took up residence in there.

I bought a free-weight set and started lifting and running after work. I used the evenings to finalize my dissertation. I submitted it in March 1973 and officially completed my PhD in aeronautics and astronautics.

I was sent on numerous temporary duty (TDY) trips to help bring me up to speed on the various programs I was assigned. On one trip to Northern California I took my family at my own expense. This was the first time our boys flew on an airplane and it proved to be a great adventure for them.

When we finally moved into our new home, we were barely making ends meet financially, so we used sheets for window coverings. This radical change in our lives brought on considerable stress. My first supervisor was Major Charles Payne – yes, I actually worked for a Major Payne. He and I became good friends and to this day I count him as one of my best friends.

I continued lifting weights in my office and ran at lunchtime. This was not the norm in those days and, in fact, created some difficulty with the branch chief, Charlie Cooke (i.e., my boss's, boss's, boss).

One day he came by my office during lunch while I was in my shorts lifting weights. He decided this would be the time to address my lack of respect for the established dress code (slacks and dress shirt with a tie). I told him it made no sense to wear a tie in the middle of the Mojave Desert and pointed out even our Air Force counterparts wore open collar uniforms.

Then, as if to emphasize my point, an overweight fellow employee walked by my office wearing a tie that was at least 15 years out of date. I turned to

Charlie and asked if that was how he wanted me to dress?

He responded, "Well no, not like that."

We reached a compromise. I could wear my collar open, but would keep a tie in the office in case we had visitors.

One such visit occurred a year or so later during an Inspecting General (IG) visit – which turned out to be a really big deal.

As all the civilians stood outside in the heat with our ties on the IG said "Why in the hell are you wearing ties in the middle of the desert?"

The dress code changed, QED.

Early on at the lab, I was told by Kathy, the branch chief's secretary, I would have to serve as the security monitor for the division. This did not set well with me, as I wanted to focus on more meaningful assignments. Acting as security monitor would be time consuming and of little added value. However, my protests went unnoticed.

When I was eventually called down for instructions concerning the walk-in security vault with its huge, tumbler-type lock, I was amazed to find the combination was simply three, six, nine. Kathy then told me, in the event of a nuclear attack, I needed to go directly into the vault, lock myself inside and begin destroying all the classified materials.

I told her, if there was a nuclear attack, I was going to get into my car and drive as far away as fast as I could. Thus ended my tenure as division security monitor.

On one occasion, the day before I was scheduled to give an important Monday morning briefing, I decided to shave off my sparse and terrible-looking facial hair. The results revealed a patchwork of light and tan skin once covered by my whiskers. Undaunted, I asked Doris to cut my hair, which had gotten long and was as unsightly as my beard.

When Doris finished, my hair was completely uneven with hunks of hair sticking out everywhere. In spite of looking as bad as I possibly could, I showed up for my presentation only to receive an "Oh, my God," look from the lab commander. This led to a visit to the barbershop the next day where I ended up with an extremely short, conventional haircut.

Toward the end of my tenure at the rocket lab, I was chosen to participate in the selection process for the Inertial Upper Stage (IUS) propulsion system. This was a huge honor, as the IUS was a large procurement and would be the last of this type for many decades. The competition had been quite keen.

The top corporate executives for the three companies, who had submitted bids, were there for the kickoff presentations, as well as a virtual Who's Who in the government hierarchy. We received strict instructions to attend all three presentations, or be disqualified from the selection process.

During the first presentation, Bill Payne, who sat right in front of Charlie Cooke, fell asleep. In spite of getting an ass chewing from Charlie during the break, Bill promptly fell asleep again during the second presentation.

At the next break, Bill took the offensive.

"Before you say anything," Bill said to Charlie, "I wanted you to know that I felt the only fair thing to do was to sleep through all three presentations." Amazing!

In all fairness to Bill, he had been diagnosed with a sleep disorder that resulted in excessive sleepiness at inappropriate times.

Little did I know that during the long commutes with fellow workers from Tehachapi to the rocket lab (more than one hour each way) I would grow to respect their opinions. Basically, these were very conservative folks – and ultimately I would also become conservative.

There is a quote which dates back to the 1800s that pretty well summarizes my experience. It goes something like this: "If you're not a liberal at 20 you have no heart, if you're not a conservative at 40 you have no brain."

This job provided an outstanding opportunity for travel, which is something I really love to do. Trips all over the U.S. and even one to Europe were part of the job. I was frequently able to turn these business trips into mini-vacations by using personal leave and paying the difference. It was a huge perk – skiing all over the Western U.S., visiting with friends, seeing new cities, etc.

One trip with Doris was to attend a technical meeting in Udine, Italy. We traveled through Germany, Switzerland, Italy and Austria. It was our first trip to Europe and was full of adventure, intrigue and suspense.

In spite of not knowing any of the languages, we traveled through strange countries by train and saw some fantastic sights. We also met colleagues in Italy and saw the sights in Florence, Rome and Venice.

I had been asked to attend the meeting by the Air Force Office of Special Investigation (AFOSI) and had the opportunity to meet some Eastern European scientists, but that turned out to be only a small part of the education we got while traveling through foreign lands. During that visit, numerous people were murdered in a shootout in a neighboring town, the Italian government collapsed and there was a national strike with crowds marching through the streets carrying red banners bearing a hammer and sickle. Otherwise, we literally knocked around Europe for nearly an entire month enjoying the adventure. We ordered food by pointing at the plates of other patrons, visited salt mines, entered huge ice caves, hiked to castles and traveled up the Rhine by boat – what a trip it was. In fact, both Doris and I felt it to be one of the all-time best trips we have ever experienced.

When we first moved to Tehachapi the weather conditions were perfect for wildflowers, which resulted in the area's best floral display in over 30 years – it was truly fantastic. One of my climbing partners from Seattle, Rick Knight, decided to move in with us for awhile that spring.

In exchange for room and board, I made an agreement with Rick that he would work two hours a day on some landscaping projects around the house. He also did some work for another rocket lab employee who was building his house from a kit. Unfortunately, Rick managed to run a tractor into the side of that house during the job. Occasionally, Rick would jump a train to Bakersfield and visit some friends he made there. On one trip, the boxcar he was riding in caught on fire – go figure.

Rick was a huge asset around our home – the ground was as hard as rock and we had a difficult time setting posts into the ground for the dog kennel.

Rick and I also managed to smoke prodigious quantities of bad pot while watching Roller Derby. We watched so much of it we could pick out the villains and heroes – scary! I would pay $100 for a one half kilo of Mexican marijuana – that should say something about the quality.

One night we were talking and I jokingly told Rick I wanted him to start digging a hole for the swimming pool we wanted in the center of our backyard – he moved out within a week.

While still with us, Rick decided to build a hang glider from a kit. When finished, every attempt to get it airborne was futile. We tried every hill in the neighborhood and finally drove to the top of a small mountain in Golden Hills. We then made a death pact (i.e., if you do it – I will do it, sort of thing) and drew straws to see who would go first. To my relief, Rick won.

A slight breeze came up and within two steps down the hill Rick was flying more than 100 feet above the ground. Holy s…, I thought, I was next.

I had recently finished an advanced degree in aeronautics and fully understood just how narrow the stall window was for the Rogallo wing design of the hang glider. I was terrified.

When my turn came, I tried to stay a few feet above the ground, but crashed at least three times just getting down that stupid hill. To the best of my knowledge, we were the first to ever hang-glide in the Tehachapi area.

Rick went on to own and fly three state-of-the-art gliders and became a good hang-glider pilot in Alaska.

Being a pothead in Tehachapi required me to maintain an interesting balancing act in my life. I was serious about my job and didn't want my private life to interfere with it, so I sort of led a double life. Our local sheriff was a real stickler when it came to the evil herb and on more than one occasion he made news for busting someone for possession or growing the stuff.

He once arrested a guy after discovering he had smoking paraphernalia in his backpack. Another was nailed for having a single roach in his car after being pulled over for a tail light violation.

Since my neighbor and I enjoyed a toke once in awhile and I had marijuana growing in my attic, I became somewhat paranoid.

Rick once observed, "Tehachapi is a town of ropers and dopers – and there are a lot more ropers than dopers."

I also learned a lesson on how not to try to set things straight with one's neighbor, no matter how loud and annoying his motorcycle was. Calling in the sheriff was not an option, but I did it anyway.

My neighbor happened to be the son of the local supermarket owner and was rather well known in town. That did not matter to the sheriff.

"Just because they are family," the sheriff announced, "I don't want you to think we are not going to enforce the law here."

I guess you can imagine how that went. Following the sheriff's visit, my neighbor and his motorcycle punk friend sought revenge by firing dirt plumes over my house. They did this by lifting the rear wheel on their bikes, revving their engines and then dropping the tire into the soft dirt – pointed directly at my house.

Lesson learned – better to suck it up and try to work things out with your neighbors.

By coincidence, I met Wayne Klinger at a Halloween costume party. Doris and I dressed as … what else, climbers. He came straight up to me and introduced himself and his lady friend, hoping I actually was a mountaineer. Once that was established, he asked if I'd take him climbing and from that point on we became good friends. Wayne proved to be a good climber right off the bat and we ended up doing many excursions together.

Interestingly enough, prior to my meeting Klinger, I had noticed a want ad in the newspaper advertising for nude models. In a small rural town, such a request can be considered a no-no. It turned out Wayne was the one running the ad and the woman who answered it happened to be his date at the costume party.

But the real irony was the lady happened to be married to someone from a prominent family in Tehachapi and her affair with Wayne wasn't going over well with the local populace. In fact, before Wayne was eventually run out of town, she told us the local married sheriff was having an affair with one of her girlfriends – small world.

Living in the foothills also allowed me the opportunity to work on some other projects, such as the fantastic coaster cart with a 4:1 reduction brake I built. It, too, proved to be great fun as we'd take it on moonlight rides doing 30 miles per hour while sitting six inches off the ground. Did I mention I built it for the kids?

We started attending the Lutheran Church in Tehachapi and I began pestering the pastors with questions that must have driven them nuts. One I remember was my inquiry as to whether or not the Virgin Mary could have been a hoax. I asked if they thought this was a young girl who found herself pregnant and then cooked up this clever story to cover her indiscretion, or did they actually believe in the Immaculate Conception? These were some of the ways I invented to entertain myself.

Long walks in the sparsely populated areas near our home were the norm. One thing I especially enjoyed in Tehachapi was watching the full moon rise over the hazy valley during the spring, summer and fall months. I also purchased a crude eight inch reflector telescope with high quality optics to do some serious star gazing, then extensively modified the mount to improve its function. The relatively dark skies over Tehachapi revealed many objects and the observations were quite rewarding.

My primary activities while living in Tehachapi were climbing, skiing and surfing. We made many family camping trips in conjunction with these activities.

Since we camped often, I searched for a used camper trailer so we would not have to sleep on the ground all the time. We eventually bought a small trailer from a fellow at work. It was a 13 foot long Serro Scotty which had been used as a dog house in his back yard for the past year or so. For a purchase price of $200, we had our first RV – the Dog Trailer.

After extensive remodeling, we spent over 75 nights per year in that thing for the next ten years and it was a big improvement over tent camping. Our camp was usually a "hippie" affair with many privacy screens consisting of airline blankets hanging on nylon lines surrounding our campsite.

During our second summer in Tehachapi, Nelson and Linda Walker re-entered our lives. Having been friends when we lived in Seattle, they had moved to the Bay Area of California and we frequently visited and climbed together.

I will never forget Wayne's 32nd birthday. He was visiting and Linda and Nelson were there as well. After hiking to some local petroglyphs, we discovered it was Wayne's birthday and the ladies decided to bake him a cake. He had always sort of hit on them and this was payback time. Arriving at the table was a cake in the shape of testicles and a penis with "F ... You 32" decorating its top.

Over the years in Tehachapi, I did a lot of bouldering around the house, cut and split many cords of firewood with Jim Townsend, took the family backpacking, sailed to Catalina Island with friends from work and poached some quail from Golden Hills. In particular, one memorable trip was a deer hunt with Durwood Trasher, a friend from work. He loaned me a 30-06 rifle and taught me how to use it. Once we arrived in the Sierra, I struck off by myself in quest of Bambi's father. Being stoned, I inadvertently discharged a round which hit a rock nearby and ricocheted all around me – I felt like I was in a bad western movie. I immediately removed the bolt and decided to hike the rest of the day. I really don't like killing things anyway.

I eventually reached a point where I wanted to quit using marijuana. I felt it had a grip on me and wasn't sure I could shake it. In the middle of all this, Shawn, who was six years old at the time, asked me if there was a God. I said I was not sure and asked him why he would ask. He responded by saying if I did not know whether or not there was a God, why were we going to church?

I told him it was a good question and I would try to find an answer. The events that followed during the next year were astounding. My immediate reaction to Shawn's question was that Jesus was not the answer. I had been going to church off and on my entire life and it did not seem obvious to me that Jesus was, indeed, God. I did not dismiss Jesus from the search; I just felt there must be more to it than that.

I truly valued the opinions of a couple of co-workers in this regard. Bob Geisler and Tuck Bohemer really did steer me in the correct direction and a lot of what they said made good sense. In addition, Pastor Marv Anderson was extremely patient with me. I would get stoned and go to adult membership class at the Lutheran Church and blast away with any question that came to mind. Jesus was hanging around in the wings, but I needed more.

I decided to venture on a spiritual quest for the truth and prayed that God would reveal himself to me in some tangible way. My thought process was, if I could be 80 percent certain on 80 percent of the issues relating to God, I would believe.

At this time, the boss of my boss came by my office and asked me to tell him a little about myself. Since I had been thinking about this for some time, I went to the blackboard and drew this sketch.

I had begun to form a vision as to where I wanted to go with my life and I came up with this four point model – Family, Career, Sports and Service. As the model shows, these four points intersected at the middle. Overarching these four items was my spiritual life. I knew when I had that part right, everything else ran more smoothly. When I operated in this mode, I felt satisfaction and at peace. In fact, these were my perfect days. When  the other four were out of balance with the spiritual, things did not seem to go right and my life became less satisfying.

On a trip to meet Reid to ski at Bend, OR in January 1976, we had a horrible car accident. It was a foggy, cold morning and Doris was driving with the Dog Trailer in tow on an ice covered road with a steep slope on the right-hand side descending 100 feet or so into a raging river. Out of nowhere, a truck towing a trailer hauling a big Caterpillar tractor slowly pulled onto the highway on the left about 100 feet in front of us. Doris stiffened up, locked her arms on the steering wheel and straight-lined braked as best she could while I turned and shoved the kids down in the back seat.

We slammed into the side of the truck and were basically wedged underneath the trailer containing the tractor. As the truck continued to pull forward, our station wagon was literally ground in half. Amazingly, we all appeared to be unhurt.

Following the accident, Doris and I agreed it was a "peaceful" event and we felt God had been in the front seat with us throughout the accident. I knew for the first time there was a God. Lesson learned when dealing with God – be careful what you pray for.

Following a quick settlement on our totaled vehicle, we bought a used low mileage Datsun 510 wagon. Little did we know Doris would suffer extreme pain from a classic whiplash scenario over the next year and, of course, since we had settled the claim before the symptoms revealed themselves, there was no recourse for medical bills or other compensation.

Right after the accident, Reid came out of his way and picked us up to take us to Portland, where we rented a car and finished the business portion of our trip to Seattle. During this trip I was introduced to Eastern Mysticism by an individual who could best be described as a "drug priest." I dove full on into the teachings of Baba Ram Dass – an ex-sidekick of LSD guru Timothy Leary. I would later meet Ram Dass face-to-face in Los Angeles, deepening my conviction there was, indeed, a spiritual otherworld out there.

By this time, I was praying for a deeper spiritual experience and the Datsun provided the perfect medium. Over several months, it fell apart piece by piece – first the head gasket, then the wheel bearings, the water pump and on and on. Finally, when it was time for our big family ski trip to Mammoth, the wheel bearings failed on the trailer - unbelievable. So while Doris and the boys skied the first day, I fixed the trailer. I was becoming a pretty good mechanic.

This whole experience turned out to be a sort of meditation type of thing and resulted in an increased internal peace.

I followed up my spiritual pursuits by studying Carlos Castaneda, Native American shamanism and virtually every form of mysticism I could uncover. The mixing of pot with these investigations led me to deeper and deeper convictions that God was quite real, co-existed with us here on earth and life was indeed eternal. I managed to get pretty far out there trying to leave my body, practicing extremely deep meditation and even attempting to change the direction of the wind.

After four years at the Rocket Propulsion Laboratory, I felt I had been successful in my career.[9]

Our home in the foothills of Tehachapi was fixed up nicely, both inside and out - an amazing achievement for our young family. We took frequent short trips to the beach for surfing, hiked along the Kern River and took extended vacations all over the USA and even to Europe. From both a professional and worldly standpoint – things were great.

As I previously pointed out, my vision circa 1967 was for a successful life based on the following prioritized goals: earn a bachelor of science degree in aerospace engineering, secure a job which paid at least $9,000 a year, achieve some sort of world-class greatness in climbing and maintain a solid, traditional family. I had really achieved these goals and felt on top of the world. I literally had it all – advanced degrees with honors, a terrific great-paying job, a decent climbing resume and a super family life. Little did I know how much I had deluded myself into believing we had arrived at the top.

I also managed to get in some serious trouble at work regarding voucher irregularities from my numerous TDY travels. That ultimately led to investigations by the Air Force Office of Special Investigation (AFOSI) and the FBI. Bottom line – the paranoia associated with being stoned most of the time combined with the recent Watergate scandal, led me to believe I was going to jail for a long time. I seriously considered taking off with the family and pets in the Dog Trailer, leaving everything behind and starting over in Canada.

The most amazing thing about all of this was that I was at the top of my game, living a double life (i.e., drug use and work) and knew none of it really mattered. It was all material stuff and as long as I had my family and some sort of relationship with God – that was all that was important. I was truly ready to give it all up and move on.

The investigation into voucher fraud was in full swing and I felt my secret clearance might be in jeopardy if they uncovered my pot use during the investigation. In the middle of it all, I received an offer of employment at the Los Alamos National Laboratory in Northern New Mexico. I had always wanted to work there – it was the top dog in research and development, as well as advanced computing techniques and I really liked the area.

I set out on a trip to interview for the position and vividly remember driving in a government car up the mesa upon which the laboratory is located while smoking a joint. I recall thinking about the ongoing investigation at the rocket lab and praying, God please show me what to do. I completely surrendered to God at that moment and told Him I would do whatever He told me to do and that I fully accepted Him in my life in whatever form he chose to manifest Himself – no conditions whatsoever.

Should I escape to Canada, stay at the rocket lab and face the music, or take the job at Los Alamos which would result in even further investigation for the required clearance?

I never did hear the thunderous voice from on high telling me to "move to Los Alamos." But I did receive absolute direction in a variety of ways, all of which could have been coincidental.

After the job interview, I skied at Taos for two days before returning home. Upon arrival, Doris said she couldn't believe what had happened. Someone wanted to buy our house and it was not even on the market at the time. And furthermore, I was unable to sell it two years prior when I was offered a rotational assignment in Washington DC. Doris and I decided to drive out to Los Alamos and check out housing and schools, etc.

Available housing was at a real premium in the area at the time, but we easily found a good home in our price range with excellent schools for our boys. We made a contingent offer and then returned home to find we had an offer of $49,000 on our house if we decided to sell. To make a long story short – every obstacle for moving to Los Alamos vanished, with the exception of the investigation issues.

I felt as if I were in a dense forest and could only see light by looking up. And while in the midst of this forest, a clear and narrow path cut through the trees leading directly to Los Alamos. So, in complete faith, I gave notice to the rocket lab and made arrangements to begin employment in early November 1976.

Once it was announced I would be leaving, a fellow employee suggested Doris and I attend a marriage encounter program offered in the Los Angeles area. I thought to myself, no way, my marriage is in great shape and I sure don't need that sort of thing. But he persisted and I decided to sign up, only to find there was a six month waiting list.

Somehow, they fit us in due to our plans to leave the area. Les and Barb Tepe volunteered to watch our boys and before I knew it, we were off to a life-changing weekend. I had been praying this would be a spiritual experience and lead us closer to God.

After the two hour drive to Los Angeles and just as we arrived at the hotel where the event was to be held, we were told we had an emergency situation with one of our boys. As it turned out, while in route, our younger son had fallen out of a tree and broken both bones in his arm right above the wrist. By the time we received the message, Todd was at the hospital.

We gave the doctor permission for the necessary surgery. After the surgery, the doctor insisted we return to the hospital as soon as possible to be with our son. I explained our situation and told him Todd was with people I had confidence in and we would not be home for two days. The doctor was very critical of my decision, but I told him the worst for Todd was over and I felt I was where I was supposed to be.

I knew some sort of spiritual warfare was going on and some entity was trying to keep us from this seminar. I was fully prepared for this encounter and had brought a one ounce lid of pot so I could stay fully stoned for the entire weekend. What followed was not at all what I expected.

By the end of the weekend, we both had experienced a miracle in our lives and had a personal encounter with Jesus Christ. Keep in mind, this was the last thing I desired – I wanted God and not some substitute. Additionally, the drug high induced by smoking a lot of pot was completely replaced by an incredible spiritual high.

Well, at this point I knew Jesus was the real deal. He was the one with whom I wanted to continue my walk. It was only after this weekend that I could see how Satan had cleverly worked his way into my life. To this day, I try not to make judgments on the path of enlightenment chosen by others, but I know "as for me and my household, we will serve the Lord. Joshua 24:15." And that means inviting Jesus into my heart and doing my best to live a life worthy of His calling.

The beauty of all this was Doris and I shared this experience together. I believe Doris has always been a Christian and, furthermore, without this conversion on my part our marriage was destined for divorce. Bottom line – I never did get 80 percent convinced on 80 percent of the issues related to God, but I did indeed find Jesus and have never looked back.

Within weeks of the seminar, we moved to Los Alamos and the vision for my life and family would undergo a major revision.

The Land of Enchantment

We stumbled into the rural mountain village of Cordova in the isolated Truchas area of New Mexico. Lo and behold, the place turned out to be the home town of one of the lab techs I knew from work, Hermanio Cordova. The friendship between our two families grew. One year they invited us up for a big celebration to be held in their village on Good Friday. It started in the morning with a pilgrimage and ended with a midnight service conducted by the Penitente in the Catholic Church. The church, complete with ten foot thick adobe walls and a dirt floor, was quite primitive.

The Penitente is a sort of moral police force that still practices un-usual forms of penitence including near-death crucifixion. So here we were, midnight in a small village attending a service where we were the only Anglos present. When the Penitente enters the church, the lights are turned out and the room is filled with the sounds of clanging chains and noise makers. During the entire time I kept thinking, let's see, if they are going to crucify someone, who would they pick – a friend or a total stranger?

In a total move of faith, we were off to New Mexico. I had accepted a job as a staff member in the Structural Analysis and Test Section of the Weapons Group (WX-3) which was contingent upon my obtaining a Department of Energy (DOE) Q clearance (essentially Top Secret).

The voucher fraud investigation was still unresolved (AFOSI and FBI). I was still smoking pot daily and was now being investigated for a new clearance by DOE, et al. Negative outcomes in these areas could have serious consequences – even to the point of making me unemployable in my chosen field of specialization. Pending my clearance, I was assigned to the "Leper Colony" holding area outside the gates of the WX site.

Todd's arm was still in a cast and we would now have to find a new doctor to continue his treatment. We bought a house in White Rock, NM (a small town five miles from Los Alamos) for $68,000. It measured 1,850 square feet and sat on a quarter acre, which served our needs quite well.

We started attending the Lutheran Church in Los Alamos. While attending a Bible study group we were introduced to Jim and Blanche Caldwell. Jim worked at the WX site and held weekly Bible studies in his home. While at work, Jim would come by on his lunch hour and visit me in the Leper Colony.

His leadership led us to a spirit filled non-denominational church in Santa Fe and to my giving up smoking pot. I was not physically addicted to marijuana, but was psychologically dependent on the substance. I found it extremely difficult to quit and had tried to quit numerous times before.

I definitely disliked my dependence on the herb as a result of my habitual use, but felt hopeless each time I tried to stop. I confided my problem to Jim and he advised me to use prayer to help in my struggle. With Jesus in my life and the desire to have the Holy Spirit alive in me, quitting pot turned out to be amazingly effortless.

A few days later, I smoked my last weed at a Dave Brubeck concert, then simply quit. The next evening, Jim and Blanche came over to check on me and see how I was doing. During their visit they noticed Doris was not feeling well and asked what was wrong.

I explained to them about the automobile accident the previous year and how the whiplash had resulted in severe migraine headaches. Each one took about a week to go away.

Jim immediately said they believed Jesus could heal Doris and asked if it would be all right to lay hands on her and pray. I was very skeptical, but reluctantly said OK. To make things worse, he asked me to lay hands on her with them as they prayed – this made me extremely uncomfortable.

Afterwards, there was no apparent change in her condition, so we bid each other goodnight and went off to bed. The next morning, while Doris was driving me up to the Leper Colony, it occurred to me to ask how she felt.

She replied, "I hadn't thought about it, but I feel fine." In fact, she has never experienced another attack of that type since. Just another coincidence, I guess!

I often contacted Jim Caldwell, especially when I needed prayer support. I truly valued his friendship and guidance.

During this period, the voucher fraud investigation faded away - another answer to prayer. The investigation and the way it was handled by the authorities involved, was truly one of the worst memories of my life. They would toy with an individual's mind and take incredible tangential paths designed to mentally torture the person in every way possible – and they were very effective. In fact, I was never officially notified when it was over – only by inference did I come to realize it had been dropped.

A close friend from the Seattle Explorer Post, Peter Flewelling, came to visit us at Christmas. Prior to giving up pot, I had asked him to bring some dope with him. I was afraid to try to score any while the investigation continued. When he arrived, I announced I had quit pot.

Peter looked puzzled. I went into considerable detail about all the events of the past year and witnessing to him was like BBs bouncing off of bulletproof glass. During our discussions we smoked one joint together.

To make a long story short: in a period of four days which included a Bible study, a New Year's Eve Christian party and a Full Gospel Businessmen's Fellowship International (FGBMFI) meeting, Peter was saved and spirit-filled. Neither of us has ever smoked pot since and we're both still serving Jesus to the best of our abilities.

After two and a half months in the Leper Colony, I received the dreaded call to come down to security to answer a few questions concerning my background. Doris came and picked me up from the remote site and drove me to the administrative area. I was very anxious and just prayed the entire trip. When we arrived, I had decided to tell the truth, period.

After reading me my rights, which was very scary as it included things like, we can and will turn anything we find in this interview over for prosecution; the young lady started a tape recorder. Immediately her countenance changed from pleasant to harsh and she said in a demanding voice, "When is the last time you smoked dope."

I was truly speechless and tried my best to put words together to answer the question. At first, all that would come out was uh, uh, uh. Then I finally said, "I quit one month ago and slipped up once two weeks ago, but haven't had any since then. Furthermore, I have friends who can independently confirm this."

She immediately turned off the tape recorder and said in a pleasant tone of voice, "I believe if you tell the truth you will get your clearance."

For over an hour they probed my entire history of marijuana usage. When it was over they informed me if I did indeed receive the clearance and if it was discovered I had been using any illegal substances from this point forward, my employment with the laboratory would be immediately terminated.

Within a week, I received my Q clearance and assumed my work assignments from the group where I was sent. Through the Freedom of Information Act, I was able to obtain the investigation reports. I determined my next-door neighbor in Tehachapi, the father of the kid who terrorized the neighborhood with his motorcycle, had told authorities he thought he'd seen me smoking pot during a party at our house.

Bottom line: I could have lied, but I didn't. This gave me a clean slate and plenty of incentive to never smoke pot again. Another coincidence – isn't it amazing how that works.

A rather funny thing happened around that same time. After the Marriage Encounter weekend, I had decided to give ten percent of my gross income to the church (i.e., tithing). We were sending the money to the Lutheran Church in Tehachapi until we found our church home in New Mexico. After several months of this tithing, I received a telephone call from Marv Anderson, the pastor in Tehachapi.

After a short conversation, he asked what was going on in our lives. I explained the events that had taken place – receiving Jesus, Doris' healing, quitting pot, baptism in the Holy Spirit and so on.

He replied, "I am excited for you both, but I wish you would be a little more Lutheran."

So I said, "Do you want me to start giving $10 per month again?"

His reply was "Well, not that Lutheran!"

I truly valued the role this man played in my walk toward the Lord – he was quite patient with me and I will never forget it.

We had a memorable experience in New Mexico when our boys participated in a church Christmas pageant. It was truly a neat program put on by Terry, a young man who ran the children's ministry, complete with kids riding on the backs of other kids dressed as donkeys. Shawn (then about seven years old) was playing the part of the angel Gabriel. As he bounded in to tell the Virgin Mary about the forthcoming Immaculate Conception, his halo fell from above his head winding up around his neck.

It was during this time Boy Scouts became an important part of our lives. Both of our boys were involved so it became a family affair. Doris was a den mother and later I became assistant scout master for the local troop. At various times I also was an assistant coach and umpire for Little League baseball.

I enjoyed the flexibility and professionalism at the lab – they were truly an enlightened employer and understood that motivation comes from within and the individual work ethic was more important than a "prescribed presence" in the office.

In the remote Los Alamos area, there were approximately 4,000 PhD's in a population of 20,000 people. The combination of an isolated community and a highly educated populace led to a rather screwed-up town. This became apparent in spades while working with the various youth groups filled with kids from broken homes and blended families. Doris drove a school bus for kindergarten through sixth grade and the stories she would relate about the students' behavior were amazing.

A lot of stuff happened about this time. We had to give away our Irish Setter, Dink, as he had developed a biting problem. I gave him to Tony Archuleta from the lab. He lived in a small Hispanic village named El Rito and said he needed a mean dog. While Dink was not actually mean, I had no option except to give him away.

Six months later, we visited Dink in El Rito and he was doing fine, but he wanted to return home with us – what a heartbreaker. We love all of our animals and they are a lot like our children. Giving one up is terribly difficult.

On a subsequent visit, we learned he had died, apparently from worms. During this second visit, we attended the local fiesta and Tony sort of took us under his wing and showed us around. There was a classic horse race – a quarter mile down a straight dirt road with lots of money changing hands in the pre-race betting scene.

One horse was a sandbag, a lower tier racehorse put in the mix and it created a huge stir. What a scene it turned out to be.

On another trip to the Truchas area, we stumbled into the rural mountain village of Cordova. This area had largely been isolated from the rest of the U.S.; in fact, National Geographic reported the villagers still spoke a long extinct Spanish dialect brought to the area centuries ago by the conquistadors.

Driving down the main street, a dirt road, we ran across a Hispanic fellow dressed in black and carrying a six-shooter in a holster. He proceeded to stare us down, big time. We avoided making eye contact with him as much as possible and detoured off on a side street where we stopped by a local wood carver's shop. Lo and behold, the shop turned out to be in the home of one of the lab techs I knew from work, Hermanio Cordova.

Unknown to us, his wife, Gloria, was a world renowned Santeria Carver. We discovered some of her work was even on display in the Smithsonian Museum.

We spent several hours visiting and bought some wood carvings. The friendship between our two families grew over the next few years and to this day, when visiting New Mexico, we always stop by to see Gloria and Hermanio. At one point they encouraged us to move to Cordova – they had a house they offered to sell us for next to nothing. We actually gave it a little thought before deciding against the move.

One year, they invited us up for a big celebration held in their village on Good Friday. It started in the morning with a pilgrimage to El Santuario, a church ten miles away held sacred by the locals. It holds special meaning because of its never-ending supply of dirt considered to have healing powers. The dirt comes from a hole in the floor of one of the sanctuary's antechambers.

Following the pilgrimage, there was a procession of sorts down the main street of Cordova to the church that involved Los Penitente carrying a sacred icon. The Penitente still practice unusual forms of penitence such as self-flagellation, covering themselves with honey and crawling through ant nests, having cactus tied to their bodies, etc. The most amazing part of this was their practice of near-death crucifixion.

It came to my attention that the Penitente was greatly feared by the local citizenry. During the procession the locals would share in the Penitente practices until they drew near. Once these men clad in white pants and hoods and whipping themselves on their bare backs came within earshot, the citizens immediately clammed up.

Following the ceremony and later, after dinner with the Cordova's, we attended a midnight service conducted by the Penitente held in the Catholic Church. The church itself was amazing. It had ten foot thick adobe walls at the base, a dirt floor and, in appearance, was both beautiful and primitive.

No Catholic priests were present during this Good Friday celebration as they do not recognize the Penitente or their practices. So here we were, midnight in a small Truchas village, attending a service where we were the only Anglos present.

In spite of my fears everything turned out fine – early in the service the moderator said in English "and we welcome our Anglo friends." This immediately made us feel at peace and it turned out to be an unforgettable and positive experience.

In fact the experiences we shared with friends in small villages surrounding Los Alamos were true treasures. Not many folks are invited to these types of events, especially laboratory workers and their families.

In general, at least back then, lab workers were viewed as being relatively wealthy and having a huge chip on their shoulders due to their self-aggrandizement. Since Doris and I were sort of out of the "hippy mold" and neither of us took ourselves seriously, we more or less fit in with the local culture.

We decided to build a custom house in White Rock. We sold our home on Brice for $74,500, moved into a rental, bought a lot, hired a designer/contractor and started building. We had signed up to do a lot of the grunt work and the construction contractor turned out to be the employer of my climbing partner Bill "Willie" Spencer. So Willie was working on the place during the day and frequently would come by to help Doris and me in the evening.

Others pitched in and, before too long, we moved into our dream home with incredible views over the Rio Grande Rift and the Sangre de Cristo Mountains. Watching the full moon rise there was something else.

On occasion, after one of the frequent summer thunderstorms, we would see spectacular rainbows – some even triple, from our deck. The 1,750 square foot house ended up costing us $95,000 and sat on one third acre. It was a passive solar design and was literally airtight – a wonderful, cozy home. We heated it with a wood-burning stove and our utility bills were next to nothing.

During the construction process, Doris bought a beautiful Irish Setter puppy for my birthday and we named her Heather Marie – she was a wonderful dog and a great running companion.

Around this time Willie asked me about a job at the lab. He had applied for a technician spot and was waiting for his clearance approval. I told him, whatever he did, tell them the truth.

When he was called in for his security interview, they asked him when was the last time he smoked dope and he replied, "About 20 minutes ago!" They told him to quit pot and come back in a couple of years.

By the way, he did finally land a job at the lab several years later and became an outstanding technician. Willie was very sharp and I am sure the lab benefited greatly from his tenure.

Work, church, climbing, skiing, skateboarding, rafting, Boy Scouts, building a house, local weekend family trips (Mesa Verde, Carlsbad Caverns, Guadalupe, White Sands, etc.) occupied our time in this remarkable area. Extended trips to Southern California to visit family and friends, camp and surf pretty much filled up the rest of our time.

In particular, skiing often at Pajarito Mountain was a wonderful recreational opportunity for the entire family. The boys had become great skiers and Shawn truly excelled in powder. Forays in the Dog Trailer to other ski resorts in the region were great fun.

On one particularly memorable trip to Southern California while towing the Dog Trailer, our Datsun burned a valve. Shortly after getting a ring and valve job and within 200 miles, a valve stem broke and destroyed the engine block. After a new engine, the car worked flawlessly until we sold it two years later. In the meantime we bought a Ford Bronco, with which we had lots of fun.

We did some local rafting[10], numerous long walks (White Rock and Los Alamos neighborhoods) and hikes. I was also able to do climbing routes in the Brazos and near Las Cruces.

In February of 1979, I decided to take the family to see the total solar eclipse in Northern Montana. Doris and the boys complained bitterly as we left White Rock in the Bronco with the Dog Trailer in tow. It was one of those - "This is stupid; it's the middle of the winter and no one wants to see this dumb thing anyway" - sort of events.

We made several stops at historical locations in transit. After the spectacular eclipse it became – "That's the neatest thing we have ever done" – all the way home. It was a fantastic family trip through frozen wastelands to see nature's greatest spectacle.

I attended technical meetings all over the USA[11]. One meeting in San Francisco took place right in the middle of the gay and lesbian protest over Dan White's manslaughter sentence for the double murder of the mayor and the gay city supervisor. This was truly amazing as we had never experienced anything of this sort. We were blown away by the open public affection between same-sex couples.

The lab and particularly the group I was assigned to, was an outstanding place to work – a totally professional and enjoyable environment. John Ruminer, my immediate supervisor, turned out to be a decent man and a great boss. By the end of my nearly four year tenure at the lab, I was made the manager of the Materials Testing Unit of the Structural Analysis and Test Section, had published several papers and even made a trip to Cambridge, England to attend a conference at the request of the CIA.

The University of Cambridge conference held August 1979 at Kings College (this is where Newton developed gravitational theory) was a fantastic experience. I was able to make contact with a high-ranking Russian academician. He was in charge of a large manufacturing operation and was negotiating with the Japanese for the purchase of Instron test frames. He even had a KGB handler with him.

After joining him for dinner in the dining hall, he invited Doris and me to his room for an after hour's party. This consisted of rounds of vodka with the standard "tva-jó zda-ró-vye" toast.

Since we don't typically drink alcohol, we became totally blasted in a few minutes and the entire evening was rather surreal. The main negotiation was over how many liters of ethyl alcohol per day would be included in the agreement. This was ostensibly for cleaning the instruments, but in reality it was a huge perk for the academician who would likely use it for his private alcoholic binges.

After the affair, when we left to go to our bed and breakfast at the home of one of the university porters, we literally could not find our way out of the college.

The following day we had dinner with the Chinese delegation – this was the first international technical meeting the communist party had supported and it was amusing to watch them attempt to use a fork. Interestingly enough after our contact with the Chinese, the Russian academician was immediately pulled from the meeting. From then on I was continually stalked by three KGB agents (heavy-set men in gray suits and, in general, quite obvious).

After the conference, we traveled through Wales and via ferry to Ireland. I had been invited by the University College, Cork, to present an honorarium lecture. Professor Mike Quinlan, who had been a post doctoral fellow for me at the rocket lab, showed us around Ireland, which was a rewarding experience. We even visited his uncle's farm and met an elderly woman whose life had been severely affected by the great famine – fascinating stories.

I received an inquiry from a headhunter regarding a position at Xerox Corporation in Webster, NY. The job description interested me because I wanted to go into management and this position would be a big increase in that type of responsibility. This was a difficult decision, since I thrived in my job at the lab and loved living in New Mexico. We had only been in the new house we built for a year. I loved our beautiful, energy-efficient home with its spectacular view.

After a preliminary interview in New Mexico, I traveled to New York for an onsite interview and gave a presentation on my research at the lab. This led to a job offer and after careful consideration and a house-hunting trip, I accepted the position as the manager of the Fusing Technology Area with a $48,000 annual salary, a $10,000 signing bonus and a June 1980 start date.

One issue which contributed to this decision was the fact Doris did not like living in the Los Alamos environment. We both felt the change in location would be beneficial by allowing us to raise our boys in a more traditional community.

Our home in White Rock sold in a single day for $125,000. We purchased a 110 year old schoolhouse in Victor, NY for $122,000.

During the New Mexico years, my vision for life changed significantly. Although never formally written down back then, the prioritized goals were clear in my mind and had become as follows: my relationship with the Lord, my relationship with my family, my job and then sports. Only later in my life would I actually construct the vision these goals support. I had the process a bit backwards.

Upstate New York

It was a Friday morning, May 15, 1981. I arrived at work as usual, about 45 minutes early. In April, we had taken a 15 day family vacation to California and I truly dreaded returning to work at Xerox. I felt the job was unreal and I had surrendered it to God's will – I did not know how I would ever be able to satisfy my employer.

My normal routine was to read a little Scripture and then start my work for the day. At 8 a.m. I was called into a meeting in my boss' office. When I arrived, there was a representative from Human Resources present and George began by asking me to resign, or accept a demotion to a Technical Specialist (35 percent pay cut). I selected resignation.

I negotiated a seven month severance package, cleared out my office and left. I was truly shocked and did not see this coming.

Moving to Victor, NY, was a mixed bag – I loved the rolling countryside and rural environment of our schoolhouse, but lamented leaving Northern New Mexico. I had left a month ahead of the family to start the job. Then I returned by air to pick them up and drive back east.

I still recall the flight back to Los Alamos; I was really choked up knowing we were leaving a very unique and spectacular area.

The move to New York with the family turned out to be a great experience. We traveled across the Northern United States and Eastern Canada and had many memorable stops along the way.[12]

In particular, spending the Fourth of July in 1980 at Mitchell, SD was a fantastic experience. The Fourth has always been one of my favorite holidays – I love pyrotechnics, especially the illegal type. In South Dakota, apparently everything is legal, so we purchased a bunch of fireworks, scoped out the Corn Palace and checked into a motel.

I asked at the desk if there was a public fireworks display nearby and was told to go out to the lake at dusk. We arrived at the lake around 7 p.m., set out a blanket and entered the "Twilight Zone."

It was like World War III – absolutely unbelievable. Armed with tons of firecrackers, rockets and aerial displays and a performance enhanced by copious quantities of alcohol, many locals proceeded to try and kill everybody within range. Shooting rockets at the boats on the lake, tossing M80's at each other and lighting off bricks of 1,000 firecrackers at a time really added to the excitement.

In the midst of this, the official aerial display started complete with the obligatory oohs and ahs. Amazingly, no one was hurt and everybody was dazzled by the experience – a truly unforgettable evening.

Once back in New York with the family, we settled into a motel for two weeks before moving into our new home. The 110 year old extensively re-modeled schoolhouse was actually a black hole. It consumed all our spare time and cash.

It had a swimming pool, which was great two months out of the year, but required lots of maintenance and attention. There was an acre of grass which you could literally hear growing at the rate of two inches a week. The property had a well that couldn't produce enough water to supply the house and much of the remodeling was improperly done.

For example, when we tossed a couple of steaks on the Jenn-Air range located on an island in the center of the kitchen, exhaust suddenly began to spew from under the cabinet. The range had never been vented to the outside – it was just dropped into the cabinet top.

Climbing down the 35 foot deep, four foot in diameter, rock lined hand-dug well was another memorable experience. After lifting the cover and discovering more than 50 garter snakes, I noticed there was a considerable amount of debris in the bottom. Donning a wetsuit and descending into this spooky, dark, wet environment was actually quite scary.

After cleaning the bottom and sending buckets of junk topside, I climbed out and now knew firsthand what the expression "colder than a well digger's ass" meant.

The house was heated by electric, baseboard heaters. With 3,500 square feet of interior floor space and 16 foot high ceilings, heating the schoolhouse this way would have bankrupted Donald Trump in a single winter.

We modified the two fireplaces to use wood-burning inserts and purchased five cords of wood the first fall. Cleaning the chimneys on the steeply pitched roof of this two-story equivalent building was very exciting, not to mention having to purchase the chimney cleaning brushes.

To deal with the grass and snow, I bought a used 16 horsepower tractor with a 48 inch mower deck, 42 inch snow blower, tire chains, wheel weights and a trailer to haul the firewood to the garage, as needed. We cleared another half acre and seeded it with grass, removed dead trees, eradicated poison ivy, fixed the small barn, repaired the water heater, etc., etc., etc. It was never ending – spending all summer getting ready for winter – and all winter getting ready for summer.

The pluses of rural Upstate living definitely outweighed the toil associated with the environment. Our neighbors were wonderful and always pitched in to help, often without asking whenever we appeared overwhelmed with fix-it tasks.

Jim Torpey and his dad, Gene, were among the nicest people on earth and ingenious regarding repairing equipment – like the tractor mower deck that gave up the ghost.

Ralph and Dorothy Baker were another amazing couple – they were about 80 years old when we moved in next door and a tenth of a mile away. The schoolhouse was located on the corner of their farm and their daughter Effie was in the last class to complete primary education in this one-room school.

In spite of the major remodeling, the home still looked exactly like an old schoolhouse – complete with the original bell and "School District 10" painted above the front door. The entry floors were original rock in which arrowheads had been embedded and there were separate girls and boys entrances. The classroom area had hardwood floors with slate sub-floors, a cobble rock foundation and solid mahogany siding.

Once the East Bloomfield schools started, our boys would ring the school bell to let the other kids in the neighborhood know the bus was arriving. We also used the school bell to call the boys home when they were out playing. Once, thinking it was still a functioning school, we had a total stranger walk right into the house to ask directions.

We first met Ralph while walking through the 90 acre field of seven foot tall corn planted on his farm that surrounded the schoolhouse. After first moving to rural New York, anytime Doris, the boys and I walked between the cornrows or on someone else's farm, Doris would say we were going to get in trouble for doing it. Right after I assured her this would not be the case, we saw Ralph walking straight for us as we emerged from the tall corn. As appropriate, Doris muttered, "I told you so."

But much to our delight, after introducing ourselves, Ralph said we could walk anywhere on his farm at any time. We subsequently made similar arrangements with our other neighbors in the area.

During the summer, we frequently took all-day family walks with the dogs going across lots and seeing many natural wonders – open fields, woods, ponds, lakes and tons of wildlife. Fall in Upstate New York is unbelievable. The colors are dazzling.

The winters amazed us. Lake effect storms were legendary and 40 inches of snow in a single storm was not uncommon. With lots of snow, we did some fantastic ski touring. Many times, we were out all day and would see lots of wildlife and very few people or cars.

Particularly memorable was Christmas Day 1980. After opening presents, which included touring skis, the boys and I skied over to Isabel's Woods and found a huge wasp nest. After obtaining permission to cut it down, we took it home where it still hangs to this day.

In the springtime, we would watch the maple syrup harvest and production. We would take long drives to see the foliage come alive. It was indeed a four season environment.

Meanwhile on the job front, the environment at Xerox was surrealistic – truly amazing. While waiting to move the family to New York to join me, I was invited by my boss's boss, to play racquetball after work. I had never played the game, but had played squash once and had played handball in college, so I agreed to go thinking it might be fun.

While driving to his club's facility, he let me know in no uncertain terms that he was a very important person at Xerox. As one of the few vice presidents, he felt he was destined to move rapidly to the top. What happened next I will never forget.

As we entered the completely enclosed court, he closed the door, folded the handle flush with the wall and said, "The battlefield." It turned out to be a memorable evening and a rude, accurate introduction to senior management at Xerox.

Right before I joined the firm, Xerox was gearing up to avoid the "Honda Syndrome" that hit the motorcycle industry. The company was attempting to stop the Japanese manufacturers from moving up the copier "food chain" into the high-volume copy business, where the big bucks were.

Both IBM and Kodak caught Xerox off guard by introducing products in the lucrative high volume market. It was a coup de grâce move that created an environment at Xerox that I could only compare to being inside an active washing machine.

There were constant changes. In nine months, I had to deal with 25 different projects with more than 50 different employees. It became impossible to stay on top of things while trying to learn each new product and function in a totally unfamiliar culture. I was trapped in an up-the-line management situation with my style of responsible delegation.

I preferred letting the people who did the work take the credit for a job well done. My job was to take on the responsibility of any problems that might arise. My way of thinking was if I would make my boss and my employees look good, then by default I'd look good also.

My boss and mentor Ron Andrews, who had both an MBA and PhD, was a great boss. In fact, while working for him my first six month review rated me as "consistently exceeds expectations in technology functions." My underlying problem at Xerox was that I was sort of set up in this particular job.

I had replaced a gentleman by the name of John Trainer, who was well liked by everyone except apparently, management. John stayed on at Xerox until he found employment elsewhere and he and I never had issues. Problems arose, however, from a senior technical specialist by the name of Rabin, who felt he should have been promoted into the position I was hired to fill.

My boss's secretary Mary Ann who said soon after her husband suffered a heart attack, "I don't get heart attacks, I give them," was very close to Rabin.

George was a director within our division and a true piece of work. He literally shook most of the time and was a non-stop cigar smoker. When he unwrapped a cigar, he could barely put it in his mouth and light it because he shook so badly. Watching him made me nervous. To escape the tension of this environment, I would take long walks during lunch to relax and help maintain my sanity.

After nine months of reorganization, I was transferred to George who was close friends with both Rabin and Mary Ann. The stage was set.

Within two months I was asked to resign, which I did after negotiating my severance package. It included full salary for seven months, budget for an office and financial support to aid in finding new employment. The request to resign caught me completely off guard. I was truly shocked.

Before this happened I had considered looking for other employment, but wanted to succeed at Xerox if possible. Unfortunately, under the circumstances I did not succeed and this turned out to be another of my worst memories.

Also during this period, we had to put our 14 year old Poodle Whiz to sleep. He had fallen off the balcony in the schoolhouse and was fighting chronic infections caused by impacted teeth. I cried terribly over it and even today always choke up thinking of our first "baby." He was a great dog and this qualified as another one of those all-time worst memories.

Amazingly, George, the person I respected least at Xerox, suggested during my separation interview that I read "What Color is Your Parachute?" by Richard Bolles. I bought the book out of spite and it turned out to be one of those life-changing decisions. I learned a great deal about myself from following the exercises contained within that gem and also learned how to find a job.

Employment offers had always come my way without any real effort on my part. But this was different – I was unemployed in a geographical region where I had no real network and during a period when there was a local downturn in the economy. Once again, I was faced with losing everything, but with Jesus in my life it did not matter.

I found satisfaction knowing I had done my best, did not compromise myself and above all, my situation was not the result of any illegal activities. Furthermore, the training I received in my employment at Xerox and the trial by fire was more valuable to me personally than any MBA program in the country. I not only knew what my management style was and that it was valid, but I also knew what I wanted to embrace and avoid in future career positions. I definitely left Xerox a better and more confident person than when I had arrived 11 months earlier.

Maintaining my sanity during all this was not easy. I had been very active in a ministry known as Full Gospel Business Men's Fellowship International (FGBMFI) and frequently served as a keynote speaker for their dinner meetings. It was a testimony type ministry and I was asked to speak all over Upstate New York and even in Montreal, Canada.

The FGBMFI experience was tremendous and kept me focused on what was truly important in life. I had noticed whenever my spiritual path was on track - reading scripture, praying and keeping priorities straight - my life and accomplishments excelled in general and vis-à-vis.

We became very close friends with Ralph and Dorothy. Often during the winter, I would ski tour through Olnie's Woods and then meet Doris at their house to play cards. Frequently Gene and Harriet Torpey would join us and our fellowship together was great.

When we first met Ralph, he told me they were Christians. As it turns out, the only fellowship they had was in the form of Pat Robertson's TV ministry. We were literally the first friends they ever had who were practicing Christians.

Ralph once told me he was not from the area, which led me to believe he was from a long ways away. Later I learned he was born and raised about ten miles away, which to him was a great distance. He had never been farther from his home than across the border in Northern Pennsylvania and he had never flown in an airplane.

Basically, Ralph was an intelligent man and committed Christian who lived a sheltered life as a hardworking farmer. On one occasion, Ralph and Dorothy invited us to attend the South Perinton United Methodist Church. This was a small rural church established in 1837. It was located near his hometown where they were raised, married and would ultimately be buried.

Talk about the frozen chosen – this church was unreal. The congregation consisted of approximately 20 octogenarians, one younger couple and a rotating pastor. During the worship, Doris and I, the pastor and the younger couple were the only ones singing. The others were standing and simply holding the hymnals. During the sermon, well over 50 percent of the congregation fell sound asleep. After that experience, we frequently brought Ralph and Dorothy to church with us.

One evening, I was invited by FGBMFI to speak inside Attica Prison, so I invited Ralph to join me. At the prison, we were carefully searched and then led inside without the accompaniment of guards. The local FGBMFI leader served as our escort as we walked long distances through common areas until we reached the auditorium where the meeting would take place. We got lots of deadly stares and even saw men cross-dressed as women – it was a scary experience.

However, the ministry went fine and I became comfortable among the inmates present. I believe many of them were sincerely interested in following Jesus, but I also had a dozen or so tell me they were innocent and needed help to get out. In fact, no one suggested to me they were indeed guilty and had received the sentence they deserved. It proved to be an eye-opener for Ralph and me.

During the following summer, Ralph and Dorothy asked us to baptize them. We arranged for our pastor to join us in our backyard pool and started the ceremony. Ralph was no problem – he entered the swimming pool and I lowered him in and out of the water with ease.

Dorothy, however, was a different situation. She was a very slight built woman and when I attempted to lower her under the water, she literally bobbed like a cork and did so for quite a while. Ultimately, it all worked when the pastor joined me in using our combined strength to push her under the water. She then resurfaced like a breaching dolphin.

The summer of 1981, we took the couple to Rochester to see the Fourth of July fireworks. The show was spectacular over the city. It was the first time in Ralph's life he had seen a major fireworks display!

After an intense job search, lasting about two months, I started to feel depressed and sorry for myself. I had done everything I could and now was in the wait-and-see mode. It is rare when a professional gets a five and a half month hiatus right in the middle of his career, but that is exactly what happened. Had I known there would be a job waiting for me at the end of this sabbatical, I would have enjoyed it much more. I was literally worried I would have to pump gas in order to feed my family if everything did not turn out right.

I had no choice but to trust God – pray about it and turn it over to the Lord, which I did. But my nature was to worry about things from time to time.

As a family, we used the time productively by taking numerous local trips. We even chaperoned for the kids at school events. We also took an extended family trip in the Dog Trailer through the Northeast United States and Canada.[13] This included a 40 mile family canoe trip from Long Lake to Tupper Lake in the Adirondacks, complete with two portages, black flies and hurricane force winds – it was quite the adventure.

I became very involved in Scouts as an assistant scout master and was able to attend scout camp with Shawn that summer – what a neat experience it turned out to be. Watching my son in this environment was a great opportunity.

Shawn also signed up to attend the National Jamboree at Fort AP Hill, VA. In conjunction, Doris, Todd and I planned a trip in the Dog Trailer through Pennsylvania Dutch Country and Washington DC to meet Shawn at the Jamboree. After picking him up, we headed home via Philadelphia, New York City, Rhode Island and Massachusetts.

Shortly after we returned home, Ralph fell and broke his hip. They had leased out 90 acres of their farm, which was planted in field corn and they had the other ten acres planted in vegetables. They planned to sell the vegetables from a small stand located in their front yard.

Ralph was released from the hospital around the time the vegetables were ready to harvest. Unfortunately, he was basically immobile, so Doris, the boys and I all worked with Dorothy to harvest the crops and run the vegetable stand. Ralph had become rather cantankerous and was barking out orders until I finally said, "Enough of this – get your butt out of bed and help us with the work that needs to be done."

After getting him up on his feet, he announced he needed a bath – so I proceeded to fill the tub and get him ready to wash. He then announced he bathed in Spic 'n Span, which is a product containing trisodium phosphate (TSP). Sure enough, after adding the TSP he got in the tub and was definitely squeaky clean upon emerging from his bath.

I put him on a small tractor and had him follow us while we harvested the vegetables. His recovery was miraculous, especially considering his advanced age.

One afternoon, while we were all standing in front of the vegetable stand, a neighbor lady who was walking her dog stopped by to say hello. As she stood there, her dog walked over to Ralph, who was leaning against a tree, lifted its leg and urinated on Ralph's shoe. Ralph said nothing, although the lady was quite embarrassed.

A few seconds later, the dog turned the other direction and proceeded to urinate on Ralph's other shoe. On the inside I was laughing hysterically and again Ralph never moved or said anything about the incident. The lady then gathered her dog and continued down the country lane on which we all lived.

On another occasion, Ralph and I were watching "60 Minutes" on television and one of the feature stories was about Northern California pot growers and how lucrative it was as a business. Ralph was a man of few words, but following that segment he looked over at me and in a deadly serious demeanor asked, "Do you know how to grow the stuff?"

He then said, next season he wanted to plant his 90 acres in pot alternated with field corn. I reminded him of the Attica visit and he rapidly changed his mind.

I took a couple of long interview trips in conjunction with my employment search and received several job offers on the West Coast. None of them were willing to buy my house from me and that closed all doors since the housing market was essentially dead in the Rochester area back then. I had the house on the market for four months without a single bite.

I had even applied as a Mission Specialist for NASA's Astronaut program. Colonel Chuck Payne was now in charge of the Vandenberg Space Shuttle facility development and was helping me in my endeavor. I really thought I had a chance, but withdrew my application after reading the fine print – considerable pay cut, ten year commitment and no guarantee of a space mission. I was deeply concerned for my family's welfare, both financial and emotional and I couldn't take the chance that something could go wrong on a mission, so I withdrew my application.

Later in the fall, I was speaking at a FGBMFI breakfast meeting in Rochester and one of the guests approached me to say he thought he might have a job for me. Gary Gustafson was the manager of the Research and Engineering Department of the Kodak Apparatus Division (KADRL). Within weeks, I was a staff member for Eastman Kodak Company.

I had to accept a pay cut relative to Xerox, but moved forward in faith that everything would all work out OK. I was fortunate enough on my first assignment to have a problem where I could rapidly move towards a solution. I took the failure rate of a complex, four element glass lens assembly from ten percent to less than one percent in a matter of a few weeks. Five weeks after joining Kodak, I was given a six and a half percent raise that brought me up to $48,000 per year – comparable to what I was making at Xerox.

Ironically, the level of security at KAD was better than at Los Alamos. Hard to believe, but true; industrial espionage is a very real threat.

During my work on the lens element, I spent some time observing the manufacturing process in order to fully assess the problem. I had no idea what type of project this was and I was intentionally kept in the dark because I did not have a "need to know." When leading me to the prototype manufacturing facility, they erected a pathway with partitions on both sides of the station. The only part of the process I was allowed access to was what I needed to see in order to do my job. In fact, I didn't learn until the product was released that I had been working on the front cell lens assembly for the Kodak Disc Camera.

When this entire unemployment situation developed, I could not see any positive benefit arising from it. Why would Jesus let it happen in the first place?

After the fact, I saw it as analogous to a complicated jigsaw puzzle in the shape of a giant triangle. As I moved forward in time, the pieces of the puzzle began to come together behind me and fall into place. Each piece fit exactly as designed and connected precisely with the other pieces that would follow.

I learned to totally trust in Jesus for our livelihood and became willing to give it all up if necessary. I experienced quality time with my family, helped neighbors in their time of need and ended up in a remarkable job with a Christian manager. Countless blessings had come my way. A priori, I would have never guessed the ending to this exceptional experience. I would not take a million dollars for the experience, but I don't ever want to go through it again.

While living in NY, the family was very active and we certainly had our share of sports injuries: Shawn a broken thumb (baseball), Todd injured his elbow (skateboarding), then broke the tip off of it in soccer and later caught a baseball with his upper lip and nose. And yours truly smacked his ankle with a surfboard fin.

We all survived, but this was the beginning of a trend that would last all through the boy's adolescence – a seemingly continuous string of injuries related to sports.

Shawn received his Eagle Scout award at 13½ years old – a local record. Both boys were very active in Boy Scouts and I continued to serve as an assistant scout master.

In May 1982, I received a call from Aerojet Solid Propulsion Company (ASPC) in Sacramento, CA to see if I would be interested in joining their company. The previous year, they had heard I was looking for employment in California and felt they had a great match for my skills. I was brutally honest and said I was not interested. My first five months at KAD had been exceptional and I was very happy with my employer and fully committed to my job at Eastman Kodak.

I had considerable success with my projects, literally saving Kodak millions of dollars on their disc camera project. I totally understood the "Golden Handcuff" syndrome often associated with employees at the Eastman Kodak Company. They went out of their way to make you feel important, provided the best training programs imaginable, offered a stellar benefits package and planned numerous family oriented events.

They even allowed me to attend a technical meeting in Hawaii that spring and I couldn't have been happier with my situation. During the 24 days we would be on the islands I would be able to work in plenty of surfing and sightseeing around my attendance at the technical meeting. Doris and I were very excited about this trip.

After several calls from ASPC, I finally agreed to come out for an interview. I told them to book the trip from Rochester to Sacramento for a Friday interview, then book me on to Los Angeles so I could surf a couple of days with Chuck John and visit my folks. I would then take the redeye flight back to Rochester on Sunday.

After the interview, I realized they were offering me a unique job as a manager in an area where I had a lot of experience. Although I was initially interested in their proposal, I declined the verbal offer they made. I returned to New York and prepared for our trip to Hawaii.

After I returned home, Aerojet called and upped the ante to their highest-level manager, but I again declined. They then asked where they could meet with me in the next week or so to give them a chance to revise the offer and, hopefully, close the loop with me. I gave them the contact information for Hawaii. Doris and I took off on our vacation/business trip.

The Hawaii trip turned out to be exceptional. The meeting was good, the sightseeing fantastic and the surfing educational. After the technical meeting, we toured all the main islands – Oahu, Maui, Hawaii and Kauai. Before leaving Oahu I had some fantastic overhead plus surf.

Sure enough, Aerojet called while we were in Hawaii, but I continued to say no and thanked them for considering me. However, I checked out the Sacramento area through friends and could find no negatives. Everyone I contacted said they loved living there and would never leave.

Finally, Aerojet offered a deal that I could not refuse: Grade 16 Senior Manager, $55,000 per year with a $10,000 signing bonus and complete moving package. The deal included purchase of our existing home at well above market value, assistance in buying a new home in California, two house-hunting trips and on and on and on. If I had wanted this job from the get-go, I would have never had the guts to negotiate this way – it is amazing how it turned out.

After accepting the job with an August 1982 start date, we purchased a new 1,910 square foot home in Roseville (near Sacramento) for $113,500. The interest rate was an incredible 14 percent, after Aerojet's buy down on the points.

Leaving KAD was very difficult. I literally felt guilty. They had been such a great employer and I loved the professionalism and the work environment.

Gary had been super to work for.

I was given a small going away luncheon. While there, they presented me something to remember them by: a newspaper doctored with a headline that read "KADRL Team Plays with Peeters Out!"

After only ten months with Kodak, we packed up the schoolhouse, said a tearful goodbye to our beloved neighbors and embarked on a memorable cross-country journey to Northern California.

During our eight travel days, we visited Canada by going over the top of the Great Lakes and then across the Northern States. We rode horses in Theodore Roosevelt National Park, visited Yellowstone National Park and dropped down through Salt Lake City and Northern Nevada before reaching our next great adventure – California.

Rick Knight hang gliding, near Tehachapi, CA

Doris and the boys in Yosemite

Jim and Blanche Caldwell
Near Santa Fe, NM

Doris, Todd and Shawn on a
summer walk around home
Upstate New York

Doris
South Carlsbad State
Beach

Doris with Ralph and Dorothy Baker
Upstate New York

Camping in Yosemite Valley

4

Being a Waterman

After several great rides while surfing at Kaisers on the South Shore of Oahu, I found I was trapped in the impact zone. The next thing I knew, I was hammered onto a coral head by a wave breaking off the tip of my surfboard and inflicting coral cuts on my feet. After returning to the lineup, I took off and managed to botch the wave, getting hit by my surfboard and cracking several ribs. It was very painful, but it was Hawaii and I might never return, so the next day I paddled out to Threes and surfed a short session.

Riding the Face of a Moving Wave

After moving back to California from Washington in 1972, the family made frequent trips to South Carlsbad State Beach for camping and body surfing. During one of those trips, we met Dick and Libby Weinberg, who in turn introduced us to their son Mike and his friends – Chuck John, Charlie Bryant and Bing Gleitsman. These guys were going to teach me how to surf – and indeed they did.

Chuck scored a used board and the plan was to take me to Salt Creek and, apparently, try to kill me – it almost worked. Their idea of a surf lesson was to paddle out for a session with me in tow and deposit me in one of the gnarliest breaks in Southern California during a big swell with the instruction, "Catch a wave."

This also started the skateboard years. With the arrival of the urethane wheel, Chuck John, who was a pioneer in this technology, started one of the first skate board factories, Silver Shadow. Armed with Chuck's products, we did street runs using the car for shuttles around Golden Hills in Tehachapi. Chuck John, who is a gifted athlete and good at a variety of sports, became a lifelong friend.

To learn how to surf, I made several trips to Laguna Beach where Chuck, Mike, Bing and Charlie had rented a house. One night after surfing, Chuck and I decided to get some fast food. I suggested we go to McDonalds and Chuck immediately said, "No!"

I asked why and he said, "The trouble with McDonalds is that if you buy a Big Mac, fries and a shake, you're hungry when you leave, but if you buy enough to be full, you're sick when you leave."

I have personally proven this theory several times since then.

Besides terrifying me in the surf at Salt Creek, we would do skateboard street-runs on Skyline Drive in Laguna Beach. Taking turns driving, we would shuttle to the top of the local hills after midnight and skate the five-mile long runs, which included lots of very neat driveways to carve on. To add to the excitement, at various times the homeowners would run out shouting obscenities at us and then sic their dogs on us.

One run in particular stood out – I was skating near the end of the pack and I noticed that everyone passed up this one neat driveway. Located directly below a street light, it had a 15 degree incline relative to the street and looked perfect.

Speeding along at 30 mph, I angled for a turn high up in the driveway and hit it with maximum speed, only to discover it had an invisible one-inch lip at the intersection with the street. Linear momentum dictates that when the board stops instantaneously, the body continues in motion until it impacts concrete. Considering the angle change, it was a full-body contact smash and it hurt so bad I was not sure if I was dead or not. Boy did that hurt – I actually laid there motionless and counted body parts to see if I was OK.

Bing was driving the car behind me and immediately stopped. He jumped out and said, "Since you're hurt, you can drive." With that, he jumped on his skateboard and proceeded down the hill.

Other pancake type falls occurred in the pools located in various skateboard parks that had become popular in the early 1970s. Bottom line, falls from skateboards to pavement involving angle changes hurt a lot.

On a positive note, skateboarding does relate well to surfing and these excursions helped improve my surfing skills. In fact, skateboarding is often referred to as "street surfing."

On the first trip to my four friends' rented house, I found the place to be pretty cool. But on subsequent trips, various utilities would be shut off due to non-payment of the bill. After a few months, there was no electricity, hot water, etc. They then moved to another place and the cycle repeated itself.

In their last rental, while smoking pot and cooking French fries, they nearly burned the place down. Chuck told me while he frantically tried to put out the massive kitchen fire, he could peripherally see Bing, Mike, et al, carrying all their belongings out of the house as the fire raged on. The result was a partially destroyed house complete with charred and burned through interior walls. Still, they continued to live in it for awhile.

The last time I saw the house was for Mike's all-night bachelor party where even more damage was done to the place. This convinced me that I never wanted to be a landlord.

While skateboarding at La Costa, Chuck John got seriously hurt on one run as he entered an intersection and was broadsided by a car. That resulted in him doing a series of cartwheels during which he went "rag doll." Wearing only swim shorts, he was badly injured with tremendous areas of road rash; both lungs collapsed; he broke all of his ribs on his left side; and popped one rib completely off his sternum. His excellent physical condition from years of swimming and diving was the only reason he survived.

He was released from the hospital after a week in intensive care and his total recovery took 18 months.

On one trip to Baja California to surf with my family, we were stopped by a rag-tag band of Federales and/or robbers – to this day we don't know which. As a heavy set guy with a big sombrero, crossed ammo belts over both shoulders and holding a big rifle approached our vehicle, he signaled for us to roll down the window. I swear, when he cracked a big smile he had a gold front tooth which reflected a star-shaped flash of light as he said "Buenos Días Señor."

He then asked if we had any pistolas and proceeded to direct his co-horts to search the car. As I rolled down the rear window of the station wagon, Dink, our large Irish Setter, went off on a barking rage. Our intruders immediately directed us to leave the scene. We thanked God for that mean-sounding dog!

In the area of water sports, body and board surfing were something I had been involved in most of my life. I loved the ocean and was anxious to see my boys enjoy it as well. On numerous trips to the excellent surfing beaches of Southern California, they gradually took up the sport of Boogie Boarding. Although neither son continued surfing as an adult, as teenagers they were both able to ride the big winter waves that break on the outer reefs of Southern California.

One particularly memorable day was in the winter with Chuck at South Garbage along the Sunset Cliffs area of San Diego. A series of huge storms had caused many sewer mains to break and/or leak raw sewage into the ocean. The beaches were all closed from the Mexican border northward along Southern California. Sunset Cliffs is normally a very popular and crowded break, especially during a big swell.

With the beach closures, Chuck and I were the only ones in the water and we had the big perfect waves with offshore winds to ourselves. We had wave after wave of incredible rides with no competition – it was truly a fantastic day of surfing.

One ride in particular stood out – it went left on a big wave so steep that I had to stabilize myself using my hand in the face of the wave. The ride was incredibly fast and long with a massive wall of water overhead – a perfect ride.

The only drawback was the water was full of feces, toilet paper and other debris. Needless to say, we were careful to not ingest any of that vile liquid.

Surfing had begun to consume me – I was in love with it. I have often said that if I could only do one sport it would probably be surfing.

I averaged 51 surfing days per year over a 12 year period ending in 2006. We made numerous trips to the beach – especially San Elijo north of San Diego. I actually started to fit in with the locals at Turtles and still maintain those friendships to this day.

Our first trip to Hawaii was in April 1992. During our first day on Oahu, I went out to test the surf on a chest-high day at Kaisers. After several super rides to the right, I decided to go left and, after a great ride, found I was trapped inside the surf line. To make matters worse, I was not in the paddling channel.

The next thing I knew, I was hammered onto a coral head by a wave breaking off the tip of my surfboard and inflicting coral cuts on my feet. I was shook up, but decided to paddle back out and catch one last wave before figuring out how to fix the board.

I took off right and, sure enough, I pearled the board and as it rebounded from the hydraulic forces it hit me in the chest cracking several of my ribs. It was very painful but I managed to paddle back to shore and walk to our hotel room on Waikiki Beach. I duct taped the tip of the board and made plans to surf the next morning.

When I awoke early to go surfing, I literally had to roll off the bed because of the pain. Undaunted, I paddled out to Threes (a hollow, powerful and fast wave) and surfed a short session. I repeated this on the third day as well, before deciding I had better let the ribs heal a bit since they hurt so much.

I took the board to a surf shop and arranged to have it repaired. Then Doris and I went for a weeklong tour of the other islands during which I surfed a session on Kauai at Horner's with a rented board.

After returning to Waikiki Beach, I was able to surf many of the breaks along the South Shore of Oahu. The ribs were sore, but it was a rare opportunity for me so I persevered and was rewarded with some great surf sessions at Threes, Paradise, Populars, Canoes and Queens.

On our last day in Hawaii, I got up at 3 a.m. and paddled out to Threes in the moonlight. I wanted to surf one last time before catching a noon flight for home. It was very scary paddling out all alone and watching the distant lights behind me receding farther and farther away.

As I approached the reef break at about a half mile off shore, I was amazed to find two other surfers out there in the middle of the night with the same idea. After several great rides, I paddled in, packed my board for the flight and then Doris and I headed for home. I not only left Hawaii a better surfer, but a much smarter one, too!

Finally, in April of 2008, I made my way back to Oahu, HI for some serious surfing. I started on the West Side where I was able to catch Makaha four times with one day being truly fantastic. The amazing thing is that break is notoriously territorial and dominated by locals – as are many breaks on the West and North Sides of Oahu. My approach was to be very humble, yield waves even if I had the right of way and engage with the locals, particularly those who appeared to be at the top of the pecking order. Bottom line: knowing that surfing these breaks was at the upper edge of my skill level, I adopted the approach of showing tremendous respect to the locals.

It worked wonderfully as most locals respected age and at 62 I must have looked ancient to those guys! They literally encouraged me to take off on waves and helped me to figure out the breaks in a hurry. I even ran into a friend, Frankie DeSilva, from Turtles in Southern California – talk about a small world.

Unfortunately, I also stepped on a sea urchin which was a painful mistake. The locals tried to help by telling me, "Eh Brah, try shi shi," which translated from Pidgin English means "Excuse me, fine sir, try peeing on it."

I chose the alternate approach of soaking it in vinegar and attempting to remove the spines. It's something that just hurts for a long time – literally weeks.

Next, I moved to Mali Point for two great sessions in overhead plus waves with really big bowls. Unfortunately, I somehow sustained an inguinal hernia and, after the trip to the hospital, I headed to the other side of the island. In spite of the injury, my experience gave me confidence in big waves and set me up to move to the North Shore – a lifelong goal.

Staying at Backpackers, a dirty but relatively inexpensive hippy sort of place, I had six days of great surf. Each day the surf would build up in size allowing me time to get used to the incredible power of the waves on that side of the island[14]. It all culminated in a great session at Sunset Beach with overhead plus surf.

My show-respect approach worked well on the North Shore. That was in part because I was really sincere and those guys were all orders of magnitude better surfers then I was or ever would be.

Paddling out through huge surf with surfers dropping down faces on big guns is very scary, but at the same time exhilarating. The locals encouraged me to take off and set me up for a couple of incredible rides that felt like a racecar accelerating down mountains of water.

I had finally ridden that classic break. Ironically the rip conditions were quite bad and, as I paddled back into the beach, the lifeguards began to stop surfers from entering the water. I had timed it perfectly.

As a reward, I immediately went to Matsumoto's Store in Haleiwa for a much deserved shaved ice. The only bad news was that during one of those surf sessions I managed to crack a bone in my foot. So I left Hawaii with sea urchin spines in my broken foot and a protruding inguinal hernia – oh well, it was a great trip!

Often in the 1990s, I would take a whitewater kayak out into the surf. It offers the advantage of a paddle and a hull speed that is considerably greater than that of a surfboard, making it is easy to catch waves. It is also exciting, since being in a sitting position every wave feels like it is overhead and rides often end in the tube! Frequently, when paddling out through waves, it was possible to literally launch the entire kayak into the air off the back side of the approaching wave.

In February 2000, on the weekend of my dad's funeral, I was surfing in huge waves at Turtles and decided to dedicate the session to my dad. Typically, I would paddle out in the dark and surf before the crowds arrived and that day was no exception. Once out, as it started to get light enough to make out the swell, I realized it was big and dangerous. The other thing I noticed was that I was the only one in the water and that lots of other surfers were standing behind the fence atop the cliff watching.

Impervious, I managed to catch two incredibly fast and big waves. My dad was frequently upset at me because, when I was in the area, I always stopped in for a brief visit and then immediately headed straight to the ocean to surf. He wanted to visit and I wanted to surf. Well, he got even!

I decided to have my dad "ride with me" in spirit and returned to the lineup for a third time. It was a kind of – "take this wave with me, dad" – sort of thing.

I took off in a really steep, hollow wave. I made a snap decision to try to back out, but I was too late. I ended up going over the falls and was driven to the bottom of this huge wave and then mercilessly pummeled along the ocean floor. Upon resurfacing, I found only the rear two feet of my surfboard still attached to the end of my leash.

Following a long and difficult swim, I retrieved the other six feet of my board and made my way back to shore. After climbing the stairs leading up from the beach, I was greeted by a throng of amazed folks. I was later able to have my surfboard repaired and still use it as a backup for really big days or when traveling to Baja.

During an early part of the new millennium, we became good friends with Joe and Becky Mettee. They own VG Bakery and Donuts. VG's, a long-time local establishment, had been voted best bakery in North County San Diego. It was located across from the San Elijo Campground and we ran into the Mettees often. The bakery was even a sponsor of my Everest expedition.

Joe is a really great guy and terrific surfer. We often surfed together and our families would get together whenever we visited the campground. We also made several trips together traveling to Costa Rica, Baja, the Southern and Central coasts of California, as well as other surfing sites.

Joe, Chuck and I took a memorable camping trip to the Wall in Baja California and had some exceptional surfing sessions. Also, for anyone who likes donuts, it's hard to beat having a bakery owner for a friend. For my 67th birthday, Joe baked me a 14 inch long maple bar with "Happy Birthday Randy" inscribed on top!

I had always wanted to surf from the tip of Baja to the California border in a single trip. I had surfed Baja many times over the years, but had never made the "big trip." Finally, in May 2006, Doris and I embarked on a two month road trip in our RV. We traveled through mainland Mexico and ferried across to La Paz and onto the East Cape located below San Jose del Cabo. The next month, we surfed our way north along the peninsula's remote and isolated Pacific Coast region.

At Shipwrecks, in big and powerful overhead surf, I broke my leash and nearly drowned during a dangerous swim to shore. I also injured the top of my left foot on some rocks.

And surfing was not the only challenge we faced. While traveling through San Jose del Cabo, a young Mexican man and I managed to run into each other. It was a minor fender-bender and I knew better than to argue who was at fault. I paid the man $30 and drove off as fast as I could. Accidents in Mexico are real bad news – better to pay up and move on.

In spite of the travails, our casual camping was often at incredible ocean-front spots and sometimes right on the beach. I could literally step out the door and into the ocean. It was awesome. There were no crowds and we had great fun.

The roads in Baja are notoriously bad. On a trip north to Cuidad Insurgentes, we left the developed roads and drove 66 miles on a paved road full of potholes. It was then another 30 miles on a dirt road rippled with washboards and covered in sand. We eventually reached Scorpion Bay near San Juanico and set up camp for a week. The chest-high waves there made it all worthwhile.

It was here I had the longest ride I had ever experienced. The surf carried me for a third of a mile in near-perfect conditions.

One day, as I was heading out to surf, Doris said, "I want you to know I will leave your hat and your flip flops, but I won't be here when you get out."

That told me it was time to move on, so after one last surfing session I returned and packed up. I let some air out of our tires to better navigate the sandy roads as we backtracked the way we came. However, after reaching the main highway and turning north, we stopped several times to surf and spend the night.

By the trips end, I had surfed 16 days in eight different locations. It was an amazing road trip and perhaps the best surfing I had ever done.

"Tow-in surfing" was also a wild dream of mine. It involves using a jet ski with a tow rope to pull a surfer into big, fast-moving waves that normally are too large to paddle into. I modified my surfboard by attaching toe straps so I could lock my feet onto the board. There was only one drawback: it's illegal to tow-in surf along the California coast.

Oceanside Harbor was where I decided to try tow-in surfing for the first time. To avoid detection, my co-conspirators and I decided to go before daylight. Joe had his jet ski, Chuck had the nerve and I had the board. Prior to the adventure, I tried to find out how others had done this under the radar but no one would give me any details.

We reached the lineup in the dark and towed in Chuck first. Then Joe and I went back through the big waves nearly going airborne on some of them. On one particular wave, we went over the top and landed with a splash on the backside just in time to see a harbor police boat approaching at a high rate of speed. Chuck had figured out the situation and surfed innocently back to shore and disappeared.

The harbor police ordered us to follow them to shore, where they wrote us out a ticket and threatened to impound Joe's jet ski. I stepped forward and told the police it was our first time and I was the instigator of the caper and deserved the citation. The police weren't impressed and proceeded to cite Joe.

As dawn approached, we could see other tow-in surf setups scattered around the parking lot. The officer told us that due to the fact we didn't try to run away from them, he would only issue us a warning ticket.

I couldn't help but wonder who in their right mind would try to outrun an armed police boat with a jet ski?

After the police left, the other would-be tow-in surfers came over and befriended us and told us how to avoid getting caught. With that knowledge, I hope to finish this project someday.

I estimate we spent over two years camping along the coastline of Southern and Central California. It was generally about a week at each campground, but we made those trips several times a year. When we bought our RV and gave up tent camping, we were able to travel during the winter months when the waves are at their biggest. It also opened up surfing along the coastline of Northern California. I have surfed more than 200 breaks, ranging from the southern tip of Baja all the way to Fort Bragg, CA.

Over the years, I was able to surf many of those breaks several times while enjoying some huge overhead waves. Doris and I made a number of these camping trips and I extended our surf outings to the East Coast, Hawaii, Bali, New Zealand, Australia, Costa Rica and South Africa.[15]

Another neat experience is paddling out in the dark during a red tide. The water fluoresces around one's hands and a luminous wake comes off the front of the surfboard. After catching a wave, it is possible to look back at the wave and see the florescent trail left by the surfboard in the face of the wave. It's a totally cool thing to see.

The amazing fact about surfing after all these years and completing thousands of rides, is that I can still remember specific all-time best rides. I have vivid memories of my ride at South Garbage, the juice of Hawaii and Baja which are legendary, and the fantastic beach breaks of Costa Rica or the reef breaks of Bali. Long rides at Scorpion Bay and Rincon were truly fantastic. But one stands out for a rather unusual reason.

While surfing Cardiff Reef in overhead surf, I saw a pod of dolphins silhouetted in the wave surfing at high speed only ten feet in front of me. Years later, at the same location, I was riding left when a dolphin 25 feet in front of me breached and cleared the water – it was truly an amazing thing to see that close up and in the wild.

Sea Snails Anyone?

In the mid-1980s, I began free diving for abalone. Abalone is a sea snail mollusk and hard to get, especially free diving – SCUBA gear is prohibited. Abalones typically live on the underside of rocks surrounded by dense kelp 15 or more feet below the surface. Also, they can only be taken in waters north of the Golden Gate, which means cold water, sharks, heavy surf and rip currents.

My first trip with Denny Swenson was a disaster. The surf was huge and Denny was washed onto the rocks and lost some of his gear. It turned out to be a survival test and neither of us scored an abalone.

Next, I went with Bill Baxley, a great free diver and a sure bet we would find abalone. The swells were 12 feet high with a surge and near zero visibility underwater. Bill did get a couple of abalone, but I don't recall even seeing one that wasn't in his possession. He did, however, give me one along with a demonstration on how to clean the sucker. My attempt to clean one nearly cost me a finger, which was stitched up during a visit to the emergency room.

Abalone is an incredible delicacy to eat, but I still wanted to get one on my own. One would be enough to make me happy.

A few weeks later, Bill and I returned with his specially designed dive kayak and my whitewater kayak. After a four hour drive along the Northern California coast, we put our kayaks into the ocean and paddled out of Anchor Bay past a rock covered with sea lions making a horrible fuss. But I was determined and eventually was paddling my way back to Anchor Bay with my first abalones.

As we approached the sea lion rookery I decided to take a closer look at what the fuss was all about.

"I, I wou, would…na not do that," said Bill, said with a stutter.

I had an opportunity to see these animals up close in the wild, so I ignored his warning and paddled to within 50 yards of the rock. At that point, a giant sea lion launched himself into the water with a huge splash and swam toward me at a high rate of speed. It turned out to be sea-lion mating season and I was invading his territory. I turned on a dime and padded as fast as I could.

I imagine I looked like the "Road Runner" cartoon character as Bill yelled out, "Pre, pre, pretend…yo, you…like it."

In spite of being challenged by a huge male sea lion during mating season, I became hooked on abalone diving. Before long, we were making diving trips with friends from the church we attended in Roseville. During those 20 plus years of abalone diving, I would also take along my surfboard for some added entertainment. We had some great memories of our trips to Anchor Bay, a beautiful and remote spot to camp and dive.

Joe Mettee introduced me to free diving at night for lobster. This, too, proved difficult and after three excursions I still came up empty-handed. I did manage to touch four of them, but they are easily frightened and very fast in getting away. Someday, I'm going to get one of those suckers!

Self Contained Underwater Breathing Apparatus

In July 1996, Doris and I decided to give SCUBA diving a try.

I was doing the "Ask the Rocket Scientist" radio show at the time and the studio gave me a SCUBA lesson package. While contemplating buying some SCUBA gear, I called Doris to get an OK and she answered in a rather sarcastic voice that this would be another activity I would be doing on my own. So I asked her to join me and to my surprise she said, "Yes." I was shocked because Doris is afraid of the open ocean.

The dive shop was having a huge sale, so I bought enough gear for the two of us and a dive lesson package for Doris as well. After bringing home the diving gear, Doris wanted to recant. But I said I had purchased the gear on sale and it couldn't be returned. I give her credit; she stuck it out and became a good SCUBA diver.

She ultimately earned her Advanced Open Water SCUBA Diver Certification and I became a Dive Master and Master SCUBA Diver. I helped our instructor Mark Embry teach the advanced course in Monterey. To date, I've had 173 dives and 111 hours underwater. Doris has made 73 dives spending 41 hours underwater.

In addition to many trips along the entire California coastline, we made numerous destination dive trips all around the world. We also did a couple of cruise trips, which allowed us to dive several islands in a single week in the Caribbean.[16]

The ultimate diving experience is a live aboard dive-boat trip and we did two – one in the Cayman Islands and the other on the Great Barrier Reef off the coast of Australia.[17]

At CoCo View Resort in Roatán, Honduras, I did 26 dives in one week. One day I managed to do six dives all deeper than 60 feet, with a total bottom time of nearly four hours. Trip highlights included sitting in our cabana-on-stilts over the water while reading and relaxing. Some days I wore only swim trunks while diving with nine pounds of weights. That was quite a pleasant contrast to the six mm neoprene wetsuit with hood, booties and gloves, plus the 30 pounds of weights necessary to dive in the frigid Pacific near our home.

When diving, we saw lots of colorful coral, fish and sponges. I did one solo night dive into a shipwreck where a huge moray eel hung out. After leaving the wreck, I descended to the bottom at 65 feet to lie on my back in the sand and turned off my dive light. I figured I would lie there for a couple of minutes and see what happened.

Well, I lasted about 20 seconds and it was amazing to see how many fish came around to check me out. It was quite scary alone on the bottom of the ocean at night with no light!

On a dive trip to Mexico, we did drift diving in Cozumel and then dove Cenotes in Akumal. The Dos Ojos Cenote was probably the best dive we've ever done – Doris was a little scared at first, but hung in there and enjoyed the experience.

The highlights of these dive trips included drift diving, swim-throughs, huge walls and arches, Cenotes, cavern diving, night dives and deep dives. The sponges, corals and sea life were amazing - particularly seeing a big Eagle Ray (15 foot wing span), octopuses, huge turtles, sharks, eels, seahorses and sand dollars.

What is a Waterman?

Being a waterman means developing stamina and learning to be at ease in the water no matter the conditions. Whether it is surfing huge waves, free diving deep into kelp beds or SCUBA diving caverns, it is imperative to remain calm. Keep in mind that does not mean never being afraid – we all get scared in difficult circumstances – but the trick is to remain calm.

Panic leads to bad decisions, which often result in the rapid loss of energy – the exact thing you can least afford when your life is at stake. Fear is healthy and respecting nature, especially in the ocean, is very important. I don't have gills, so I pay close attention to whatever situation I find myself in and never take safety for granted.

As far as water sports injuries are concerned, I've had cracked ribs, shoulder impingement issues, neck injuries, tooth (root canal) issues, leg, ankle and body cuts, plus bruises from being hit by fins. I've ripped out a toenail on a piece of coral (surgically removed); coral cuts; embedded sea urchin spines; inguinal hernia and a broken foot.

It kind of makes you want to sign up to be a waterman, doesn't it?

Todd, Shawn and Randy, San Elijo State Beach

Randy
Oceanside, CA

Camping at Punta San Isidro
Baja California, Mexico

Manu Bay, Raglan, Tasman Sea, New Zealand

Joe Mettee and Randy in Costa Rica

Randy and Doris, Caribbean Sea

Paddling out

Getting stuck in search of good surf, Costa Rica

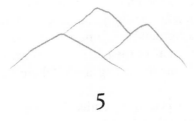

5

UP THE CORPORATE LADDER

PLUS A FEW DOGS, PUNK ROCKERS AND RADIO

Back Home to California – The Flat Lands – Roseville

Unbelievable! I had been directed by US Customs agents to serve as the point man in an ongoing investigation to bust one of my top R&D scientists. Acting as the eyes and ears of the investigation team, I was required to not divulge details of the assignment with any personnel, including my boss. After weeks of my knowing he was likely going to prison, the day finally came. I had planned to be gone that day to attend an entrance interview at the California Maritime Academy with my younger son Todd. Sure enough it happened – the scientist was literally hauled off in chains and it made the national news. He had sold missile parts to hostile foreign governments.

After arriving in Northern California in late August 1982, we lived in a Holiday Inn for a month with two dogs and two cats, while our home was being completed in Roseville. While there, the boys and I learned a valuable lesson – never submerge your entire head in a public hot tub. We awoke the next morning unable to open our eyes – they were actually glued shut from the mucus associated with pinkeye.

My job at Aerojet as the manager of the Propellant Characterization and Analysis Department was enjoyable right from the start. My technical and management background was a perfect fit and I got along well with my boss Dick Lou; in spite of the fact not more than 20 minutes into the job, one manager told me the saying around there was, "Dick Lou, before he dicks you."

After nearly eight years working under Dr. Lou's leadership, I can honestly say I felt he was one of the fairest managers I have ever worked for. Many at Aerojet did not understand him or his management style. In general, he did not play favorites, demanded a lot from his direct reports and was even handed overall. He was, however, blind to the chaos created by some of his actions, and this did impact his effectiveness. I truly liked his personal secretary, Ruth Stetler, and over the years we became good friends.

I had learned from previous situations that the boss's secretary could make you or break you. Bottom line: they can aid in your communication with your boss, or screen you out totally. Worse yet, they can selectively screen information and perform character assassination behind the scenes. It is best to make the secretary your friend. To aid in this process, I had learned from previous employment to pray earnestly for the secretary and her family – not that she would change, but rather that she would be richly blessed. When I did this, the dynamic immediately changed – you cannot earnestly pray for someone without thinking kind thoughts toward the person and that changes everything.

We had heard about Warehouse Ministries from the worship leader in our church in Upstate New York, so shortly after moving, we decided to check it out. It was a large inter-denominational church body loosely connected with Chuck Smith and his Calvary Chapel organization. We attended there several years before moving to a new branch of the church which started in Rocklin, much closer to our home.

Over the years I attended several men's retreats and enjoyed this dynamic ministry. The family also regularly attended Christian rock concerts held at the church and saw many top quality performances. During this period of time, I was also the guest speaker at a half dozen or so Northern California FGBMFI dinner meetings.

I shared my testimony and ministered through this organization for four years before it came to a conclusion and sort of faded away. I was blessed to have had this unique opportunity and felt satisfied with the entire ministry.

Two months after moving to California, we contacted Ralph and Dorothy Baker and asked them to fly out to California to visit over Thanksgiving and amazingly enough, they accepted.

We paid for their airfare and when they arrived, we showed them all over Northern California, including camping at the beach and Yosemite. This was a real once-in-a-lifetime experience for them and we thoroughly enjoyed their visit. In fact, it was not only Ralph's first time in an airplane, it was also the first time he had gone farther from his home than the adjoining state of Pennsylvania.

In the first few years after relocating to Northern California, we saw them several more times on business trips to the East Coast before they passed away. We count them among our closest friends, ever. They were such gracious and unassuming people and knowing them truly enriched our lives.

On the home front, after moving into our new house, the boys joined the local Boy Scout troop and I signed on as an assistant scout master. A short time later I took over the local Order of the Arrow (OA) chapter and started an Explorer Post. I served as the advisor for both.

Scouting played a major part of our lives for over ten years. Both boys earned the rank of Eagle Scout with multiple palms. Things we did during those busy years were Philmont Scout Ranch, the National Jamboree, Indian dance team, scout camp, ski trips, ocean trips, career nights, whitewater rafting, skydiving and many others.

By the end of my adult leadership in the Boy Scouts, I was quite honored to have received the Wood Badge, Vigil Honor in the OA, the Silver Bear and Silver Beaver awards. I virtually gave up climbing during those years and fully dedicated myself to working with the boys as they grew up. It was a great decision and I have many incredible memories from this period.

In particular, as I was preparing to step down from adult leadership, I attended a local Camporee in April 1986. During that weekend, I was given a clock with the inscription, "Thanks ... Leader – Counselor – Friend." I treasure the gracious gesture on behalf of my adult scouting co-worker and friend, Monrad Monsen.

The Aerojet employment certainly had its ups and downs. Overall, the work was quite rewarding and I thoroughly enjoyed it. Occasionally, horrible things happened. For example, an MX Missile incident at Tullahoma, TN resulted in the death of three Aerojet employees. Another employee death resulted from a propellant accident in the research facilities at Aerojet. And if that was not enough, one of my top propellant technical principals burned down his brand new laboratory.

These and other incidents, combined with the constant threat of unemployment due to the uncertainties of government-sponsored contracts, took their toll over the years. The question of being able to survive until retirement age was always in the back of my mind.

On one occasion, Dick Lou had emergency gallbladder surgery. I was left in charge of the entire Chemical Research and Development organization. To my horror, the executive vice president for the Aerojet Propulsion Division decided it was an ideal time to clean up the research facilities. To accomplish this, he would make impromptu visits to the laboratories and make a huge fuss.

Once he got right in my face and yelled that someone was going to be fired over what he had found. It was pretty hard not to take that personally!

As a form of relaxation to counteract the stress, I frequently took long walks with Doris at lunchtime. We would walk along the South Fork of the American River for six miles or so and often I would take a quick swim before returning to work. Long walks had always allowed me to think out loud and even today provide me with a very enjoyable form of relaxation.

The commute from Roseville was about 20 minutes and I enjoyed the drive. On one trip in to work, I noticed a license plate frame that said, "All blondes aren't dumb." It was on upside down. Oh well!

We definitely missed the open spaces of Upstate New York, the slower pace of life and our friends. But overall, our transition to Northern California was smooth.

Some of the management perks at Aerojet included access to company tickets for events such as baseball and basketball games, concerts, shows, etc. On one occasion, I obtained box seats to the Giants game in San Francisco, which even included a preferred parking pass. I'll never forget our younger son's response to the event when he commented, "This is what it is like to be rich."

I learned early on that women can size up one another. Case in point was a young lady working in the research facilities. She always dressed right on the edge of what could be considered inappropriate work attire (short skirts, low cut tops, etc.).

Well, at the annual company-wide Christmas party, she dressed rather provocatively. Although nothing was said, people definitely noticed.

During the door prize drawing she won a $100 gift certificate to a local department store. I was seated at a table with several other ladies who she had to walk past in order to claim her prize. Just as she approached, one woman in our group couldn't resist and said in a rather loud voice, "Oh good, now she can buy the rest of her dress."

On one business trip to Monterey, CA, I looked up an old high school buddy named Ernie Lorts. After getting reacquainted, he insisted we come to dinner that night at the Sardine Factory where he waited tables. This was one of the best restaurants in California at the time. I told Ernie I could not afford it. He said to show up and he would work it out so it would be $25 or less.

We took him up on it and visited the restaurant that evening. We were seated in the atrium room right next to the owner's immediate family. Our dinner included nearly every hors d'oeuvre they offered, two very nice entrees and dessert. In fact, the meal lasted over three hours as we were instructed not to leave until after the owner's family left. Once they were gone, Ernie presented us with the bill, which indeed did total less than $25. Amazing!

Another outstanding business trip was an American Chemical Society (ACS) recruiting trip in Florida. By coincidence, there was to be a space shuttle launch while we were there. I contacted Colonel Chuck Payne, who was then in charge of the Vandenberg AFB shuttle facility development and asked for the VIP tour.

Like Ernie, the colonel came through and we had fantastic seats for the launch. Incredibly, we were seated with four-star generals and the astronauts' families.

After the ACS meeting, I surfed Cocoa Beach. We went sightseeing all over Florida and took a side trip to Nassau.

On a business trip to San Diego with Doris, we ran into our old friend Les Tepe, while walking along one of the area's beaches. His wife, Barb, had recently died from breast cancer. We expressed our deepest sympathies and continued to talk. That's when Les said something I have never forgotten.

"The one redeeming thing about cancer," Les said, "is that you have the chance to say goodbye."

Even in the untimely death of his spouse, he found a positive aspect. To this day he is a committed Christian and his comment has completely changed my thinking regarding cancer.

Another real treat was the opportunity to attend a propellant meeting in Karlsruhe, Germany. I took a vacation in conjunction with the week-long meeting. Doris and I traveled for a month through Spain, Portugal, Morocco, Gibraltar, France, Switzerland and Germany. We visited with friends, experienced the Alps, enjoyed the meeting and, in general, had a memorable time.

Other business/vacation trips during this period were numerous and varied.[18] Many involved multiple trips to each location and, as always, I did my best to leverage them into interesting experiences, often bringing Doris with me. In fact, I rarely traveled anywhere without figuring out a way to parlay the trip into a surfing, sightseeing, visiting friends, etc. type of adventure. I never ignored the primary reason for the trip, i.e., work, but found great joy in turning it into a mini vacation. From my perspective, this was a huge perk. I not only made full use of it, but encouraged my employees to do so as well.

Together, Doris and I traveled throughout most of the United States. We particularly enjoyed the East Coast and Washington, DC areas.

During our family vacations, we traveled to virtually every part of California and most of the Western USA. This included frequent, extended camping trips in the Dog Trailer to various beach and mountain locations. Among our favorite places to camp were San Elijo and South Carlsbad State Beach parks, which also allowed us to see our families and friends still located in Southern California.

During this period virtually every Christmas and Easter were spent camping at the beach and surfing. Aerojet shut down over Christmas and the kids were out of school during Easter break. Since our first campout at South Carlsbad in 1966, we have spent the equivalent of more than two years total at California's state beach parks. Other vacations included Lassen National Park, Redwoods National Park, a weeklong Caribbean cruise and many other trips across the USA.

When the kids weren't able to travel with us, returning home was occasionally filled with surprises. On one arrival, we were met at the curb by Todd, who announced Shawn had chicken pox. We immediately called our parents to see if we had had the illness as children; fortunately, we had. Two weeks later, Todd came down with it as well.

On another trip, we spent Halloween back East without Todd and Shawn. When we returned home everything seemed in order and we didn't think anymore about it until the following year. The next Halloween, as the neighbors came to the door trick or treating, many of them commented on how much they enjoyed last year's haunted house.

Over the years, the boys were active in many sports – soccer, baseball, basketball, football, horseback riding, water skiing, skiing, rafting, boogie boarding, etc. They also became involved in skateboarding - building and using ramps all around the area. It was amazing how often they were injured. For a few years, we were on a first-name basis with the local orthopedic surgeon. Either Shawn or Todd was always in a cast with broken thumbs, leg injuries and so on. However, I disliked the skate-punk attitude which accompanied the activity.

In the 1980s, snowboards started showing up at some of the local ski areas and the punk attitude followed. Of course, both boys immediately started snowboarding and over the years became very good at it.

With work, travel and vacations, we managed to stay quite busy. Although climbing was largely out of the picture during this time, I remained very active in any sport or activity involving the family. They primarily centered on snow and water activities. I did, however, maintain my training regimen with the same intensity as if I was going to climb a huge mountain by week's end. Stretching, weight training, running, and walking were involved in daily routines that took approximately two hours.

I also started riding my bicycle back and forth to work on a regular basis. The 11 mile ride took about 40 minutes each way and was great, except for the traffic. This fitness program proved to be the key to my success in sports and the big climbs which would eventually come.

One morning as I returned home from my daily run, I noticed the Ford Bronco was missing from the driveway. After checking and discovering everyone was home, I realized it had been stolen, complete with all my tools. I reported it to the police and my insurance company, AAA. I was told it was gone for good.

With the insurance money, I bought a used Chrysler LeBaron station wagon and outfitted it for rafting and camping trips (heavy-duty shocks, trailer hitch, etc.).

Amazingly, a few months later I received a call from the police asking me to pick up my Bronco. It had been recovered the day it was stolen from a chop shop as a part of a sting operation funded by AAA – unbelievable!

AAA sold the Bronco back to me at a low price and I immediately sold the LeBaron that I had grown to hate. Every trip with the Chrysler involved a mechanical breakdown.

I did compete a few times in sporting events: kayak down river, wild water and slalom races, Epies Great Race Triathlon (eighth place, senior iron man), Chili Bar white water rodeo (second place – novice), California International Marathon (3:18:56, top one third of all men), etc.

Meanwhile back on the home front, we sold the Dog Trailer and bought an 1985 Toyota pickup with a cab-height camper shell. It was difficult to let go of the Dog Trailer after so many years of great memories. But now, it was largely just Doris and me on trips. The time had come.

We camped many times in the pickup/camper shell combination and it served us well for over ten years. This was a particularly effective unit for illegal casual camping in places such as Yosemite, since it did not draw unwanted attention and we were basically out of sight as we slept in the back of the truck.

In the summer of 1983, Doris and I attended our 20 year high school reunion and it was genuinely a great experience. As usual, I had combined it with a business trip to Southern California visiting family and friends and camping at the beach. I saw many classmates and friends and, of all the reunions before or since, this one was the best. My boys met several of our good friends at the picnic portion of the reunion.

In August of 1988, in conjunction with a 25 year high school reunion, I planned and organized an Explorer Post reunion with the guys from my high school. It was quite special and five of the original members showed up. We had a memorable time.

The boys always did pretty well in school, so in June of 1984, when Shawn came home with an F in Spanish, we were caught completely off-guard. I asked Doris to go to the school and find out exactly what was going on since he had had a B-minus at the quarter.

The counselor said this was to be expected as he had a D-minus at the quarter and then produced a signed deficiency notice complete with Doris' signature on it. Shawn had doctored the D-minus to look like a B-minus and forged Doris' signature on the deficiency notice. Hmmm! Well, this was a true shocker.

Although we did not like it too much, Shawn drifted further into the skater scene. By this time the boys had formed a four piece band (Shawn on base, Todd on drums, a guitar player and a lead singer) named the "Team Urinals." Now I like just about any type of music, except punk rock. You guessed it – a punk rock band – and their first album was "Where the Dicks Hang Out."

They were actually pretty good with gigs in Sacramento (opening for some rather well-known bands) and in the Berkeley area. One member of the band was a talented graphic artist and they sold quite a few T-shirts featuring a urinal for the letter "U" in Team Urinals.

Their first album caught on regionally and they later released their second album "Push Them Lies." The cover consisted of the letters PTL, a sketch of Oral Roberts with his fist raised and a cross with a dollar sign on it in the background.

Some might recall the Jim Bakker (PTL Club) scandal and Roberts saying that if he did not raise millions he would be called to heaven.

Truly, these boys knew how to push my buttons. They even threatened to audition for a spot at the Aerojet family picnic (I threatened to kill them if they did) and asked me if I would manage their band. Bet you can guess. I said, "NO!"

One time when we were camping at the beach over Christmas, the boys came home a few days before us since they had a gig involving their band. We had planned to arrive home after New Year's, but decided to return a few days early.

Everything appeared to be in order except for a dozen empty wine cooler bottles neatly placed in the garage and an ashtray with cigarette butts on the patio table. I made a few calls and located the boys at different locations and told them to come home immediately.

Shawn, the older son, arrived first and I asked him what happened while we were gone. He said he had invited a few people over, including his girl-friend, for New Year's Eve. Since he was 18 and his girlfriend was 17, he further explained he thought it was best to be at home rather than out driving. Alcohol and cigarettes were involved and he also said his brother and some of his friends were there as well.

I told him I was upset, but appreciated him telling me the truth. I sent him off to his room. Moments later, Todd entered.

I asked him what went on and he immediately blurted out, "We found those empty bottles on the front lawn and figured you would be mad if we didn't pick them up."

Without breaking his speech cadence he asked, "Has Shawn come home yet?"

Doris was behind Todd and putting her hands to her head as I told him that Shawn was indeed home and that I had just sent him to his room. We put Todd on restriction for several months.

Later they wrote a song entitled, "Three Days Early," which was about their experience when the parents arrived home early.

Back on the job front, I was selected to attend the Aerojet Advanced Management Training Workshop and then the UC Davis Executive Program. These were both excellent programs. I not only learned a lot, but made several long-term friends. I attended the UC Davis reunion dinners for many years after I completed that program.

Later on, Dick Lou asked me to help recruit Gerry Manser and Dick Cornea, a couple of key employees from Thiokol.

On a visit with Gerry Manser in Brigham City, Utah, I will always remember his comment that "This is not the edge of the world … but you can see it from here." This made recruiting Gerry a little easier.

We also brought Dick Cornea out to Sacramento and my boss planned a special banquet at a local Chinese restaurant.

During dinner, I decided some comedy might break the ice so I announced that I had been eating more Chinese food lately.

Dick Lou looked surprised and said, "Really?"

I replied "Yeah, in fact, just this morning I had Ho Ho's and Ding Dongs for breakfast!"

Everyone roared, except Dr. Lou – I don't think he understood the humor of the situation. And yes, we were successful in recruiting those key Thiokol employees, both of whom became good friends at work.

Since the boys were essentially grown up at this juncture, I decided to reapply for an astronaut position as a mission specialist. With my technical background, expedition experience and excellent physical condition, I thought I had a good chance. I was turned down and felt quite disappointed.

We were then in an era when NASA intensely recruited female and minority candidates and my age worked against me. Still, this remains a real disappointment – I truly would love to go into space – perhaps someday.

During a 12 month period of 1988/1989 I experienced what could only be described as a great year. With over 182 activity days during this period, I completed some amazing achievements: climbing Denali, running a marathon, completing a mountain-bike race, biking a century, skiing a trans-Sierra, etc.[19]

During this time several big changes occurred in our lives. On the job front, I was promoted to Director of Research and Development at Aerojet, replacing my boss Dick Lou, who retired in May 1990. This was a huge promotion and I was afraid that I could not handle the increased responsibility.

In addition, we bought a new home in Folsom in order to be closer to work, as the commute became a hassle. In the process of moving and trying to sell our Roseville house, the housing market tumbled and we became landlords.

The job worked out fine. I was able to double the size of the Chemical Research and Development Division to 150 employees. I kept the Roseville house for about five years before selling it to Todd.

Adventures in Yuppieville (Folsom, CA)

> *Imagine that one day you're vice president of engineering in charge of 1,050 people and the next day the only one you're in charge of is yourself! To most, that might come as a kind of a shock.*
>
> *But when you discover your boss and mentor had retired the day before and his arch enemy is now the boss, it helps explain why you were suddenly given a lateral transfer to chief scientist. Well, it doesn't take a rocket scientist to figure out your days are numbered and it has now become of paramount importance to keep your integrity intact.*

We enjoyed our new home and the town of Folsom very much. The house itself was a high-end, customized tract home we had built with a nice, low-maintenance landscape. It was a significant upgrade from our Roseville home and my commute to work was much shorter and easier. However, it did have the feel of a yuppie community. In fact, I once spotted in the neighborhood a license-plate frame which said, "Die Yuppie Scum."

I had been chipping away at visiting all 50 states and in October of 1990 I finally completed the quest. Our country is so beautiful that I just wanted to see all of it.

The family also started an annual trip to Capitola, CA in the fall of 1990. We stayed in some funky condominiums known as Venetian Village located right on the beach. Typically, we would stay for three nights and visit the

Santa Cruz boardwalk. There we played air hockey and walked the beaches and piers at both Santa Cruz and Capitola, when we weren't watching football on TV.

Each morning, I would head out before daylight to surf local spots. I particularly enjoy surfing early in the morning and it has the added advantage of not interfering with other family activities. This Capitola tradition continued for 20 years.

The family also made numerous trips in the spring to places such as Yosemite; Lake Shasta, Trinity Lake and the California Delta (houseboat rentals); camping at the beach, etc. On one of our Yosemite trips, Todd and I hiked the old "Ledge Trail" to the top of Glacier Point. I had wanted to hike the trail since the bicycle trip to Yosemite with my brother in 1963. The trail had been closed since 1952 and turned out to be a pretty exciting "hike," involving the use of hands and difficult route finding on this long abandoned route. We watched the hang gliders launch off Glacier Point. It was such a sight that I decided I wanted to do it someday.

It was also a milestone year for Doris and me as we celebrated our 45th birthdays and our 25th wedding anniversary.

Over Christmas break, Doris and I took a winter trip to Yellowstone where we rode a snowmobile 160 miles through the park and spent a night at the Old Faithful Winter Lodge. We saw more buffalo than one could possibly imagine. At one point on our trip, we moved to the side of the groomed road to allow a herd of buffalo to pass.

As I pulled to the side, our snowmobile rolled over the embankment. Doris and I crouched down behind the overturned machine as the herd passed. They came so close, we could see each individual hair of their coats. We were also rather scared as those large animals can become dangerous if aggravated. We shared a sigh of relief when they passed by without incident. We rolled the machine back over, climbed aboard and continued on our way.

I had a great experience when the boys and I attended the 1991 Bill Graham Memorial concert at the Polo Grounds in Golden Gate Park, San Francisco. It was a mini-Woodstock with over 300,000 people. There were superb performances by Santana, Los Lobos, Grateful Dead, Crosby, Stills, Nash and Young, Joan Baez; and even comedian Robin Williams. I thoroughly enjoyed that day.

Denny Swenson, a local chiropractor, became one of my closest friends. Over our 25 plus years of friendship, we hiked, climbed, skied, ski-toured, kayaked, rafted, dove for abalone and went SCUBA diving together. We also held each other accountable regarding "walking the talk" of our Christian faith.

Denny was one of those rare friends who comes along in life one at a time; the kind you can share everything with – no secrets. As amazing as it may seem, Doris too has been that type of friend during the entire course of our marriage. I have been truly blessed.

I settled into my new job as director of research and development. My work involved a lot of travel so, as always, I turned trips into fun mini-vacations for Doris and me. I also started teaching courses for Aerojet, including training in "Frontline Leadership."

I had great assignments, like serving on the Highly Filled Materials Institute Board at the Stevens Institute of Technology located in Hoboken, NJ. I enjoyed the appointment and made several great trips to the New York City area with Doris. We stayed at Weehawken, NJ and could see the city across the Hudson River. It was spectacular and the views from Hoxie House, the college president's residence, were equally impressive.

On one trip, the New York Rangers had just won the Stanley Cup and we attended the ticker tape parade thrown in their honor – an exciting experience. We also managed to see several Broadway plays, walked through every Manhattan district and, in general, got a feel for the big city. New York City is truly a remarkable place and totally deserving of its world class status.

On one Seattle trip, we arranged reunions with all our friends there: Boeing colleagues, professors and friends at the University of Washington and members of the Explorer Post. Other trips included Indiana (Amish areas) and Upstate New York to visit friends and see the old school house – now a bed and breakfast.

On another occasion, I traveled to Washington DC for the World Space Conference. While there, Doris and I toured Williamsburg, Mount Vernon, the National Mall with its museums and toured the White House. After leaving DC, we traveled along the East Coast and I surfed the outer banks of North Carolina.

One summer, our younger son Todd worked at Aerojet for two weeks as an intern. The internship was required for his engineering degree at the California Maritime Academy. We commuted together to work and I enjoyed watching him complete his short tenure at the "rocket ranch."

Years later, our older son hired on at Aerojet in the procurement department and it was a joy when I occasionally saw him at work. It was a rare opportunity for me to share my work location with my sons and I thoroughly enjoyed the experience.

The big negative at Aerojet was the constant uncertainty of continued employment. Money was always an issue because of defense cutbacks in aerospace funding. Over the years, Aerojet experienced a continuous cycle of hiring followed by layoffs.

I had indeed hoped to reach financial independence before turning 50, but would continue working because that's what I wanted to do. My secondary objective was to qualify for early retirement at age 55 and receive the associated free medical insurance.

On one occasion, as I was walking down the hallway at work, I passed one of my managers who had recently turned 55. I commented that I wished I was 55 and his reply really struck home.

He said, "Randy, don't wish your life away." That comment changed my entire attitude.

Throughout the years at Aerojet, I continued to kayak, skydive, surf and ski at every opportunity. I thrived on intense sports. However, I learned early that if Doris or the kids were not with me during those activities, I simply wanted to finish and return home. Some folks did these outings for the social benefits, but personally, I did not. My focus, consistent with my vision, was to be with my family whenever possible. I enjoyed the intensity of sports, but valued my family life more.

In April 1992, I decided to put together what I called a "Sports Classic" weekend. It was to include a wide range of athletic events to be done in a single weekend. Because of our unique location in Northern California, I felt I could pull it off. I enlisted Todd's help and we came up with a plan involving hiking, surfing, skydiving, rock climbing, whitewater kayaking, cycling, running and skiing. We did everything in a day and a half.[20]

I enjoyed doing such a wide variety of activities at relatively high levels of proficiency in a single weekend – it gave me great satisfaction. I strive to be multi-dimensional and proficient in my sports and this was a great test piece.

I doubt anyone else has ever put this combination of sports together in such a short time, but who knows?

In the fall of 1992, I was approached by a local disc jockey and asked to do a radio segment entitled, "Ask the Rocket Scientist." The idea was Jeff McMurray's of the popular classic-rock station known as the "Eagle" in the Sacramento area. It was to be a takeoff on the popular cliché "It doesn't take a rocket scientist to figure that out." The spot would air once a week during the morning rush hour when lots of Aerojet folks would be listening.

I declined his offer, although he called several times to try to convince me to do it. I felt I had everything to lose and nothing to gain. As a director, if I made any mistakes they could easily fall on the ears of both my employees and the management.

However, because of Jeff's persistence, I finally agreed to ask the company CEO, Dick Simonsen, what he thought of the idea. I was sure he would say no and that would be the end of it. I was actually shocked when Simonsen thought the idea was a good one and could even result in a positive image for Aerojet. Thus began a 20 year stint on several different radio stations around the country.

The weekly ten minute segment aired live in Sacramento. Callers to the show would ask questions and I would answer from home via telephone hook-up to the DJ at the radio station. It was amazing and scary, but a lot of fun.

Jeff and the other DJs were incredibly clever in making the show work. Jeff had one of the brightest minds I have ever encountered – smart, witty and lightning fast. The callers' questions were all over the map – some serious and others frivolous.

I'll never forget one caller asking, "What is a training bra training for?"

Jeff quickly clued me in. I answered live on the air, "It's like training bird dogs. You're trying to make pointers out of setters."

On another occasion, I had a tough one when asked, "If you're in your car and somehow you can go the speed of light, what would you see if you turned on your headlights?"

I had just seen Stephen Hawking's biographical movie entitled *A Brief History of Time* and felt confident when I answered that you would be surrounded by a field of light – wrong!

Twenty minutes later, I arrived at work and had half a dozen voice mails telling me I had screwed up on that one. The correct answer was, of course, the headlights would propagate out just like normal.

Based on Einstein's theory of relativity, it is platform dependent. It can give you a headache if you give it serious thought – doesn't this mean the headlights would be traveling at twice the speed of light? A paradox in relativity?

I was fired from that job five times; Sacramento, Las Vegas, Houston twice and Atlanta.

When the station was reorganized and Jeff was let go, I was unceremoniously let go as well. After Jeff landed at another location, he brought me back on the air with him. When Jeff quit being a DJ, Steve Robison picked up the segment in Houston and we were still working together until 2012 when the station was reorganized.

I liked it better not being local – a lot less pressure. Over time, the questions were being submitted by email and I could pick and choose which ones I wanted to answer.

When I started, the station gave me tickets to concerts, football games, amusement parks and so on. Eventually, I developed sponsors and would trade out 30 second commercial spots for sporting gear, ski-lift tickets, etc., which I would incorporate into the show. Towards the end, it became a paid position.

I grew to love doing the program and learned a lot by researching the questions. It also helped to keep me sharp mentally and I enjoyed both the challenge and the perks. Because of the "Ask the Rocket Scientist" gig, Doris and I saw some incredible concerts (Elton John, Rolling Stones, Grateful Dead, Eagles, Eric Clapton, Tom Petty, etc.), went to several 49ers games and attended radio station Christmas parties and a media weekend at Heavenly Valley.

Heavenly Valley became a sponsor for many years and I was able to barter for lots of equipment from several sporting goods stores in the Sacramento area and Houston.

In 1998, Jeff sent me the following email, which I appreciated a great deal.

Hey Doc, Thanks again for the great time today. You are about the only person I know that can pack an adventure into something as mundane as "lunch." If everyone followed your example and lived their lives to the fullest, we'd be too exhausted to fight wars. You are an amazing man, not just because of the level of physical fitness and endurance you possess, but because of the person you are. You are a fine role model for kids. The world could use a few more men such as yourself. It was great spending some time with you today. Thanks so much for carving out such a block for me. I look forward to getting together again soon, be it skiing, star gazing, etc. My best to you and Doris.

Back on the job front, in order to be better prepared for my duties as a director at Aerojet, I went back to graduate school at UC Davis. Aerojet was deemed a "super fund" site and I had to understand what was required to clean up the trichloroethene (TCE) contaminated soil and aquifer.

When I talked to the guidance counselor, she suggested I first take an undergraduate course since it had been over 20 years since I had done any course work at the university level. I told her I was not that naive – I knew upper division undergraduate courses are much harder than graduate courses.

Furthermore, I told her, "After all it's not rocket science; it's only civil engineering!" Big mistake.

I suspect she told the professor of the three unit graduate level water quality course I took to make my life a living hell – which he did. Worst of all, two other Aerojet engineers were also enrolled and I felt I had to do better than they did or everyone at work would know. As fate would have it – I had to learn a whole new arsenal of tools and tricks in order to complete the homework.

The exams were difficult and the course also required an in-depth term paper. I did manage to earn a solid A, but it was really a tough course. I did indeed learn a lot: one thing was to not take another graduate course anytime soon.

Instead, I opted for 31½ units of extension courses and earned two certificates at UC Davis: Hazardous Materials Management in 1995 and Site Assessment and Remediation in 1996. This gave me the knowledge I needed to cope with escalating responsibilities.

I prepared for a bigger role at Aerojet by taking numerous management courses (more than 400 contact hours) in various programs (UC Davis Executive Program, Cal Tech Management Program, NTL Institute, Aerojet Advanced Management Program, Aerojet Leadership 2000, etc.).

In July of 1993, I was promoted to director of engineering, which included chemical research and development, chemical operations, the environmental laboratory and development engineering to include a total of 300 people. This was a big promotion involving the consolidation of several diverse operations and management positions.

With the increased responsibility, I took on community volunteer activities connected with Aerojet, i.e., organizing the Junior Achievement Bowl-A-Thon fundraiser, serving on the Cal Poly Industry Advisory Council and the University of Washington Aeronautics and Astronautics Visiting Committee.

An amazing thing happened in March of 1995. Along with the rest of the project team, I signed the Near Earth Asteroid Rendezvous (NEAR) spacecraft with a gold, permanent-marker pen. Six years later, this satellite soft landed on the surface of the asteroid Eros. Bottom line, my name is on an object sitting on the surface of another body in our solar system – way too cool!

Prototypical of my style of mixing work, sports and family is what transpired following a big climb in Yosemite.

Doris and I met in Fresno, CA, drove to South Carlsbad Beach State Park and camped overnight with my folks. The next day, we picked up our younger son in Long Beach. As a part of his requirements for graduation from the California Maritime Academy, Todd had to spend a year at sea as part of his education.

He had just completed a 72 day assignment as a cadet on the Arco Independence, a huge oil tanker, making five round trips between Long Beach, CA and Alaska. After a short reunion, we returned to the beach to camp and surf for another three days. We then drove to La Jolla where I worked a day at a contractor facility while Doris and Todd toured the area. I also managed to surf near there at Wind and Sea in beautiful overhead waves.

We next traveled to Rialto, CA to visit with Doris' folks and attend a 30 year high school reunion. Then Doris and I left for a five day business trip to attend a board meeting at Stevens Institute of Technology in Hoboken, NJ. As usual, we had a great time together walking all through New York

City to see the sights and the people.[21]

On the home front, our boys branched out on their own. Shawn married Annika in April 1990 and in June of 1995 our first grandson, Tyler, was born. Shawn also managed to finish his BA with a double major in philosophy and media communications from California State University Sacramento. Later, he and Annika added another son Cameron and a daughter Chloe to their family.

Todd graduated from the California Maritime Academy with a double major in marine engineering technology and mechanical engineering. In May 1997, he married Tanja and they had two daughters, Emily and Olivia. Our five grandchildren span an eight year range. We have enjoyed our grandkids and still attempt to do annual family trips.

During the 1990s, we often spent the night at Shawn and Annika's home just to hang out and visit, or perhaps watch a movie or some football. We also spent a lot of the holidays and birthdays with the kids and their families.

Aerojet would shut down between Christmas and New Year's, resulting in slightly more than a week off each year. This allowed for quite a few vacation opportunities.[22]

When we bought a 34 foot Bounder in March 1995, our first class-A motor home, I was truly in pig heaven. With that unit, we could camp with impunity in virtually any conditions. It was incredible camping on a bluff right above the surf and see seagulls soaring below as the waves were breaking in the background.

My interest in astronomy was rekindled when the Schumacher-Levy Comet struck Jupiter in 1994. I decided to purchase a used Celestron 11 inch telescope and others would follow. Denny became my regular observing partner. We had many rewarding sessions together.

Typically, we would go to Blue Canyon and use the scope on a Friday night and then sleep out under the stars. The following morning, we would go climbing at Donner Summit followed by an afternoon swim in Donner Lake. Saturday night, we would use the scope again, sleep out and get up early enough to drive home and go to church.

Over the years, I bought and sold many astronomical instruments.[23]

Later in 1997, when comet Hale-Bopp arrived, my first visual sighting impressed me, which further sparked interest in more intense observing sessions. Finally in 1999, I saw Pluto – extremely faint and a real challenge. It is two thirds the size of our moon and two billion miles away! I plotted it for two nights to confirm the sighting.

I also made a pilgrimage to Kitt Peak National Observatory in Arizona that year and participated in a night observing session with their 16 inch Meade Schmidt Cassegrain.

The Solar Eclipse Cruise on the Dawn Princess in 1998 was one of the top five vacations of all time! The boys immediately dubbed it the "Nerd Cruise" and actually that was a pretty good description! Of the 1,100 passengers aboard the ship, I would estimate 600 of them fit this category in the truest sense of the word.

We had booked a standard cruise with an itinerary which included seeing the solar eclipse at sea near Aruba. There were lectures daily and guest celebrities aboard, including Apollo 11 moonwalker Buzz Aldrin. There had been announcements all week in the ship's newsletter describing the eclipse, what to expect and how to observe the event.

On eclipse day, as we were at sea and nearing the start of the eclipse, the deck was littered with a plethora of telescopes, cameras, binoculars, tripods, etc. and a whole lot of nerds. During the partial phases when it began to get dark outside, sort of like twilight, hundreds of dolphins began to ride the ships wake and breach the surface of the ocean – truly breathtaking. Shortly after, while I was setting up my instruments to view the progressing eclipse, a young, attractive blonde woman walked up to me and asked "What's going on anyway?" Amazing, utterly amazing!

The eclipse itself was sensational – during totality several planets, stars and of course the sun's corona can be seen – it was beautiful. It shakes you to the core to witness this type of primal event. Other highlights of the trip included touring San Juan on our own, seeing Carnival at Dominica, doing several great SCUBA dives with Doris (especially at Dominica) and just being aboard the ship.

In June of 1997, I received a huge promotion at Aerojet to vice president of engineering. Over the prior seven years I had absorbed several directorships and integrated the personnel into my organization. The head count in my organization had grown to 1,050 personnel.

I reported directly to the CEO at first. In November of 1997, as the Northern and Southern California facilities were combined, I ended up reporting to the vice president of operations, Bob Harris, which was fine with me as I really respected him.

These were truly exciting times and the projects were numerous and varied. They covered a broad spectrum of interdisciplinary activities which included liquid rocket engines, solid rocket motors, satellites, armaments, metrological and spy satellites, weapon systems, environmental remediation, resource recovery, chemical synthesis and pharmaceuticals. The personnel were amazing – intelligent, motivated and enjoyable.

The challenges were equally daunting, however, and as reorganizations occurred, I found myself working for Joe Carleone, Vice President of Operations, which personally was difficult. Our philosophical approach to handling the constant aerospace cycle of hire and layoff was fundamentally different. He had also come from the Southern California organization and that impacted our relationship as well.

To Joe's credit, I felt the operations vision statement developed under his leadership was one of the best ever: "Make Every Customer Successful." This is one of those easy-to-remember statements that has the potential to positively affect the operation and culture. As I rolled out this vision to small groups of Aerojet employees, I often asked how many of them had a personal vision for their life. The positive response was always sparse, which started me thinking this was an often overlooked aspect of life.

An excerpt from our 1997 Christmas letter pretty well summed up the job situation.

> As the vice president of engineering for Aerojet, the new CEO has passed on his wisdom with comments like 'Screw up and I won't kill you, I'll just shoot you in the knees' and 'If you lose a key program, you better plan to fall on your sword.' Well now ain't that special – I feel so motivated! The bummer is that I really love my job, I am excited about what I do and I need to make it to retirement. Somehow Aerojet is stronger than ever – but faces the constant threat of immediate annihilation – go figure. The future will always be uncertain – today I am at the top of my game and tomorrow I may be unemployed.

I also received this nice note from one of our secretaries as we were going through a major reorganization – it let me know I still mattered to some folks:

> Randy – just wanted to take a moment to thank you for the Christmas gift certificate from engineering. Duane and I enjoyed a wonderful dinner at Mikuni's, which is one of our very favorite places. Most of all I want to thank you for bringing me into your organization. The people are wonderful to work with and I am so happy to be back in a 'professional' environment. I hear you are doing a good job – if anyone can make things work, it is you. I remember those two rafting trips where you said, 'Just keep paddling and don't ever lose the paddle.' With the reorganization, we just need to 'keep moving and don't ever lose sight of our objectives' (even in the rough spots). Thanks for being there to guide us through the rapids (changes), keep us out of the whirlpools (going around in circles) and watching out for those hidden rocks just below the surface. Connie Magill.

Doris and I continued to have interesting vacations and in April of 1997, we toured Central America. While visiting Tikal, an incredible Mayan site in the jungles of Guatemala, we planned to see a sunset from the pyramids. After the park closed at sunset, they required visitors to have a guide if they wished to remain inside. I did not want a guide, so the first night we chose a rather obscure location and watched the sunset on our own. We then immediately slipped out of the park as it got dark.

On the second night, figuring I had the system worked out, we chose the famous Astronomical Pyramid and planned to stay until well after dark to avoid detection. Well, that plan did not work out too well. Caught inside Tikal without the obligatory guide, I offered a $5 bribe to a guard and he allowed us to remain in the ruins atop the Astronomical Pyramid. As the sun set, the green parrots and toucans begin to fly around and the howler monkeys started making a raucous noise. It was truly amazing.

After dark, we saw comet Hale-Bopp over the jungle canopy – what a sight. Since we only had a small penlight between us, we were glad there were other groups. It would have been nearly impossible to descend from the pyramid on our own in the pitch-black conditions and finding our way out of the park through the jungle would have been extremely difficult. It was scary out there alone in the dark.

On this trip, we even rode a collectiva bus with locals traveling with their food, chickens and kids. We also took a collectiva boat to visit San Andrés village across the lake from Flores. To return to the airport, we flagged down a mini bus. I love traveling that way – spontaneous and just like the locals.

Besides stops in Belize City, Copan and San Pedro Sula, we spent a week in Roatan (Honduras) SCUBA diving at CoCo View Resort.

On a regular basis, we went with our friends from church to abalone dive the North Coast of California (Anchor Bay, Dillon's Beach, Manchester, etc.). I was fairly proficient at getting abalone and enjoyed the free-diving experience along the rugged Northern California coast.

Business trips continued and I always enjoyed them. In 1997 we returned to Europe – Paris Air Show and attended a technical meeting in Germany. It was a great trip as we traveled by train and rental car across much of Europe.[24]

In May of 1998, I had a pleasant surprise when I received the Outstanding Alumni Award from the Aerospace Engineering Department at Cal Poly, Pomona. They had a nice banquet and I gave an after-dinner talk that was well received.

The following year, I received the California State Polytechnic University College of Engineering Distinguished Alumni Award. The ceremony was quite a nice affair, complete with a short acceptance speech and a wonderful trophy commemorating the event.

Holidays often included our kids. Easter, Fourth of July, Halloween and Christmas were frequently shared with family and I cherished those events, even though they were stressful at times. I tend to be very nostalgic about this sort of thing and always looked forward to being together as a family.

In June of 1998, I had a wonderful Father's Day with Shawn and Todd. They took me to Reno, NV to see the IMAX film "Everest." We then played nine holes of golf at a course near Auburn, CA. It was a great day with just the three of us. The kids also gave me a book about Everest with a nice card. This was sort of the pinnacle of our father-son relationship.

At Annika's suggestion, we took a family RV trip in August 1998 and it was really quite nice. We traveled to Mount Lassen Volcanic National Park in the RV for two nights. We camped at Manzanita Lake and North Summit Lake Campgrounds, hiked to the top of Lassen and enjoyed swimming and sightseeing. Later that year, we took a five day RV trip to Anchor Bay with our grandson, Tyler, to dive for abalone with the warehouse group. It was Tyler's first trip with us away from home.

Great Britain in September of 1998 was another unforgettable journey as we traveled by car all over England, Scotland and Wales. We often traveled on small narrow roads with hedgerows. It was magnificent, beautiful, exciting and scary all at the same time.[25]

Spending a week in London, I attended the Farnborough Air Show and visited most of the sights in the area. Other highlights were punting on Cherwell River, overnight and dinner with the Baroness at Kilravock Castle (dates back to 1460) and touring the Isle of Skye.

I was also involved with the GenCorp Cross Technology Team and the GenCorp Technology Steering Committee. I visited virtually all of the research facilities and became involved in new and ongoing research for the company. I also saw some great rocket launches – Titan II and Peacekeeper from Vandenberg Air Force Base and a Titan IV B from Cape Kennedy, complete with a tour of Space Launch Complex 40 with the next Titan and Mil Star payload in place on the pad.

Cruises had become one of our favorite ways to travel. In February 1999, we launched on a super vacation through the Panama Canal. We spent several days in Acapulco and took a local bus to Taxco. Taxco is an historic silver town where we stayed at the Los Arcos Hotel, the very same place my folks stayed in 1948. We watched the cliff divers and visited the central market.

Next, we boarded the Sun Princess and set sail for a ten day cruise which included stops at Puntarenas, Costa Rica, while transiting the entire length of the Panama Canal. We visited Cartagena, Columbia, Aruba, Saint Thomas and San Juan, Puerto Rico. It was a nice two week trip – quite relaxing with a lot of days at sea enjoying massages, reading, sightseeing and shopping.

Shortly after this trip, we were off to SCUBA dive in Mexico, beginning with a day and a half in Mexico City before traveling on to Cozumel. Sites visited along the way included Teotihuacan, Tulum, Coba, Chichen Itza and Cancun. Our ranking for the Aztec and Mayan sites is Tikal, Chichen Itza, Teotihuacan, Copan, Coba, Tulum and Altun Ha.

Our pets became part of the family and their loss was always traumatic. During this period, the first to pass away was Molly (a gentle and lovely Brittany Spaniel) at 16 years old. She was followed by Wiggles (an affectionate tabby cat) at 18 years; Heather (a lovable well-behaved Irish Setter) at 13 years of age; and Boots (an aloof black cat) at 17 years old.

Next was our poodle Ebbie at 15½ years while we were on a houseboat trip at Lake Shasta. He was truly the love of Doris' life. His death caught us off guard because he had perked up that day and wanted to walk with us on the trail to Shasta Caverns. In fact, the evening before he died, he ate everything in sight (chips, hot dog, chicken sausage, etc.) and seemed fine.

After a rough night, during which Ebbie had a stroke, his condition worsened at 5:30 a.m. Doris held him in her arms and we said goodbye on the back of the houseboat during a beautiful dawn of subdued light and a mist over the lake surrounded by a verdant forest. Ebbie looked around several times and we gave him numerous kisses as he passed away.

That precious, little dog will never be forgotten. Doris, of course, was extremely upset and I still miss him terribly. He was incredibly loyal to Doris and would always wait in the hallway for her to return. He loved to run and would bark while chasing after Heather or Daisy during our runs. Eating was a big event and he would cause a great stir with his bark when Doris got up in the mornings. He also would sit patiently at the table whenever I ate Cheerios or pizza and wait for some cereal or a piece of crust. What a wonderful dog.

In April of 1999, when my mentor Dick Simonsen retired from Aerojet and his arch rival Carl Fisher took over, work went to hell in a hurry. Carl had been Joe's boss before the reorganization and I did not have a prayer. Within 24 hours of the new CEO taking over, I was called in and told I had been given a new assignment. In a lateral transfer, I was to become chief scientist and be in charge of strategic planning for the organization and would have no direct reports.

Well, it didn't take a rocket scientist to figure out my days were numbered. I immediately started to negotiate my separation from Aerojet, but was repeatedly told mine was an important position and they were counting on me to handle it. I am not a strategic person by nature, but rather tend to converge on solutions rapidly. I felt it to be of paramount importance to keep my integrity intact by giving this my very best effort.

On the home front, as the Folsom area was growing and houses were built around us, I felt a need to escape suburban life. I recall taking our

Cocker Spaniel, Daisy, on long runs near the end of her life and running among the horses and cows near our home. It was a sad time when we lost her in 1999. That year, I did a dedication run for her (our normal run with all the spots I had named) – Out of the Blocks, Ebbie's Schoolyard Run, Daisy's Backside Run, Daisy Dog Shadow Hill, Pee Bush and Home Run.

June 1999, was a turning point in our relationship with Shawn and Annika. Things started to go south when we told them we were not planning to be full-time babysitters for their kids any longer. Doris just wanted to be grandma.

During our 1999 Capitola trip, Shawn was a pud. He said he wasn't having fun and did not want to come again next year. We eventually got over it, but it was a downer. Bottom line, he was under a lot of stress (financial and work). Add to that mix, I am somewhat obnoxious and you have the makings of a weekend from hell!

In spite of this, Doris and I, as well as Todd and Tanja, all had a good time.

In July 1999, I turned my last overseas trip for Aerojet into a 19 day vacation. I traveled there to attend the Unispace III Conference in Vienna. As we drove across Europe, I managed to visit Christian Gabl in Austria before squeezing in a climb with him in Chamonix, France.[26]

We were anxious to return home and pick up our new puppy, Sarah, but I did not want to go back to work.

Truly, my heart was not in this assignment as chief scientist and when budget crunches eventually came, Joe asked me if I was still interested in negotiating a settlement. I said I was and so I did. I left the company after more than 17 years, taking a separation package and early retirement. My last day at Aerojet was March 31, 2000.[27]

I learned some valuable lessons from Aerojet. My philosophy was always to objectively try to evaluate my weak points, as well as strong points, by frequently seeking feedback. I would surround myself with the best people possible and especially those who complemented my weak areas. I fully believe in delegating assignments to the lowest level possible. If projects were on track or turning out well, I avoided micromanaging and generally only interacted when they wanted direction.

I never took credit for work my reports had performed – I always let them pitch their own results. If things turned out well, I let them take the credit. On the other hand, if something went wrong, it was always my responsibility for any mistakes and I took the blame. Bottom line, as mentioned in an earlier chapter, if I could make my employees look good as well as my boss, I felt I would look good by default. Furthermore, I never felt threatened by my direct reports and, in fact, always tried to have several reports trained and qualified to take over my job. I learned a long time ago that you won't get promoted unless you have someone ready to assume your responsibilities.

Bottom line: don't be afraid to groom your replacement. You will never move up unless your replacement is ready to assume your job. If you are replaced, as I was at Aerojet, move on.

Other great lessons:

• When receiving feedback, the only acceptable answer is, "Thank you." Never rationalize away input by countering with "But, you don't understand." Take time to evaluate the feedback and, if appropriate, make some changes.

• In a male dominated work environment, like Aerojet was in the 1980s, a woman wanting to succeed had to take on the attributes of a man. She was then considered a pushy bitch.

• Pareto principle, also known as the 80/20 rule, states that for many events roughly 80 percent of the effects come from 20 percent of the causes. For example, 80 percent of the sales come from 20 percent of the customers. Use this principle to figure out what to focus on to get the most from your efforts.

• Work on important, but not urgent, tasks – this is strategic in nature. When you are attacking important and urgent tasks you are essentially fighting forest fires.

Because the job and associated daily commute would no longer be an issue, Doris and I decided to relocate. We did a lot of research and carefully considered the beach areas in Southern California, the Reno and Carson City areas of Nevada and the foothills around Sacramento. Our decision was made on the basis of our personal vision and it basically came down to where our kids were at the time and how we would feel if they relocated.

We decided on Foresthill, CA.

We bought a lot located one hour northeast of Sacramento at an elevation of 2,300 feet at the base of the Sierra Nevada Mountains and hired a builder. The small, rural community of Foresthill was perfect for us. My plan was to do consulting after retiring, which would likely mean commuting to and from the Sacramento Airport (about an hour away). Of course, the move brought on the stress of selling our home, packing, moving, temporary living arrangements, unpacking and so on. Fortunately, our home in Folsom sold quickly and we were off to a new millennium.

Top right - Todd and Doris
Yosemite, CA

Top left - In the Bounder at Sand
Dollar Beach Central California
Coast

Left - Moving West
Yellowstone National Park

Bottom left - Venetian Village
Capitola, CA

Bottom right - Camping at the beach
Southern California

Ask the Rocket Scientist, Houston, TX

Randy as vice president of engineering, GenCorp Aerojet

Punting on the Cherwell River, Oxford, England

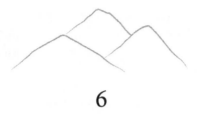

6

WORLD CLASS RAPIDS

As Willie stepped out of his raft, he tore an "L"-shaped hole in the pressurized tube and it immediately went flat. Realizing what he had done, he broke down and cried over the gravity of the situation. There were still 100 miles of river remaining including Lava Falls at flood stage. Steve tried to console Willie by telling him things were going to be all right – in a macho sort of way.

"Stop crying and duct tape the damn tube," Steve said, "and we'll fix it tomorrow."

With tensions running quite high, Papillon, a fiery redheaded woman about five feet tall, ran over to Steve, looked up at him and said, "Who told you you're the river god?" With her head coming up to about his naval, I thought for certain he was going to pile-drive her right into the wet sand.

In February 1983, I purchased a used, 14 foot Miwok raft setup from Wayne Klinger for $1,000. Rafting became a passion for several years during which I ran virtually all the rivers in the Western U.S., many at extreme flows. A number of the trips involved family and ultimately my son, Shawn, became quite an accomplished oarsman. Local trips on the various forks of the American River at flood stage were definitely Class V and plenty scary.

Off to a Rough Start

On the first raft trip to California's Merced River in a used vehicle I had recently purchased, I immediately ran into some difficulties. Son Shawn and Dick McCamey, a friend from work, were with me and the vehicle started acting up 30 miles from home near Galt. I changed the sparkplugs and we reached El Portal before the transmission seized up. I called around and discovered the nearest transmission shop was in Merced, more than 65 miles away. Unfortunately, my insurance did not cover towing a vehicle more than just a few miles.

I pulled the driveline. Luckily, I met Wayne that day on the river. After his run, he towed me more than 40 miles over winding mountainous roads using an old climbing rope before the highway patrol stopped us. Fortunately, we were near the top of the pass near Cathy's Valley. We talked our way out of a citation, said goodbye to Wayne and then crashed for the night alongside the road.

The next morning was Sunday and I talked a guy in a pickup into towing me to the top of the pass. From there, we coasted all the way into Planada, nearly 18 miles away. The guy in the pickup followed us and then towed us the last few miles to the transmission shop in Merced. Shawn and Dick rode the wino express (i.e., Greyhound Bus) back to Sacramento and I stayed and had the transmission rebuilt the next day.

On one 75 mile rafting run down the Yampa and Green rivers in Colorado and Utah, with flows of over 20,000 CFS (Class V at flood stage), Wayne Klinger and I had a nasty confrontation. When we came to Warm Springs rapid, definitely the test piece at this extreme flow, I snuck my raft down the right-hand side. Wayne chose to run his straight down the middle.

He flipped his raft resulting in a very dangerous swim for its occupants and the loss of a lot of our food. In the process, the oar pin hit Wayne in the small of his back causing an injury that would plague him for many years afterward. That night at camp, Wayne and I literally went nose-to-nose yelling at each other regarding the plan for the next day. We were nearly at the fist-fighting stage when we disengaged.

I had the good fortune of meeting Mike Doyle and Steve Ellberg on the North Fork of the Yuba River during a high-runoff spring trip. As I chased around Northern California in search of new whitewater challenges, I kept crossing paths with these guys and we ultimately became good friends. Steve was a walk-on and Mike had a full scholarship on the UC Berkeley swim team.

Mike even participated in the 1980 Olympic Trials. Had the Soviets not invaded Afghanistan, which in turn led to the USA boycotting the Summer Games, Mike would have been quite competitive. They were incredible athletes and made a formable rafting team. They had also been involved in the design and testing of the first self-bailing rafts called State-of-the-Art Rafts (commonly known as SOTAR's) and in 1982 started their own rafting company, "Beyond Limits Adventures."

A classic raft trip was our first one down the Grand Canyon in Arizona in early summer 1984. In preparation for the journey, Doris and I ran the Merced River from El Portal at flood stage (6,000 CFS) with our good friend Elvis McCann. It turned out to be a real disaster as we flipped just below Red Bud campground and took a half mile swim in solid Class IV-V whitewater.

After nearly drowning, we recovered the raft. I sent Doris along with Elvis' wife, Melissa, in their car and Elvis and I continued another 20 miles downstream before taking out below Briceburg. Doris was very upset that we continued in those dangerous conditions and the entire experience really traumatized her.

The Granddaddy of Them All

I was not discouraged by our less-than-satisfactory training run, so we left two weeks later as June 1984 was drawing to a close. We did casual camping on the way to the Colorado River to break up the long drive. We were about to embark on a 16 day trip through the Grand Canyon from Lees Ferry to Diamond Creek. It would involve traveling 226 miles on the river and include over 50 major rapids.

What makes the Grand Canyon so great is it not only has some of the best big water rapids in the world, but also has dozens of spectacular hikes and attractions.[28]

At the site where we put in, we were told the flow was a steady 40,000 CFS. They discouraged any rafts smaller than 18 feet in length from attempting the river under these extremely dangerous conditions.

Doris and I were in our 14 foot Miwok; Mike and Steve showed up with a 16 foot SOTAR (the first self-bailing raft to ever attempt the Grand Canyon). Willie had his World War II vintage landing craft named the "House Rock" that was in the process of falling apart. In fact the only big raft we had in the entire group was an 18 foot Havasu which belonged to George Cogorno, the permit holder. Mike also had a kayak, which he was planning to use in some of the bigger rapids.

I told Mike I was unaware he even knew how to kayak. He responded, "This will be my second day in a kayak."

To add to the mix, Willie brought along a couple, Wally and Papillon, who had never camped or run any whitewater before. In spite of the park service recommendation, we quickly launched and moved downstream. We soon discovered exactly how powerful the river was at this flow. In the Roaring 20s, Steve flipped the SOTAR in what did not even look like a rapid.

Starting on day one, Mike and Steve chose to get drunk every night and as a result practiced questionable hygiene. One night in particular, they decided to cook their fully defrosted now green steaks over a small fire consisting of their garbage!

Eating the partially cooked meat did not seem to bother them and when it came time to clean dishes they had a rather unique technique. They would gather the dirty utensils in the center of their raft and then throw buckets of water at them before putting them away. Amazingly, neither of them ever got sick.

Even more amazing was how they handled their turn on the toilet detail. As a group, we had several 55 mm rocket boxes to use as toilets. Each was lined with a plastic garbage bag, fitted with a toilet seat and used until full – then the next rocket box was put into operation.

Each morning, it was necessary to sprinkle quick lime over the feces and force the air out of the plastic bag by submerging it under water and then sealing it before returning it to the rocket box. Steve and Mike were in charge of the first toilet kit used on the trip and, in their somewhat hung-over state, they simply sealed up the rocket box and tied it to their raft.

Well, after a few days, the darn thing over pressurized resulting in a minor explosion. It caught fire and smoldered for the rest of the trip. From that point on, it wasn't necessary to look for Mike and Steve on the river; we just followed the smell.

One night while sitting around, Steve started talking about how he had been turned down twice for a job as a stuntman in Hollywood by a Jewish individual. He was living in Beverly Hills at the time and was quite bitter because of the rejections. He certainly looked the part – six feet, six inches tall, solid muscle and quite a good-looking guy.

In his inebriated state he blurted out, "I sure hope no one here is a Jew."

Immediately Papillon, a five foot tall fiery redhead woman complete with tattoos, stood up and said "Well I am." So began World War III.

Mary Cogorno, a veteran of many whitewater trips, told me later that on any extended trip where tension is created by extreme conditions, there is always some sort of confrontation after about five days. This has proved true in a variety of sports. Her insight has served me well over the years.

When tension causes conflict, I try not to take it personally, back off a little and just go with the flow as much as possible. I tell myself that everyone is here to have a good time and that includes me. Unless it is an issue of safety, I try not to push any issues to a point that causes confrontation.

It wasn't long before we had our first encounter with the "Nudies." While hiking up the Little Colorado River, we noticed a half dozen naked people caked in mud acting like apes beneath an overhanging rock. As so often works out on a river trip, we frequently ran into each other during the next two weeks. Other river friends included "Skirt Man and the dory people." This commercial dory trip was led by a full-bearded man who chose to wear a skirt.

The test piece for the river at these high flows was definitely Crystal Rapid. Normally, the rapids in the Grand Canyon are rated on a scale of one to ten, ten being equivalent to big water Class V. At 40,000 CFS, Crystal was rated a solid 11 plus. Doris, having already been tossed out of the raft at Hermit Rapid, was not interested in running Crystal in our small raft. In fact, I could not talk anyone else into climbing aboard to help in high siding as I oared through it.

I ended up soloing the thing and had a perfect run. After witnessing this, George asked me to pilot his 18 foot raft down Crystal Rapid. With the extra size and weight I had to run it differently, resulting in the entire raft disappearing under water for several seconds. I still remember George yelling "Oh shit" as the front of the raft entered the huge 20 foot crashing wave. The run turned out fine, but for a moment, as we surfed underwater, I was not sure if we were going to come out of it right-side up or not.

In fact, Willie did manage to flip his raft in Crystal, but Mike had a flawless kayak run in the huge waves rolling up twice. Go figure!

At one point we pulled into a potential camp only to find the nudies had already decided to stay there. As we began pulling out, Skirt Man's group arrived. One of his clients, an older woman, said to the nude man on shore, "Excuse me for staring, but it has been so long since I have seen one of those that I can't help myself!"

Stopping at Shimumo Creek, Willie tore a foot long "L" shaped hole in the tube of his raft as he stepped off. Of course, the raft immediately went flat and Willie stressed out. He was beside himself in tears as he fully realized the gravity of the situation. We still had more than 100 miles to go and he would have to run Lava Falls at flood stage with a damaged raft.

Steve, in an effort to assure him everything would be all right, walked over to the raft and told Willie to "Stop crying, duct tape the damn tube and we will fix it tomorrow."

Papillon immediately ran over and with her head at about the level of Steve's navel, looked up at him and yelled, "Who told you you're the river god?"

I fully expected Steve to pile drive her straight down into the wet sand!

The next day was the Fourth of July and we spent the entire day repairing

Willie's raft. Mike and Steve indulged in drinking once again and managed to pass out about midday with their faces down in the sand. With surface temperatures in excess of 120 degrees Fahrenheit, we just left them lying in their vomit for awhile before finally waking them up.

Later that night, we celebrated the successful repair by lighting off some fireworks.

We all hiked up Tapeats Creek to its source, Thunder Springs. Willie and I had heard rumors that with climbing gear it was possible to enter the spring and explore the cave inside the cliff. This spring was several hundred feet above the creek on a sheer wall and all the water gushed out of a single six foot elliptical hole with incredible force. After several attempts to climb through the opening, we chickened out, but told ourselves some day we will get inside that cave.

Another hike up Havasu Creek to Beaver Tail Falls ended with Willie and me going into the Green Room. This small cave, complete with stalagmites and stalactites, was located under the waterfall and required swimming underwater through a narrow, five foot long dark passage to enter the cave. Willie went first and then showed me the way inside – it was quite scary and I could have never gone first.

Once inside, it was awesome. You could look out and see the green light filtering into the cave from under the waterfall. We also did some 40 foot jumps into Havasu Creek from ledges high above the creek.

Farther downstream, we inadvertently learned our river names. As we pulled into Lava Falls, Skirt Man said to the Nudies, "Here come the Crazies!" Our runs through Lava Falls were all good and everyone was relieved the worst rapids were finally behind us.

Later, while camped at Whitmore Wash, we would experience a massive flash flood. The thunderstorm that caused the flood occurred miles from the river, but the accompanying roar was close and very loud. Once we heard it we ran towards the drainage and what we witnessed was very humbling. Rocks the size of small cars moved around in a riverbed that was dry only minutes before and the Colorado River became murky and choked with debris.

At mile 205, I managed to flip our raft resulting in a terrifying experience for Doris and me. At these extreme flows, as the river bends to the left, a series of massive waves lead directly into a huge boiling pillow of water on a house-sized rock. To the left, the main river continues; to the right, is real trouble. We flipped on the pillow and entered the Room of Doom on the right – a huge eddy at the base of a cliff face more than one quarter mile long and 100 feet wide, complete with a four foot high eddy fence keeping us from re-entering the main river.

With our heavily loaded overturned raft and just Doris and me, we couldn't flip it back over. We helplessly watched as our entire party moved swiftly through the rapid disappearing downriver and out of sight. We tried everything we could think of to right the raft and paddle out of the eddy. We literally tore the skin off our hands in the process and ripped the only tree on the cliff face out by its roots trying to leverage it to flip the raft back over.

I attempted to tie the oars to the bottom side of the raft and oar out. Nothing worked. And to make the situation worse, commercial raft companies were signaling for a helicopter rescue and I was signaling back – "NO!"

After more than an hour, Doris was crying and I was losing it just as Mike, Steve and Willie came climbing down the cliff to our rescue. Within minutes we had righted the raft, cleaned out the debris trapped inside, broke through the eddy fence to the open river and rejoined our group a few miles downstream.

It was finally someone else's turn to prepare the meals. We had organized into cook groups and Doris and I had taken the first week. Then Willie, who had the second week, asked us to help since he was cooking alone. It was now up to Wally and Papillon for the last week. This is when Papillon announced they did not know how to cook. We basically just grazed through the food boxes for the rest of the trip eating whatever we fancied.

When we reached the takeout at Diamond Creek, we found out the thunderstorms had damaged the road causing a delay in getting our vehicle to the river. In the end, it was a fantastic adventure and I think Doris' last entry in her diary sums it up best: "I have said my farewell to the Colorado River. It had enriched my life and terrified me with its strength!"

On the way home we spent a night in Las Vegas.

Pirates - California Style

Mike Doyle decided to do the first commercial run of Giant Gap on the North Fork of the American River (Class V) and asked me to captain the second self-bailing paddle raft. This was an interesting challenge since I had always used oars. I had never commanded a paddle craft before and had never used a self-bailer.

I still remember the night before the run when we camped on the top of the canyon and one of the clients asked Mike and me how many times we had run Giant Gap. Mike answered, many times, which was an exaggeration since neither of us had ever run it before!

The next day, I only flipped the raft once and by the end of this two day trip I was pretty good at running a paddle craft. Following the run, the rented SOTAR I used was sold to me at a big discount and I now owned my first self-bailer.

I was also fortunate enough to be invited on several first-rafting descents of rivers with Mike and Steve. These runs, made possible by the advent of the self-bailing rafts, included some incredible never-before run sections of rivers.[29]

These years also ushered in what is known in the rafting industry as "Pirate Trips." It is not legal to charge for raft trips without a commercial permit, but in my case it all began innocently enough.

Basically, I was taking many friends on day and multiday raft trips on local rivers and in the process spent several thousand dollars a year on equipment, vehicle wear, fuel costs, permits, put-in and shuttle fees, etc. I decided to charge $5 per person per day to help offset these costs and, amazingly, the people I had taken the most times protested this modest charge.

I immediately said, "Screw it, from now on its $25 per day per person, period!"

This charge was still a fraction of the costs for commercial raft trips on the same rivers, so once the word got out, I was overwhelmed with requests for family trips, day trips and so on. Before long, this escalated and I was putting together multiday, class V river trips while pocketing some pretty good cash in the process.

Because I was totally upfront with any participants, I was able to fly under the radar for several years before I decided to sell all my rafting gear and exit this activity. Basically, I was able to completely pay for all my equipment and trips through this dubious approach.

Several of my friends also pirated and the results were not always positive. On one trip in particular, two friends had an outdated private permit for the Tuolumne and had arranged for several clients to join them on the trip. They carefully changed the date on the permit to the current year and launched above the normal put-in at Meryl's Pool.

As they passed the pool, a ranger ordered them to come over so he could check their permit. After looking at the permit, he told them the ranger that had signed the permit had left the service a year ago. He informed them their permit had been doctored and was not valid. He then asked for everyone's ID.

Several of the clients protested and announced they were merely paying customers and why were they being cited. Busted big time!

Ironically, these guys went on to form a totally legitimate rafting company that has since prospered greatly. In fact, years later I even guided a few times for them and still on occasion borrow raft gear from them.

For six years in the mid-1980s, I averaged over 30 rafting days per year and literally did hundreds of different runs throughout California and the USA.[30]

Kayaking

In July of 1984, we purchased two used kayaks completely outfitted for $215 each. Shawn and I began kayaking rivers together. Over the years, many other kayaks would follow.[31]

Learning how to roll and read whitewater from a small boat were new challenges. We soon had it dialed in and did several runs before Shawn decided it was not something he wanted to get hurt doing. I was totally hooked, however, and continued running more and more difficult rivers.

Kayaking picked up in the mid 1980s and I averaged 42 kayaking days per year for over a decade. Both numerous and varied runs were successfully completed.[32]

I particularly enjoyed putting together long stretches of rivers by combining several sections, or runs. My idea here was to run entire rivers from dam to dam wherever possible. We also often ran these rivers at flood stage, which increased the difficulty considerably.

While kayaking, I did many moonlight runs on the South Fork of the American and particularly enjoyed solo runs. These solo kayak runs included seven onsite solo runs (i.e., rivers I had never run before) as well as dozens of solo runs on the North and South Forks of the American River. Shawn and I even managed to boogie board the South Fork American well before river boards were even invented.

I was fortunate enough to meet Chuck Stanley and later helped hire him at Aerojet. Chuck had been the 1980 National Salmon Kayaking Champion, was one of the top boaters in the U.S. and had recently co-authored *A Guide to the Best Whitewater in the State of California*. This allowed me to kayak regularly with Chuck and he was a fantastic teacher.

We often kayaked one night a week after work from April to October over a period of several years (North and South Forks of the American River). In addition, Chuck took me on some incredible runs – way beyond my ability. Under his tutelage, my skills greatly improved.

As with many of the sports I have been involved in, hanging out with the best of the best results in rapid advances in your skill level, or results in death!

Rafting with Mike Doyle and kayaking with Chuck Stanley were genuine high points in these sports. In addition, as with surfing, even after thousands of rapids, individual runs are forever burned in my memory.

Examples included the first rafting runs through Crystal and Lava Falls on the Grand Canyon at flood stage in July 1984, getting repeated kayak endos on the North Fork of the American on my birthday in December of 1984, running my first oar boat down Cherry Creek's miracle mile in

October 1985, inadvertently side surfing Clavey Falls on the Tuolumne in my kayak in June 1988 and having to crawl out along the bottom in order to escape the violent melee above.

Not all trips went well. On a trip to kayak the Merced River at high flows in May of 1987, I managed to cut my left eyelid in the lower stretch by going over a small waterfall upside down. The next day, I seriously sprained my ankle at Ned's Gulch as I slammed upside down into the wall.

I remember Chuck Stanley's comment – "It's a good thing this was not a three day weekend or you would have killed yourself!"

Later, Chuck taught me a new more compact roll technique, which I mastered on both sides.

Back to the Canyon

In May of 1990, I obtained a private permit for the Grand Canyon and put together a small team consisting of five people: Willie Spencer in his 16 foot, self-bailing raft with Glenn Larson; Bill solo in his 15 foot cataraft; Tom Hoskin of Canada and myself in kayaks. The flow varied between 4-17K CFS, but was predominately between 10-15K CFS.

We did encounter low flows and strong headwinds through the Marble Canyon section which made it difficult for the rafts. The 226 mile trip from Lee's Ferry to Diamond Creek was completed in 15 days. We took many great side hikes and ran some fantastic rapids, especially in the area known as the Jewels.

In a small party, everyone must work together in order to accomplish all the tasks associated with a long wilderness experience of this type. If anyone does not do his or her share of the work it is obvious immediately.

Well, Bill was basically a slug with little or no rafting skills! He started the trip with a sound system powered by batteries and solar cells complete with hundreds of cassette tapes and amplified speakers. Each night, after we arrived at camp, Tom and I would unload his raft while he reclined in a lawn chair and watched us do all the camp chores. He was so lazy, he didn't even bother to drain the water from the ammo cans that housed his stereo system.

After several days on the river and listening to his loud music echo through the canyons, completely destroying the peace and calm of this beautiful environment, the stereo system suddenly made a growling sound and died. What a relief! He continually slopped his way through rapid after rapid, a real testament to the river-worthy cataraft design.

After two weeks of this no-work ethic, one evening when dinner was ready, I yelled down to Bill and said, "It's safe to come up now, all the work is done."

His response was rather surprising.

As he ran up to the hill in a rage to where the dining area was set up, he was yelling at the top of his lungs, "Are you saying I am not doing my share of the work?"

The four of us just roared with laughter. Even with him as a drawback, it was a super trip.

I have many vivid memories of being washed back down the face of big rapids by the breaking waves as we negotiated our way through this unbelievable canyon with its melee of world-class rapids. As always, being in the wilderness with Willie was great – he is a true outdoorsman and friend.

The Hardcore Stuff

Once kayaking replaced rafting, on rare occasions I would still take friends downriver on a raft. However, in 1991, I got an invitation from Mike Doyle to do the Upper Kings Canyon run – 14½ miles of V-plus river recommended for "teams of seasoned experts only!" How could I pass up that?

Just getting there required grit and determination. We had to travel 50 dusty miles of dirt road and then hike with the rafts two miles down a steep hill to the put-in site.

Garlic Falls is one of the all-time classic rapids offered on this run. Surrounded by vertical cliffs, this was a half mile of unforgettable whitewater. Our run would be later immortalized in the film *California Whitewater*, produced by Camera One and Beyond Limits Adventures.

We only flipped once and rode the river all the way with the exception of one portage.

I did manage to terrify myself while kayaking with Al Albright and Doug Jones on a trip down Robe Canyon on the South Fork Stillaguamish in Washington State. It's a solid class V run. Other difficult runs would follow.[33]

I also got in over my head joining Chuck Stanley to make the Golden Gate run on the South Fork of the American River, another solid class V. I still think I was invited to provide entertainment for the others.

The run is described as "a novel substitute for jumping off the Golden Gate Bridge." As luck would have it, Lars Holbek was there making a movie titled *Wild Americans* (Watershed Films, 1992). As one might guess, in some incredible footage I was featured being thoroughly trashed by one of those terrifying rapids.

At flood stage, the South Fork of the American from Chili Bar to Salmon Falls is a scary river. John Stoffel and I made two exciting runs with one at 8,000 CFS and the other at 13,000 CFS.

Many times during these intense kayak runs, I would think of a T-shirt

I once saw relating to the movie Deliverance – It read, "Paddle faster ... I hear banjos playing." That thought always helped to calm me down.

Another strategy I used to overcome anxiety when running extremely difficult rapids was to tell myself that when I arrived at the rapid I would simply portage. Then, when I actually got there, I would scout the sucker and run it. For some inexplicable reason that always worked.

There were some terrifying times kayaking – even after a particular run. Kiwi and I planned to do Webber Creek in the winter of 1993. We were told there was a watermark on the Lotus Road Bridge and not to put in if the water was above that mark – or even close. In winter, these small streams can rise and fall rapidly in a rainstorm.

We checked the bridge pier and determined the watermark was the seam in the bridge pier. Fortunately, the water was below that mark so we felt safe to put in. Webber Creek is a classic class IV-plus mixed with trees and brush that made the run particularly dangerous.

Kiwi managed to get dumped a couple of times causing him to lose his paddle and pogies. However, we made the run without any major setbacks and we returned to where we put in. As we approached where our car was parked, we noticed the water level had dropped – exposing the reason we had such a difficult time.

The lower water level revealed the watermark on the bridge we were supposed to use as a danger reference. When we arrived several hours earlier, the water had already risen past the watermark unbeknownst to us – no wonder the run was so hard!

I passed the test in administering first aid on a river trip down the Cosumnes with my nephew Mike DeMarco. The Cosumnes is a class IV that is a little over 20 miles long and we fared well for the first half of it. After coming to a rather treacherous stretch, we went ashore to scout the best route through it.

After re-entering the water, we worked our way through the rapids and did well until the last waterfall. Mike did not negotiate the area well and went over the waterfall upside down and landed with his face striking a submerged rock. The blow broke his nose and opened a gushing facial wound.

After stopping the bleeding and calming him down, I applied some butterfly strips to his wound. Feeling much better after the blood flow had stopped, Mike and I pressed on.

After completing the last eight miles, we drove straight to the hospital to have a doctor look at his injury. After assessing Mike's wound, the doctor said he couldn't do any better than what I had done and sent us home.

Dislocated shoulders are also a hazard of running the rivers. I had to reset one kayaker's shoulder during a trip down the South Fork of the American River and assisted with resetting another one on a Grand Canyon run.

We saw some interesting vehicles while running rivers. While taking out on the Cosumnes during one trip, we saw an old beater with the roof caved in. It turned out that the concave roof was a perfect fit for a kayak with no roof rack needed. The car belonged to a member of the Tattooed Love Dogs, a local rock group.

I saw another trashed vehicle on the North Fork of the American that had a bumper sticker reading, "My other car is a piece of shit."

Chuck Stanley decided his bachelor party would consist of a run down Cherry Creek on the Tuolumne River. It's a dangerous, nine mile, class V hurdle that all macho boaters must overcome. One either struts his or her stuff or gets stuffed attempting it.

Having already gone down it a couple times in a raft, I knew it was going to be a tough run for me in a kayak. I decided I would be OK if I simply followed the leaders knowing they were all first-class kayakers. Unfortunately, they all went different directions leaving me trying to decide who would take the path least terrifying.

I managed to hold my own until we came to a rapid known as Coffin Rock. I couldn't help thinking how aptly it was named. Rounding a blind corner, I caught the bottom of an eddy full of fellow kayakers just above a series of steep drops. As I struggled to stay in the eddy above the first drop, Chuck grabbed the bow loop of my kayak right before I started over the edge – backward.

Knowing I would pull him over with me, I shouted "Better let go!" With that, I went over the falls backward and capsized in a small pool below. I quickly rolled upright just as I went over the next drop – only this time going forward. From that point on, I negotiated the rest of the run successfully, but it was scary.

After that day, I made two awesome runs down Cherry Creek with Chuck and in 1991 had a perfect run. The water was flowing at 1,200 CFS and I had to make only one portage.

Back to the Grand Canyon

It always amazes me when I go from the local rivers to the Grand Canyon; I never tire of running that river.

My third trip down the Grand Canyon came in July 2001. A 16 day run by kayak and the group included son Shawn, nephew Grant Peeters and other friends on rafts.

During this trip, Shawn suffered a scorpion sting while sleeping on the beach that proved quite painful. His buddy Jeff Varin started calling him

Scorpio after that, but Shawn had another name in mind.

"You might as well start calling me f ... ing Tom Sawyer," Shawn said, "because I am sleeping on the raft for the rest of the trip."

The trip also included having lunch in the rain at Red Wall Cavern and riding the water slide at the Little Colorado River.

When we reached the notorious Hance Rapid, a 30 foot drop rated as a nine with the flows we were experiencing, there was a group camping where we pulled in to scout the rapids. I asked permission to leave our kayaks and rafts on the beach by the camp and climbed above the site to scout the river. I returned 20 minutes later, put back into the river and made a flawless run too focused to notice two 20 something attractive ladies taking a shower totally in the nude along the bank.

However, Chuck John noticed and said he wanted the job of "soaper" for the next "titty" party we encounter.

My excitement peaked at mile 95 while being hammered in Hermit Rapid. I surfed, endoed, rolled back up, took two huge waves backward, went airborne over the next wave, was slammed over by the following one, attempted two rolls and swam the final third of the way to complete the run.

We decided to take a group picture at mile 213 and the process was delayed by our friend Peter. Peter is a fine athlete and a great oarsman, but walks with an awkward gait and exemplifies the term "nerd." To hurry him along, the others were calling for him to run.

That's when Shawn shouted, "Run, Forrest, run!"

We encountered some spectacular storms as well. One afternoon, we were hit with wind gusts up to 100 miles per hour; that combined with the rain resulted in some two to three foot rolling waves and waterfalls in every direction. The evening lightning storms entertained us.

Elves Chasm was fantastic, as was the hike from Deer Creek Falls to Tapeats via Surprise Valley. Although a little hurried, I hiked with Al, Kiwi and Tom to Whispering Falls and also made a trip up Havasu Creek to Beaver Tail Falls with Denny. Both were super hikes.

There were some low points involving brief confrontations. One in particular was with Bob, an extremely laid-back type individual. I had to pull him off the oars at mile 131 after several serious screw-ups. Breaking an oar, taking the wrong lines down rapids without wearing a life jacket and serious errors in judgment don't mix well in life-threatening situations. I was sure glad Al and Tom came along as they are very strong kayakers.

In fact, the best part of the entire trip was being in the Canyon with my great friends Al, Rick, Denny, Chuck John, Kiwi, Wayne and Tom – many I hadn't been on an adventure with in years. But best of all, I enjoyed sharing the experience with my son Shawn and nephew Grant.

In July 2003, I returned to the Grand Canyon with Al Albright to join my friend Craig Horangic and his group. Al and I were the only kayakers and most of the group's members were rather young. But we enjoyed the kayaking and I especially enjoyed not being the leader on that trip.

I had to roll up four times, but had several great runs in big rapids on Horn, Granite and Hermit. I ran Crystal three times. I experienced another mess-up at the bottom of Lava Falls where I couldn't roll up and had to swim out of my kayak.

The group included some good climbers and we pulled off the difficult moves to get through the entrance of Thunder Springs. From there we climbed another quarter mile into an incredible cave with an exposed underground waterfall. I had wanted to do this adventure since Willie and I first attempted it 13 years earlier.

We also climbed into the Blue and Thunder rooms after locating them under Upper Beaver Tail Falls on Havasu Creek.

With the exception of being at political odds with this liberal group, it was an enjoyable trip overall.

After four trips down Grand Canyon, I found it was easier to obtain permits for smaller groups. Also, small groups were easier to manage.

In May 2008, Doug Williscroft, Al Albright, Kiwi and Shawn Wood, Tom Farren, Peter Elder, Eric Stroud and I made another fantastic voyage. Al, Kiwi and I kayaked while the rest traveled in rafts. The eight person group proved to be the ideal size for the 16 day journey.

We returned to old campsites and attractions such as Red Wall Cavern. I often would hang behind the group and then kayak solo – a déjà vu type experience. The Jewels were great and included a rear-ender-to-brace move and I made the Lava Falls run with only one roll.

The downside to this trip was having broken my left foot surfing in Hawaii the week before, plus I was suffering from an inguinal hernia. The broken foot was a real handicap and the hernia worsened as the trip progressed.

On top of that, I broke my new paddle in Horn and I ended up chickening out of running Granite and Hermit. I have since regretted being psyched out and not running those rapids on this trip. There was also the incident where I thought a rattlesnake was swimming alongside me in one of the whirlpools. While negotiating the turbulent water, several people on rafts pointed out that there was a snake next to me. Catching only a peripheral view of the critter, I did my best not to get knocked over and be involved in the impending doom. It turned out to only be a stick that looked like a snake. Whew!

Some good news: the hernia surgically was repaired after my return and the foot healed without further complications.

It is hell growing old, as my sixth trip down the Grand Canyon in 2011 was scheduled to take place just three months after I had broken my hip skiing. I felt up to making the trip, but thought I'd better email my travel companions with the following note.

Subject: Grand Canyon SLACKER!!! Hello everyone, My hip is coming along great and I am confident that I will be able to actually kayak part of the run. I may have to ride in a raft most of the way – just have to see how everything goes. The surgery will have been three months to the day as we launch on May 20th, 2011. Probably can do some limited hiking as well. Overall the prognosis is excellent and the Doctor and Physical Therapist both say it is a go. BUT ... they also said I cannot lift stuff until about four months and won't be full strength until around six months. This could change for the better, but I need to prepare as if it won't. So here is the deal – if I cannot lift much, I really cannot do my fair share of the work (loading and unloading, getting my kayak into and out of the river, lifting or beaching/launching the rafts, carrying the pooper, heavy set up items like the dining fly, etc.). This is a bummer in a small group because there is a lot of work to be done every day on a trip like this and a slacker really stands out. I want to go on this trip – but I need to know that it is OK with all of you considering it is likely that I can't do my fair share of the work. I will go with the absolute per person vote rather than a majority vote – this means that if any one individual would rather I not go; I will withdraw from the trip and try to find a replacement. Please let me know what you want in this regards ASAP so I can take any necessary action. Thanks for your consideration in this matter. Randy

Tom Dancs replied:

Randy, Well considering your age, I was planning on carrying you around the whole time, reminding you every ten minutes where we are and what time it is, making your tea, helping to put your dentures in, etc. so I don't see how this makes matters any worse... I wouldn't want to go without you there dude!

Shawn Wood's reply (Note this is Kiwi's wife and he was the group permit holder):

Randy: This is Shawn. If anyone says they don't want you on the trip then they're out, not you. I know I can make this happen because I know the guy with the permit and I hold the sex and other favors card. Getting this whole thing organized isn't just a fill-out-a-form-and-down-the-river-we-go deal. You're putting much brain work (okay, so you figured this all out long ago and it's easy pickings now)

*into getting everything coordinated and the right people together for
a rare adventure. Not only that, Kiwi needs someone to watch out
for him. You and Allan will do that. It is a good thing there aren't
any woman on the trip though. I suspect you'll be a bit too slow for
the skinny-dipping. If you could do the last trip with a hernia and
broken foot, what's a busted hip with three months recovery time? We
all nominate you for the soaper.... sorry Chuck.*

I recovered fast enough after the hip surgery to carry my full body weight
in just over five weeks. To assure myself I could do the Grand Canyon, I
made three kayak runs on the South Fork of the American. I didn't want to
miss this trip because we planned to do the bottom section all the way to
Pierce Ferry to a total of 279½ miles. It would take us 18 days and I would
be with my friends Kiwi, Bob Carey, Al, Peter, Tom Dancs, Ed Rhinehart
and Stuart Williscroft.

We had our disagreements at times, but we were disciplined and had
organized good crews to get the work done.

The flow ran at 23,500 CFS the entire time. I kayaked all the rapids with
the exception of Lava Falls. I was concerned that if I had to swim in Lava,
going over some bad drops with my hip could make me a serious liability
to the group. However, I did run the rapid in the raft.

It was the first time I had been on the Colorado River below Diamond
Creek. The new rapids, great scenery and hikes were amazing. The weather
was close to perfect, a little cool to start and some rain, but it was hot by
the trips end.

I had to swim four times, twice on boil lines and again at Hance and
Ruby rapids. I also rolled up twice running Doris Rapids. Kiwi took the
plunge three times, twice on boil lines and once at Bridge Canyon. Bob had
to swim at Lava Falls.

The biggest bummer was a private group of 16 led by a very aggressive
woman who was the leader. They launched at the same time we did. They
had a couple of women who spent time in the nude and we were accused
of ogling them – that did not happen – period!

After our return home to California, I ran the South Fork American
numerous times at high flows and also caught the Middle Fork American
at a decent flow the summer of 2011.

On one trip down the South Fork at flood stage, I flipped upside down
at Troublemaker and hit my head hard. I had to swim and was glad I wore
a helmet. I'm sure it saved my life. My neck remained sore for six months
after that incident. Recently I sustained another injury at Troublemaker. I
cracked ribs at low flow by hitting a submerged rock while attempting to
roll up. It amazes me that even after hundreds of runs through this rapid I

still get surprised occasionally.

Déjà vu all over again. We have secured another permit for the Grand Canyon in late Spring 2015. This time Kiwi, Bob Carey, Doug Jones and I will Kayak while Al, Peter, Eric Stroud and Matt Wood (Kiwi's Brother) raft. Maybe this will be my last trip through the canyon - or maybe not!

Over the years, I tried some kayaking wild water and slalom competitions like Epies Great Race Triathlon. In the triathalon, I placed eighth for Senior Iron Man. I also did Chili Bar White Water Rodeo and took second as Novice. But what I really enjoy is focusing on the superb adventure that whitewater offers. It is a dynamic environment.

Rafting and kayaking are uniquely different from most sports. Regardless of how thoroughly you scout the rapid and carefully plan out the run, it doesn't always work out. Once you enter a rapid and are captured in its current, you are committed and in real time have to figure out how to react and pull it off. I think that's why it appeals to me so much.

I am often scared. But amazingly enough, when things get screwed up, I somehow get my boat aimed downstream and by sitting up straight and paddling really hard – it works out - usually.

Randy Oaring Crystal Rapid,
Grand Canyon, AZ

Haunted House
Stanislaus River, Northern California

Tunnel Chute, Middle Fork American
River, Northern California

Top right - Randy, Sourgrass Ravine, North Fork Stanislaus River, Northern California

Top left - Getting endos on the North Fork American River Northern California

Upper left - Chuck John, Kiwi Wood and Grant Peeters heading to the Grand Canyon

Lower left - Red Wall Cavern, Grand Canyon, AZ

Bottom left - Al Albright, Rick Knight and Randy, Nankoweap Granaries, Grand Canyon, AZ

Bottom right - Randy in the Grand Canyon

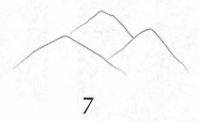

7

The Vertical World

Sean Baker and I were on an after-work practice session for an up-coming climb in Yosemite. We had chosen the cliffs of basalt located below our home on White Rock Mesa. It offered a thin vertical crack requiring small stoppers in an area known as the Playground. This would be a good test.

Taking the lead, I had gone out about eight placements when the pitch zippered. Sean was belaying and was yanked off the ground in a big arc when the fourth stopper caught hold. As he came back to the ground I was left hanging with my feet level with his head; his eyes were as large as silver dollars.

As he stood staring, I calmly said, "I think you can let me down now."

With that little episode behind us, I climbed back up and finished the pitch.

To build on my rock-climbing experiences of the early years, I began to do more serious forays into the vertical world. The scrambling trips I took in high school with the Explorer Post eventually led to frequent climbs in the Northwest as a graduate student. While at the University of Washington, I climbed at many rock climbing areas throughout the state.[34]

As my skills increased toward the end of my graduate school education, I started making trips to Yosemite National Park and doing some of the great routes there.[35] My favorite was Lost Arrow Spire, a climb I made with

Bob Odom. Lost Arrow Spire is a detached finger of a rock near the top of Yosemite Falls often referred to as the "view climb." It is an unbelievable experience to be perched on a small area atop this rock and look down a couple thousand feet to the valley floor.

The Love Affair with Yosemite Continues!

Ever since the first family trip to Yosemite as a child, I felt there was something special about the place. The bicycle trip with my brother right after graduating from high school reaffirmed these feelings and my first climbs in the valley while a graduate student sealed the deal. I would devote a great deal of time in Yosemite perfecting the rock climbing craft over the next 40 plus years.

Yosemite Valley is a glacial valley, located within Yosemite National Park, at an elevation of 4,000 feet in the Western Sierra Nevada Mountains of California. It is approximately eight miles long, one mile wide and a half mile deep and is surrounded by massive sheer granite walls. El Capitan dominates the west end of the valley while Half Dome dominates the east end. Lining the valley between these two dominate features are numerous other sheer walls. On the south side are Leaning Tower, the Cathedrals, Sentinel and Glacier Point. To the north are the Brothers, the Yosemite Falls area, Royal Arches and Washington Column. The valley is drained by the Merced River and a multitude of streams form some of the highest waterfalls in the world. It is an area of outstanding scenic beauty, is on the U.S. National Register of Historic Places and is listed as a UNESCO World Heritage Center.

For me, El Capitan dominated the scene. I desperately wanted to climb that huge granite monolith. By the early 1970s there were already a dozen grade VI routes attacking nearly every major face of El Cap. Over the years, I would return again and again to the valley to attempt various routes on this prominent feature.

Preparation for Bigger Things

To prepare for the Grade VI routes that would later follow, I climbed and trained with a variety of partners at numerous areas around California.[36]

After moving to Tehachapi in December 1972, Rick Knight, one of my climbing partners from Seattle, moved in with us for three months. He was an excellent climber and we made good use of his time spent in the area. We made numerous trips to local climbing areas and bagged quite a few great routes. One that stands out for me was the East Face of Mount Whitney, the highest point in the contiguous United States.

We arrived near Whitney about 2 p.m. and hiked and scrambled toward the base. We bivouacked near a small lake, got up early the next morning and basically free soloed the class 5.3 face. Roping up for just one 5.6 pitch, it didn't take us long to reach the summit and we were soon making a rapid descent via the Mountaineers Route. By 10 a.m., we arrived back at our cars having traveled 16 miles with a 6,000 foot altitude gain in less than a day.

Rick and I also did the El Cap Tree Route together in Yosemite, a relatively short climb near the base of this great monolith – complete with a pendulum and a 100 degree overhanging wall nail-up.

On one particularly eventful Yosemite Valley camping trip with my family, Chuck Payne and other friends, I dutifully warned everyone not to leave out any food on account of bears. As we sat around the campfire that night, myself stoned as usual in those days, someone asked if it would be all right to sleep in the back of our station wagon. I said sure – no problem. I then took the ice chest out of the car and put it on the table only a few feet in front of the tent door.

During the night, Doris woke me up in a panic. There was a bear outside the tent and she said in a low voice "Randy, do something!"

I opened the flap of the tent door to see the rear end of a huge bear wiping out the contents of our ice chest. He had carefully opened the unit without damaging the latch, was drinking milk from the carton and eating potato salad from a Tupperware bowl.

As I watched in disbelief, it occurred to me there was no way out of the tent. To add to the dilemma, Doris whispered she had cookies in the tent. This was not good news. I immediately went to the back of the tent and through a small window woke up the others asking someone to scare the bear away before he entered our tent and killed us.

Their advice was to cut a hole in the back of the tent and escape. I said no way. This was a good tent. After much debate, Lee Stamentz, butt naked, got up and chased off the bear. Wow – that was scary.

Doris usually had the unfortunate task of packing for our various weekend trips and on two occasions that didn't go so well.

On one trip to Yosemite she forgot our pots and pans. We had lots of food, but no way to cook it. During one winter trip to Joshua Tree in Southern California's high desert, we discovered we had left the tent at home which made for some cold camping.

Who says pot doesn't impair your judgment!?

Half Dome

Perhaps the most recognizable mountainous feature in the world is Half

Dome. The 2,000 foot vertical face, which looms over the far end of the valley, was created when this granite dome was sheared in half by glacial activity.

To prepare for the Northwest Face of Half Dome (grade VI, 5.8, A3) in Yosemite, Bob Odom trained in Seattle while Rick and I did the same in California. After hauling our gear (including food and water) to the base of the wall, I took a long look at the huge vertical face looming above – big mistake. I turned and asked Bob what he thought and he said he would rather not climb it.

Lesson learned – never look at the top of a route while still at the bottom. It brings on an incredible sense of defeat. I learned to focus on one or two pitches at a time to keep from being psyched out before even getting started.

While Rick hauled our gear back to the valley floor, Bob and I hiked to Tuolumne Meadows. Years later, I would return to finish this impressive route.

Back to the Drawing Board

In the fall of 1973, I managed to complete the 13th ascent of the east face of Mount Muir with Jim Trout as my climbing partner. It was something I really wanted to do and I felt a great sense of accomplishment completing a rarely climbed route on a 14,000 foot peak.

I also had a 17 year old climbing partner named Bruce Harrington during this time. He was from Lancaster and the son of one of my coworkers at the rocket lab. He was a terrific climber and for the next three years we did many routes together.

One of my more memorable scrambles I would also like to forget was with Bruce at Ski Tracks on Tahquitz Rock. The "Ski Tracks" are a pair of vertical cracks in the south face of the rock.

I was leading over the last pitch when my stomach cramped. I was in the middle of a steep, awkward chute about 15 feet off the belay. I felt if I could just pass a little gas, the cramps would cease and I'd be all right. Unfortunately, the gas turned out to be dysentery-induced diarrhea.

Although I managed to stop my mistake in mid flow, I now had wet feces running down my legs and into my climbing shoes. In a moment of panic-driven inspiration, I literally sprinted to the top, quickly released my rope and dropped my pants to finish the job, but that wouldn't be the end of it.

While finishing my business and thinking I was alone, a woman in her 30s walked over to where I was and began staring at me – surprise!

In spite of my rather uncomfortable situation, I couldn't help but notice she wore tennis shoes and had no climbing gear with her. Tahquitz's easiest route is class 3 and there are no walk-up paths to the summit. This occurred well before free soloing was in vogue and this truly amazed me, especially considering the predicament I was in!

On one climb of Royal Arches in Yosemite with Rick and my friend Nelson Walker, his wife, Linda, had asked me to please be careful as she did not want him hurt. Lacking better judgment, Rick and I were having way too much fun to take seriously such a request.

While leading the pendulum halfway up the route, Nelson fell from the far side of the traverse with no protection in place. Although the fall wasn't life threatening, he did some serious damage to his forearms and elbows as he scraped to a halt across the steep, slab face. Despite the injuries, we decided to continue.

As we topped out a couple thousand feet above the valley floor, a big lightning storm rolled in, so we quickly prepared for our descent. We racked our gear of pitons, chocks and runners for Rick to carry. I then coiled the ropes, which I carried as we raced across the dome-like terrain. While working our way along the rim of the arches, we could see lightning strikes across the valley on Glacier Point. The exploding thunder clearly frightened Rick and his paranoia was growing.

He asked me "Where would the lightning strike next?"

I told him "It always takes the path of least resistance."

Then, taking notice of the metal pitons he carried, I shouted to him, "Please stay away from me. With all that iron around your neck I don't want to get hit by lightning when it strikes you."

The words were like magic. Rick literally ducked out from under the entire rack and let it fall to the ground as he ran as fast as he could to escape the impending doom.

Rick then asked, "How are we going to get down from here?"

Like lightning, I told him the best way would be to take the path of least resistance.

As I reached the valley floor with Nelson a short distance behind, Linda came up and asked me if Nelson was OK. No matter how hard I tried, I could not keep a straight face. It took over 50 stitches to sew up Nelson's wounds.

To this day, I don't know if Linda ever forgave me for that incident.

One winter evening, while climbing in Southern California at Joshua Tree, we all huddled in the Dog Trailer to escape the cold. We played games with 13 people crammed into the tiny trailer.

On the same Joshua Tree trip, while rappelling off of a climbing route, Doris suddenly burst into tears. I had no clue as to why.

She and I had just finished climbing the Bong, a moderate 5.6 route on the Blob and were rappelling the 100 foot vertical face of the formation directly into our campsite. She explained, her tears were in response to seeing our boys way below and realized if we fell to our deaths our kids would be without parents. Doris never made another rock climb.

Falls are not the only dangers of climbing. Once, while scrambling over some boulders near our house in Tehachapi imagining I was 1,000 feet above the deck, I went over the top of a coiled Mojave green rattlesnake. This aggressive snake is considered to have some of the most neurologically toxic venom in the New World. It got my attention.

One highlight of climbing was some of the graffiti I found. On one trip to the Yosemite, I stopped to use the restroom at a gas station and was annoyed to find it had a forced air hand dryer as opposed to paper towels.

The instructions read:

Press button to start dryer
Hold hands under dryer
Shake excess water form hands
Rapidly rub hands together.

And just below, someone had scratched in:

Wipe hands on pants.

After an aborted climb of the East Buttress of El Capitan in Yosemite with Wayne Klinger and Bruce, they spent the afternoon together while I was stuck watching the gear and feeling left out. After the retreat, I was discouraged and in my mind, I blamed Wayne for the withdrawal from El Cap. Wayne was edgy as well.

The next day on a subsequent climb farther up the valley, while I was preparing to lead the difficult friction traverse on Arches Terrace, I turned to Wayne to put some large hexes and slings over his head.

We were on a ledge 100 feet above the valley floor and he looked me straight in the eyes and said, "If you put those on me I am going to hit you."

Ironically, Bruce and I were both anchored, but Wayne was still standing on the ledge un-roped. I told Wayne, if he hit me I would be the last person he would ever hit.

The intensity of our respect for one another has endured several tenuous confrontations similar to that one and to this day we are still the best of friends.

Once, while climbing Point Beyond on Glacier Point Apron in Yosemite, I sat on a small ledge 300 feet above the valley floor belaying up Bruce. Another climber on the ledge was belaying his partner on the pitch above me, so we struck up a conversation about the type of work we each did.

After I finished bellyaching about some aspect of my employment, the other fellow said "Well, I guess that is why they pay us and call it work."

This exchange really changed the way I looked at my job. Whenever I became discouraged at work, I realized it was all part of why I was paid. Ninety five percent of the time my job was fun, which more than made up for the five percent of the time it wasn't – that's pretty darn good.

Land of Enchantment - New Mexico

Shortly after our move to White Rock, NM, I started climbing on the cliffs of basalt that formed the mesa upon which our community was situated. Within a mile of our home, there were literally hundreds of high-grade (5.8-plus) routes about 100 feet in length. While climbing, I met Bill "Willie" Spencer. I got to know Willie and we started climbing together regularly. It became a great partnership.

Willie was quite a talented climber, but lacked big route experience. My technical skills weren't as good as Willie's, but I had a lot of experience climbing in the Northwest and California. We climbed an average of four times a week, more if preparing for a big Yosemite climb and less during the winter.

The flextime work schedule at the lab enabled us to meet at various climbing areas about 4 p.m. and we would climb until dark. Between us, we led most of the routes in the area, all of which had previously only been top roped. I have never really enjoyed top roping routes; for me, leading is much more intense. We even managed to climb a couple of first ascents together with Willie on the sharp end of the rope.

Todd, who was five years old at the time, often went climbing with us. He was a natural, top roping hard routes and impressing lots of onlookers. I never encouraged Todd to climb, out of respect for Doris. She was afraid he would get hurt.

In May of 1977, I planned a trip from New Mexico to Yosemite in conjunction with a business meeting in Los Gatos, CA, I needed to attend for the laboratory. During the previous winter, Bill Stronge, a climbing acquaintance from China Lake, CA, visited White Rock. After climbing together on the mesa near our home, he invited me to join him for a Grade V climb on the South Face of Washington Column in Yosemite. Rick Knight and I had tried that classic route several years before and made it only halfway before jamming our lead rope. A twist in the rope, as it ran under a roof and wedged itself firmly in place, took over an hour to dislodge. After that, we chickened out and retreated.

In the course of climbing together in New Mexico, Bill told me about his climbs, his work at the Naval Weapons Center and his girlfriend. Since he had done numerous hard routes in the valley (the Nose of El Cap, Half

Dome, etc.), I was very excited to join him for what could be my first completed big wall climb in Yosemite.

We planned to meet in Fresno. He offered to bring all the climbing gear and told me not to bring a thing. We were to go in his VW camper. With my briefcase, sleeping bag and clothing, I flew to California with great anticipation. I had made arrangements to be picked up a week later in Yosemite by a friend working in the Bay Area.

After two hours of waiting on the curb outside the terminal, Bill arrived in an old beat-up VW bus that lurched to an abrupt stop right in front of me. As Bill got out of the car to greet me, it was obvious he was drunk. I thought, "Oh well, here goes nothing."

There was a woman in the front seat of the bus, so I introduced myself and asked if she was Bill's girlfriend.

"No," she replied, "I am not that whore. I am his wife."

In spite of the rocky start, I climbed into the back seat of the bus for a silent and scary ride to the valley.

Upon arriving in Yosemite, Bill said we were going to casual camp (illegally) in the Camp Curry parking lot. It was raining hard and Bill announced he and his wife would sleep in the camper and I could sleep on the ground next to it. Not having much choice, I put my sleeping bag on a small tarp in a puddle without benefit of a tent.

The next day, we met with a climbing-ranger friend of Bill's and climbed Commitment (II, 5.9) in the Yosemite Falls area. During that climb, the rain started again and Bill announced he was not going to hang around for a week of rainy weather. After the climb, he left to go home leaving me with no car, no gear and no tent with a full week to wait before for my ride was to arrive.

I hiked over to Camp 4, the local gathering place for climbers and arranged to climb Washington Column with a 16 year old runaway who had a tent and gear. He had been looking for a partner and I happened to come along at exactly the right moment. He even kicked out his girlfriend so I could share his tent with him.

After several days of on-again off-again rain, we started the South Face of Washington Column (V, 5.8, A3). Amazingly, it went off without a hitch.

It threatened to rain the entire climb and I was continually praying – we never even got wet. Pitch after pitch we competently worked our way up this fine, steep route. I don't remember the kid's name, but I do remember he constantly sang, "Don't want a pickle, just want to ride on my motorcycle."

It nearly drove me nuts and I truly welcomed the distance between us when either he or I was far out on a lead.

I saw some good graffiti on this trip that I think may be the best I have ever seen. It was written on the wall of the rather primitive toilet facility, typical of the time period, in Camp 4 and went like this:

"What does the starship Enterprise and toilet paper have in common?" The answer inscribed below read "They are both circling Uranus looking for Klingons!"

After the climb, my ride arrived. The technical meeting in Los Gatos went great and I returned home with a Yosemite Grade V under my belt.

I again had a chance in April 1978 to go to Yosemite with Bill Stronge, who promised he would behave himself this time. So once again, in conjunction with a Bay Area business trip for the lab, I met up with Bill in Yosemite. This time, he was indeed with his girlfriend and we had three days of great climbing in the valley doing many short routes on Glacier Point and in the Cookie Area.

A Grade VI Climb, at Last

In the spring of 1978, Willie and I prepared for a climb of Half Dome's Northwest Face (VI, A3, 5.8). I had attempted that route in 1973, only to turn around at the start – it was unfinished business and I badly wanted a grade VI.

To prepare for big climbs, such as this one, I maintained a rigorous schedule of weight training, running and local climbing. Willie was still doing carpentry and in excellent shape. On Saturdays, I would typically lift weights for an hour, run three miles, lead six routes and follow as many.

In June 1978, Willie and I left for Yosemite on what turned out to be one of my all-time favorite climbs. It was Willie's first real climb – everything else had been on the basalt cliffs near our homes in New Mexico and he had never done a multipitch route. His leading standard was somewhere in the 5.11 range – and at a time when very few even led a 5.10.

Arriving in the valley after dark and camping with other New Mexico climbers, I told Willie, "Don't talk to anyone about our route or they will scare you half to death with hyped beta."

Sure enough, that's exactly what happened. Even so, before dawn the next morning we were on the way up the trail to Half Dome.

Mark Rislove and Willie's brother Kevin helped carry our gear to the base and took our extra stuff back to the valley floor after we started the route. Before dropping down to the base of the climb, we left a sign at the start of the cable route saying, "Climbers on face of Half Dome. Please don't throw rocks. Thanks Randy and Willie"

After drawing lots, Willie started up the first pitch (A2, 5.9), which he proceeded to climb free. When I jugged up the pitch, I asked what he thought.

He said, "I think we have bitten off more than we can chew."

After I told him he had just led a 5.11 pitch rather than the 5.9 he thought, he immediately looked relieved.

I led off on the next pitch and within a few moves knew we had this climb in the bag. For the next two days, we experienced some of the most memorable climbing of our lives. We managed pitch after pitch of cracks, laybacks, under clings, blank walls and friction with two incredible bivouacs (top of pitch 12 and Sandy Ledge).

That night at Sandy Ledge, we attempted to contact Willie's brother with a small CB transceiver. After repeated attempts as it was getting dark, I grabbed the radio and jokingly said, "This is Randy and Willie on Half Dome. Anyone there? Over."

To our surprise, we received a reply from someone and started a series of ongoing conversations with several CB operators camping in the valley.

At one point, we responded to the question, "What do you mean Randy and Willie on Half Dome?" by sweeping our AA battery penlights in the direction of their campsites. Our contacts spotted us high up on the wall.

I had the lead on the infamous Thank God Ledge Pitch and had managed to fall several times before somehow climbing up the last section. At that point, we could see people looking over the edge at us from the top.

Having seen our sign near the start of the cables, they would say, "Look, there's Randy and Willie."

Several even waited until we topped out to take pictures. One fellow carried our haul bag down the cables – a gracious and welcome gesture.

After returning to the valley floor that night, I woke up the next morning and took Mark up Royal Arches in return for his help earlier in the week. I was so tired, I actually fell asleep several times on the route and during the long descent down the North Dome Gulley. I can remember thinking it would be my last climb, ever. I had promised Doris, if I was successful I would give it up and spend more time with her and the boys.

Following the climb, I met the family in Barstow and we went camping at the beach for two weeks before returning to New Mexico.

El Cap?

We planned a relocation/career move to Upstate New York and I had been thinking of climbing the Nose of El Capitan since graduate school. It was the first grade VI ever completed and it had great appeal to me. Even though I had planned to give up climbing, I just could not get it out of my system. There was so much I truly loved about the sport – especially the focus and logistics associated with big walls.

Willie was a great climber and I genuinely enjoyed his company. We were good friends. With the pending move, I knew it was unlikely I would ever find another suitable climbing partner for the Nose, let alone the ability to properly train for such an undertaking in the relatively flat lands of Upstate New York.

Willie and I decided to take on this project with a plan to climb the route in May 1980. Doris was agreeable with the plan, even though I had promised to give up climbing after Half Dome. She knew how driven I was about the sport and was quite supportive and considerate of my desire to complete this goal.

We trained with a vengeance and planned out every aspect of the climb. The only real problem we had was finding reliable transportation to Yosemite. Doris needed the Bronco in my absence and that left me with the Datsun.

Willie's car was equally unreliable. In fact, we often referred to our vehicles as 100 mile radius transportation. We actually considered going out on Willie's motorcycle – bad idea. Instead we talked our friend Dave Baggett into joining us on the trip and traveled in his car.

After arriving in Yosemite, we went straight to work on the Nose of El Cap. Because of bad weather, we fixed to Cycle Ledge and rappelled back to the valley floor. Snow had fallen high on the rim of Yosemite Valley. In general, it was cold, windy and wet.

Jugging back up the next day, we pushed all the way into the Stove Legs crack system before bailing out due to threatening weather and plain old fear. It is an intimidating route. Discouraged, but not willing to sit around and feel sorry for ourselves, Willie and I did three consecutive days of great climbing in the valley. We knocked off the East Buttress of Middle Cathedral (IV, 5.9, A1), Nut Cracker (III, 5.8) and Arrowhead Arête (III, 5.8), all during mixed weather.

Even though bad weather and fear caused us to back off of the Nose of El Cap, I was quite confident Arrowhead Arête would be my last climb. Considering the quality of the route and climbing it with a great friend, I was quite content with this conclusion of my climbing.

From Rural Farm Life to Climbing Mecca - Northern California

We moved to Upstate New York in June 1980 and I gave up climbing for several years. Rural life was great fun and as a family we really enjoyed living in the area. We had great neighbors and many wonderful memories. Two years later after relocating to Roseville, CA, I made a gradual move back into rock climbing.

One particularly memorable climb on Royal Arches (5.6, Grade III,

16 pitches long) in Yosemite involved Todd (then 11 years old) and Scott Brown from work. I had climbed this route several times before and it felt great being back on rock after a three and a half year hiatus. It was Todd's first real multi pitch climb and he did the route effortlessly in a pair of checkered Vans slip-on tennis shoes – he really was a natural climber!

It was a great experience and Todd, Scott and I enjoyed the climb. It would be the last time I climbed the famous "Rotten Log" pitch. This was always the scariest part of this route and involved climbing up to a ledge on a precariously balanced and barely intact log which spanned a huge chasm. Shortly after our climb, an idiot tossed it off and forever changed this classic climb.

I continued to climb a trad (i.e., placing the projection while on lead) route in Yosemite every year or so. I wanted to be sure I could still lead on the sharp end of the rope.

Back to El Capitan

I decided to take care of some unfinished business – the Nose of El Capitan. Knowing that rain and snow spoiled my attempt in 1980, I hated not having completed this goal. I had chased El Cap since graduate school and it was time to make it happen.

My climbing partners for this climb were Willie Spencer and Jonathan Boland. We met in Yosemite in May 1992. After Willie and Jonathon hauled to Cycle Ledge and fixed lines, we jugged up to the ledge early the next day. As we moved up the route, we were slowed by a group from Texas climbing ahead of us and we did not make it to Dolt Tower that day. That meant spending a sleepless night hanging in slings in the Stove Legs crack system.

The next day, Willie, tired from a sleepless night, fell while attempting to free climb the 5.9 layback pitch just below El Cap Tower. Falling down the face, he did OK for 50 feet or so until the outer edge of his boot caught on a small ledge breaking his ankle in three places. We had to retreat to Dolt Tower, where we gave Willie Tylenol III containing codeine and 800 mg of Ibuprofen.

When the drugs took effect, Willie got up and began walking around the ledge.

"I think I can do this," he said. "I think I can do this." Painkillers can be amazing.

Realizing his ankle was broken, we made plans to do a self-rescue the next morning. It took us a half day to get back down and we left the valley defeated.

Back to the Drawing Board Again

On my third attempt, I managed to climb the East Buttress of El Cap in July 1992 (grade V, 5.10) and repeated the climb again in 1994. It's a great route, but not considered a true ascent of El Cap. The Nose still dominated my thoughts.

I continued my free climbing and became comfortable leading 5.9 trad and following on much harder pitches. Five days a week, I worked out on climbing walls during my lunch break, which really helped. During those hour breaks, John Sup and I would challenge ourselves. We would lead six or more routes, each of 5.10 difficulty or greater. I added stretching, weight lifting, walking, running and cycling to work and got into pretty good shape.

During this time, Greg Sullivan of Fresno and I climbed the Chouinard-Herbert Route on Sentinel (V, 5.9, A2) in Yosemite. We completed it in good style and I was pleased after having tried it twice before. I completed some unfinished business and had put a number of Yosemite's hard routes behind me as well as other fine routes in California.[37]

Finally the Nose

In June 1993, it was once again time to attempt the Nose in Yosemite. This time, I met up with Greg Sullivan. We fixed to Cycle Ledge and the next afternoon jugged and hauled up to it where we spent the night. The second day, we climbed to Dolt Tower and fixed another pitch. While there, news reached us that a climber doing a free solo on Sentinel across the valley had fallen to his death.

The TV news bulletin said, "Experienced climber in his 40s dies in Yosemite – details at 11." Doris and many of our friends assumed the climber was me. This was totally irresponsible on the part of the broadcast company and caused a lot of unnecessary concern.

We pressed on and by the end of the day we made it to one and a half pitches below Camp IV. While there, we spent a miserable night in slings on a narrow, sloping ridge.

The following day, I led to the Camp IV ledge in a downpour accompanied by 40 mph winds. The water literally ran down my sleeves and exited through my pant legs. At 9 a.m., we decided to retreat and reached the valley floor by 2 p.m. It got so cold that ice began to form. One party held up at the Camp V ledges had to be rescued later that afternoon.

"That's it, damn it," I said to Greg. "We're coming back next weekend to finish this bastard."

Three weeks later, we returned and I suggested we rappel from the top down the route to below Camp IV where we left off and continue our climb from there. Greg was game only if I agreed to rappel first down the radically overhanging headwall sections of the Nose. After a false start, we cached our gear and water near the top of El Cap.

Two weeks later we climbed to the summit via the East Ledges route where we recovered our cache. At 11 a.m., I did the first rappel and it was extremely difficult and scary. There was no build-up to the exposure as I lowered myself over the edge with nothing but 3,000 feet of air beneath me. I must have looked like a spider hanging from a strand of web where in places I was as much as 30 feet out from the wall.

My landing point was 30 feet to my left and I had to initiate a pendulum-type motion from side to side to reach it. Starting this maneuver with nothing to push off of was difficult indeed. With great trial and tribulation, I was finally able to hook the chain link of the bolted station with my pinky finger.

Several rappels later, we reached a spot one pitch below Camp IV at four in the afternoon. We then climbed and fixed to the base of the Great Roof and settled down for a beautiful moon-lit night on the sloping ledges of Camp IV.

The next morning, I led the fantastic Great Roof pitch and totally loved it. It was an amazing curving crack that trailed out to the right under that huge roof. Transitioning from aid to free climbing is always difficult and this was no exception. I had to make some memorable free moves in order to reach the belay station. With only enough room for two climbers, we spent the night on the small, triangular ledge of Camp VI tucked under a huge, overhanging section of the Nose.

It was the Fourth of July 1993 when we topped out around 4 p.m. the next day. At long last, I had completed the Nose, one of the most famous rock climbs in the world. Essentially, we had to do it by siege climbing, not the style I would have liked, but at least it was done.

California's Classic Fifties

I came across a book published in 1979 written by Steve Roper and Allen Steck. It was titled *Fifty Classic Climbs of North America*. I was captivated by the idea of doing as many of these routes as possible and set a goal of doing all 12 climbs located in California. That list was impressive, with seven of the routes located in Yosemite Valley and the rest scattered throughout the state.[38]

The easiest of California's Classic Fifties is Royal Arches. I had done this route many times over the years, since first climbing it in 1973. On the same trip, Bob Odom and I also did Lost Arrow Spire so that one was behind me as well. With Rick Knight I did the East Face of Mount Whitney in 1974. I had done the Northwest Face of Half Dome in 1978 and the East Buttress of Middle Cathedral in 1980, both with Willie.

Next, in 1992, came Fairview Dome in Tuolumne and Travelers Buttress at Lover's Leap. And, of course, the Nose of El Cap was completed with Greg in 1993. I was indeed chipping away at the list with eight of these exceptionally fine routes under my belt, but I still had four real biggies to go.

While looking at the big walls I still wanted to climb, I always tried to push my limits of endurance. On one trip to Yosemite in 1994 with my nephew Ryan, I decided to repeat three Classic Fifties in three days. I led all 38 pitches of the combined routes of Royal Arches, East Buttress of Middle Cathedral and Fairview Dome. I was exhausted afterwards, but I really enjoyed climbing those routes with Ryan.

Unfinished Business – El Capitan

I never felt satisfied with the siege tactics Greg and I used to complete the Nose of El Cap in 1993. I had been looking for an opportunity to try to do the route in a more conventional manner. This opportunity came in July 1994.

After meeting and forming a climbing partnership with Rich Travis, a Christian man in his 30s, we made plans to do the Nose of El Cap. We did a fix to the top of the sixth pitch and then rappelled back down and returned to work. Three days later, I jugged and hauled up to Cycle Ledge with Charlie Fox to spend the night. Sleeping on Cycle Ledge is difficult because of its slope, but that didn't alter our plans. The next morning, before sunrise, Rich caught up with us.

Charlie rappelled back down retrieving our fixed lines leaving Rich and me to begin our ascent of this fantastic route. It was nearly 11 p.m. when we reached El Cap Tower, but we thought we had climbed into a super market. El Cap Tower is where many parties bail out and most just leave their food behind. Rich and I literally had our pick of entrees for our late-night supper.

A number of the cans of food were labeled in languages we couldn't read, so we would just open the can and taste the food inside. Some of it was flat out awful. We eventually settled on shrimp cocktail, Chef Boyardee ravioli, vegetarian baked beans and tapioca pudding. Served cold, this became our favorite wall-food meal.

Although this meal sounds awful, I suggest trying it. This combination of foods is actually quite tasty, even when unheated.

El Cap Tower is a long, flat ledge about two feet wide located about 1,000 feet above the valley floor and a great place to bivy.

On Saturday we moved up the wall to Camp IV and fixed to pitch 22. I have to say that Camp IV sucks. If it rains, it is literally like sitting under a waterfall; something I had experienced before. The area is not flat and quite uncomfortable.

We reached Camp VI on Sunday and fixed to pitch 29. In contrast to Camp IV, Camp VI is a small flat triangular ledge large enough for two to sleep comfortably under an overhang about 800 feet from the top. It is an amazing spot.

The next day, we topped out at 4:45 p.m., completing this fine route in good style. We then packed our haul bag and hiked to the East Ledges where we rappelled down to the valley floor, reaching it before dark. It was an excellent climb and immensely satisfying for us both.

A Radical Overhanging Wall

Leaning Tower is an amazing feature across from El Capitan. It captured our attention so later in the summer of 1994 Rich and I tackled this imposing 1,000 foot overhanging wall (V, 5.7, A3-). It took us two days with a bivy on Ahwahnee Ledge. Ahwahnee is a massive flat, sandy ledge right in the middle of this massive overhanging wall – really a cool place.

I fell twice en route when pieces pulled as I used direct aid. Although scary, they were mid-air drops with nothing to hit.

More Classic Fifties

Together, Rich and I also tackled several Classic Fifties in August 1995. The South Face of Charlotte Dome was a great wilderness experience on a big wall, while Clyde Minaret was a very stout climb. That gave me ten of the 12 California Classic Fifties and a determination to finish the rest.

Salathé Wall on El Capitan

I began to focus my attention on Salathé Wall on El Capitan in Yosemite, another of the Classic Fifty climbs. I had it squarely in my sights. In September 1995, Rich and I started up the route. We finished Free Blast (i.e., the first 11 pitches) in a day and hauled to Heart Ledges. There was a team of four Europeans (all Swiss guides) ahead of us moving fast using two separate rope teams.

There's an old saying in Yosemite which states "You haven't led until you lead the Hollow Flake ... and it's just as hard to follow."

We discovered that saying was true as it was scary to both lead and follow.

As we finished the Hollow Flake pitch, the top Euro team was only a few pitches above us climbing the Ear – a bomb-bay chimney. I suddenly heard a loud "Merde," as the Euro team leader's fixed pin pulled and he fell backward down the vertical wall for more than 100 feet. There was a sound like a watermelon hitting pavement when he came to a halt slamming against the wall.

He came to rest upside down below his belayer and between the members of the second team. That team immediately reached the fallen climber. As his rescuers turned him upright, it was discovered he had a broken hip and ankle. He had only minor head trauma, thanks to the fact he wore a climbing helmet. Without that helmet, he would likely have been killed.

The Euro team immediately started their retreat and we helped them reverse the Hollow Flake pitch. From there, Rich and I climbed up to the top of pitch 15, an unprotected chimney. There I realized witnessing that fall had unnerved me and I simply couldn't continue. Together, we retreated to the valley floor. We had bailed on Salathé Wall.

In June of 1996 I returned with Bill Sitkin of Truckee to try and finish the route. After making it up to Heart Ledge, Bill said he felt too much pressure knowing he would have to lead the hardest pitches and couldn't go on – my heart sank.

Ironically, two climbers from Austria had joined us that evening on Heart Ledge. The next morning, as Bill and I prepared to retreat, the two Austrians asked if they could borrow our No. 5 Camelot (an absolute necessity for climbing the Hollow Flake). Bill said they could, but only if they would let me go with them. The two, Christian Gabl and Rudy, agreed and once again I was on my way up.

Climbing this difficult wall with two total strangers was quite a unique experience. Christian spoke reasonable English, however Rudy did not. Both were certified guides in Chamonix, France and competent climbers. I quickly adapted to the Euro style of aid climbing.

We spent three more nights on that climb and they allowed me to lead on a few pitches. During one of our bivouacs, a BASE jumper went off El Cap near our sleeping site. I especially enjoyed the last night knowing the ascent was in the bag.

I was quite satisfied to have completed another incredible Classic Fifties route – hallelujah! I felt sure it would be my last big wall. It was harder than either Half Dome or the Nose and my leads took both a physical and mental toll on my 50 year old body.

The Last California Classic Fifty

My first try in 1992 on the Steck-Salathé route on Cathedral in Yosemite was unsuccessful. Unable to make the first pitch, I realized this climb was considerably underrated. Still, when Rich Travis and I returned four years later, we nailed it!

Rich had not been doing a lot of climbing and basically attacked this route "off the couch," as he put it. He led the hardest pitches and we made great progress. But by the end of the first day, Rich began to run out of gas and was fading fast. However, after washing down a packet of goo with water, he took off like a rocket. We bivouacked one night about halfway up and finished the route the next day.

It was an exceptional climb on a big wall and extremely physical requiring free climbing in numerous chimney systems. While climbing the claustrophobic "narrows," I started imagining someone discovering my skeleton jammed into that crack and began to doubt my ability to finish. Still, I led some great pitches, including a hard jam crack and an unbelievable chimney pitch – a major coup de grâce.

That completed my 12 California Classic Fifties. A real difficult and challenging goal ... all world class climbs.

Is It Always So Serious?

Some of the interesting things I've seen on my climbing expeditions weren't always on the mountain. On one return trip from Yosemite with Denny Swenson, a great friend, climber and outdoorsman, we stopped at a Taco Bell for our victory dinner. As we crossed the parking lot, we saw a bumper sticker that read "Earth First ... Then We Will Log the Other Planets." It was particularly amusing since it also happened to be Earth Day.

Other things of interest were often our conversations while above the maddening crowd.

In 1996, John Sup and I took along my church pastor Kent Carlson to climb Corrugation Corner at Lover's Leap near Echo Summit. While Carlson and I sat on a ledge about 1,000 feet above the highway, I noticed the pastor wore a Harley Davidson T-shirt. I asked if he rode motorcycles and he said he did, but he did not own one. I then mentioned just how dangerous motorcycles were. I will not soon forget the stunned look on his face considering where we were sitting.

It was Pastor Carlson's first climbing experience and needless to say it was the topic of his sermon on faith the following Sunday.

During that time, Tim Money and I climbed the Southeast Buttress of

Cathedral Peak (10,940 feet, III, 5.6) and West Crack on Daff Dome (III, 5.8) in Tuolumne Meadows – both are great climbs.

Over the years, I usually led all pitches during climbs. Since I was doing a lot of climbing, I felt it best to stay on the sharp end of the rope and my partners didn't complain. However, when the climbing got serious I would revert to swinging leads and selecting the pitches I preferred.

Becoming an El Cap Veteran

To be considered a veteran, it was necessary to complete five different grade VI routes on El Capitan. By the mid 1990s there were more than 50 grade VI routes on El Cap of various difficulty and danger levels. Having done the Nose and Salathé Wall, I decided to go for three more big wall climbs to gain that distinction.

In May of 1997, I had turned 51 and teamed up with Dan Osmond to climb the West Face of El Cap (grade VI). We did this multiday route in 16 hours. I was primarily the belayer, but did lead a few pitches.

Dan was an amazing climber. He was gentle and soft spoken while living a bohemian lifestyle. He rarely worked and lived in a tree house for several months at a time. He was also the star of several rock-climbing videos. He had pioneered routes of 5.14 difficulty and on site (i.e., had never seen the route before) free-soloed (i.e., no ropes or safety gear) routes of 5.11 difficulty.

Sadly, 18 months later, Dan lost his life doing a 1,100 foot rope jump off Leaning Tower.

In May 1997, Rich Travis and I climbed Zodiac on El Cap (5.9, A3, grade IV) in four and a half days - perhaps my best climb ever. It was exceptional with overhangs, scary weather and included the coolest bivy on a double portaledge 2,000 feet up on a perfectly vertical wall under an overhang. That was two grade VIs in 24 days, leaving one to go for veteran status.

In 1998, I did a lot of short routes with various partners at several climbing areas around California.[39] On a trip to New Mexico, Willie and I did our last climb together at Las Conchas in the Jemez Mountains near his home.

In October 1998, Dave Morrison, a talented 19 year old from Washington (son of a coworker of Bob Odom) and I did the Prow on Washington Column (5.10b, A2, IV) in Yosemite. I enjoyed the climb, including fixing a pitch in the dark. The second night, we spent at pitch eight in a portaledge (Terrace Ledges) and topped out the next day around 2 p.m.

Dave was an excellent climber, intelligent and someone I planned to do bigger climbs with in the future.

In the meantime, I became climbing partners with Sacramento area resident Brad Hart. I met Brad during a trip to Yosemite and we did a lot of good routes together in the valley and other Sierra Nevada climbing areas.[40]

On one ascent at Lover's Leap below Echo Summit with Brad, I decided to free solo the last pitch of Corrugation Corner. Not bothering to tell Brad of my plan, after topping out, he took in the rope only to find I wasn't on the other end of it. Somewhat alarmed, he leaned over the edge calling out for me. That's when he saw me some 30 feet below soloing up the last 5.4 pitch.

There was another "oops" occasion during one cold, winter day as Brad and I were at Phantom Spires climbing Over Easy (5.7) on Middle Spire. At an elevation above 4,000 feet, there was a considerable amount of snow on the approach hike. Leading the first pitch, I went out over a roof and around a corner to set up the belay. The wind made communication difficult, but I was sure I heard Brad yell "slack." I quickly let out the rope only to hear a loud scream. I then caught a glimpse of Brad staggering backward down the steep, snow-covered slope at the base of the spire. Like I said, "oops!"

In April 1999, Dave Morrison and I linked Serenity Crack (5.10d) and Sons of Yesterday (5.10a). These two combined are probably the best and most sustained 5.10 crack climbing route in Yosemite. I really enjoy crack climbing.

That spring of 1999, Denny Swenson and I did the Center route on the Grack (5.6) in Yosemite Valley. I have repeated this route several times over the years and it is one of my favorites.

El Cap Veteran Status

I made El Cap veteran status in May 1999 when Dave Morrison and I climbed Lurking Fear (5.10, A2, grade VI) on El Cap. It took us three and a half days and was an enjoyable climb.

In June 1999, Dave and I attempted North American Wall on El Cap, but backed off one quarter of the way up. The climb started out well, but about a fourth of the way up the wall things went badly.

We spent the first night on a portaledge at pitch six. We had fixed pitch seven and had plenty of food and water and were making good progress. In the lead, I had to do a pendulum pitch to my left, but couldn't make the move.

I decided to hook several small flakes and then free climb a face that led to a small belay ledge. Hook moves are accomplished by using a chromalloy hook on small flakes on the rock face. Hook moves are scary, because after you move off it you don't have it as protection.

After leaving the hook moves and free climbing a fair distance, the rope jammed at the belay station and left me clinging to small holds about 50 feet above my last protection. I knew if I fell it would result in a lot of body damage.

It felt like Dave was taking forever to free the rope and I was starting to tremble. It's a motion called "sewing machine legs" and my stitching was going to come undone. Just when I thought all was lost, Dave freed the rope and I scrambled to the ledge. It was this incident that lead to our retreat.

Early in the game, I learned when you finish leading a pitch your job is not done. It is imperative to immediately manage the rope and gear and complete the hauling process. This allows your climbing partner to reach the belay station and quickly change over to lead the next pitch. Efficiency and safety is of paramount importance.

After that incident, I realized Dave's inexperience with big wall climbing on a dangerous route was probably not a good situation for us and I did not want to spend a week's vacation practically killing myself. The fear factor coupled with the amount of work we had to do was taking all the fun out of it. Dave had mixed feelings as well, so we agreed to bail.

Again, I had second thoughts about it afterward and wondered if it was to be my last wall.

Hanging Around Yosemite

I did experience a terrific weekend in Camp IV when Christian Gabl returned to Yosemite. We did several short routes in the valley and the Dike on Pywiack Dome in Tuolumne. Christian introduced me to Heinz Zac, a famous Austrian photographer and climber. I also met Dean Potter, who soloed Half Dome in two hours. Earl Redfern, who I knew from my skydiving days, was there planning several BASE jumps.

Over the years I practiced several forms of "casual camping" in Yosemite. It was something climbers did in the valley. My refined technique was to wait until dark to enter a campground and ask a site occupant if it was OK to roll out my sleeping bag for the night.

On one particular occasion in Camp 4, I slept next to a young man from Seattle named Tom Dancs. He and I became good friends after that. I also met Nate Sears, a climber and surfer from Santa Cruz the same way.

Zion and the Desert Southwest

In April 2000, I met Tom Dancs and his friend Marcus Donaldson in Zion National Park. We climbed part of Touchstone Wall (III, 5.9, C2) and all of Moonlight Buttress (V, 5.9, C1-plus). Next, Marcus and I did Olive Oil (II, 5.7) on Rose Tower in Red Rocks, Nevada.

Triple Direct

Tom and I then returned to Yosemite to attempt Triple Direct (VI, 5.9, A2-plus) on El Cap. This is a fine route which combines the first one third of Salathé Wall with the second one third of the Muir Wall and the last one third of the Nose. I first learned of it when Bruce Carson did the first solo ascent in 1972 while he was with us in Yosemite with the Seattle Explorer Post. It had captured my imagination and we went back to tackle it 18 years later.

We climbed to the top of pitch 16 about halfway up and then spent a cold, wet night on Grey Ledges. A heavy rainstorm rolled in and literally washed us off the route. After bailing from there, Tom and I climbed the Arches Terrace (II, 5.8R) together before leaving the valley.

Tom later wrote this account of our El Cap attempt.

Dear Friends and Climbing Partners,

I just got back from Yosemite National Park where Randy Peeters and I attempted to do my fifth and his seventh route on El Capitan. We chose the route called Triple Direct for its relative easiness as a good spring warm-up big wall climb.

We climbed the first 16 pitches in good style after fixing only the first two pitches. The one mistake we made was to haul the "Free Blast" part of the Salathé. While this was a purist approach to doing the wall, the low angle of those first ten pitches and the wandering nature of the route made hauling a real pain in the rear. Try moving 170 pounds of food, water and gear up 80 degree slabs and you will know what I mean.

We spent our second night on the Grey Ledges Bivi. Where all hell broke loose! You know that storm that has been flooding central California? Well we got the first act of that world-class performance from mother nature/God (depending on your convictions and/or beliefs). We spent the next ten hours trying to get what sleep we could in a massive down pour. Those of you who do big wall climbing, know that this includes all the run-off water from the upper portions of El Cap as well.

Needless to say, by morning our two pound synthetic sleeping bags weighed about 12 pounds from being saturated ... all that straight through the Gore-Tex bivi sacks ... my suggestion: if you ever do a route with sleeping ledges on it, bring a portaledge with a good fly and bivi sacks! This combination would have made the night a bit more on the damp side, rather than the saturated side.

After toughing out the night, we left our water and non-perishable food on the ledge and began the long series of rappels needed to get back to the safety of terra firma.

Sleep, food, sleep, water and more sleep got us back to our usual confident (sometimes cocky) selves. We proceeded to rack up for some trad/free climbing as if nothing had happened.

CARPE DIEM!!! Tom Dancs

PS: Randy's wife Doris makes the best Tomato Soup in the world! She played a key (and perhaps the most important role) in keeping Randy and me healthy, energized and motivated to pick ourselves up after failure. Thanx Doris!

I returned in October 2000 with Rich Travis and Nate Sears to give Triple Direct another try, only to get snowed off the route above the Grey Ledges. It proved to be a bad weather year for me on big walls. More unfinished business – ugh!

In May 2001, Rich and I returned to Yosemite to finish Triple Direct. It was my third attempt of this route.

The first day, we fixed and hauled before returning to our jobs. A week later, it took us six days to finish the climb. It was the longest period of time I had ever spent on a wall. Although held up by slower parties, the good weather made the extra time rather pleasant and relaxing.

One cool thing happened high up on the route while I led the pitch above Camp VI. We planned to fix two pitches and rappel back down to the perfectly flat triangular ledge to spend the night. At 4 p.m., when we heard climbers approaching our camp, it disappointed us to think we would have to spend the night sitting up because there wasn't enough space on the ledge to bivy four comfortably.

I had finished my lead and Rich was jugging up when I called out to the climbers below and ask where they planned to spend the night.

They yelled back, "At the Mountain Room Bar. Why?"

They were two young climbers, Jason "Singer" Smith (24) and Leo Houlding (20). Leo, a British citizen, had recently been active in Baffin Island and later on Everest. The year before, while doing a big wall in Kyrgyzstan's Kara Su Valley, Singer, along with two other climbers had been held hostage for six days by Islamic rebels from Uzbekistan. In order to escape, they had to shove one of their captors off a ledge and then run away.

As they passed by us, we had a short but amazing conversation. I asked when they had begun their climb and Singer replied, "At 12:40."

I then asked if they had started in the middle of the night.

Singer said, "No, at noon!" They finished the Nose in a total of seven hours and two minutes.

We watched as they block climbed using a combination of normal belays and static fixed rope belays. They took chances neither Rich nor I would have found acceptable. However, what we learned from watching them cut our time per pitch in half after that.

Rich is a wonderful man and a solid Christian. We still climb together and are good friends to this day.

Winding Down and Skipping Around

Over the next six years, my rock climbing forays were limited. I chose instead to focus on big expeditions and limited my climbs to Royal Arches in Yosemite and quick trips to Donner Summit in the Sierras near home. However, while traveling through Thailand in October 2001, I did stop in Phuket at Railay Beach to climb a fine limestone route at Krabi.

In June 2006, I climbed with Wayne Klinger on Royal Arches. It had been 25 years since Wayne and I had done a route together and it was a joy to climb with him again.

That September of 2006, I took a road trip and while in Wyoming snuck in another Classic Fifties route on Devil's Tower with Andy Petefish, the owner of Tower Guides. We did the Durance Route – Direct Finish (5.7, six pitches).

In August 2007, I again focused on rock climbing and with Tom Dancs knocked off a couple of Classic Fifties located in Wyoming's Wind River Range in an area known as the Cirque of the Towers. It is one of the most beautiful areas I've ever visited – post card stuff.

First, was Wolf's Head (III, 5.6) and it was one of my best climbs. Then, the next day, Tom and I did Northeast Ridge of Pingora (IV, 5.8). It was a difficult climb and Tom led all the pitches.

The following year, Bob Odom and I climbed East Buttress of Middle Cathedral in Yosemite. This time, I led on less than half the pitches and fell three times. All my falls were more than ten feet and on one I managed to sprain my ankle and bruise my left side.

After completing that route, Bob and I hiked back to the car, barbecued a couple rib-eye steaks and casual camped near Upper Pines. About 2 a.m., I was awakened by a bright light shining in my face.

"Do you own a Rav4?" someone asked.

The intruder was a volunteer ranger, so I confessed I had such a vehicle.

"Well," he continued, "a bear just ripped your door off."

That got my attention and soon I was up and headed in the direction of my car. The volunteer ranger then informed me I would have to report the fact that I had left food in my car to a ranger and there would be a $1,000 fine for doing so. He then asked if we were camping legally – amazing, since we weren't. Of course I answered yes.

I assured the ranger I would take care of it. As soon as he left, Bob and I packed up and returned to the car. The badly damaged door was still attached by the hinges, so I body slammed it back in place and we were out of the park in less than 30 minutes.

In the more than 55 years I had been coming to Yosemite, this was the first time a bear had broken into my car. The bear had been attracted to the barbecue I had cooked the steaks on, as my food had been well hidden.

In a reunion with Rick Knight, we climbed at Peshastin Pinnacles and Castle Rock on the east slope of the Washington Cascades. Rick had not climbed in years, so I did the leading. It was August 2009 and a true déjà vu experience, especially on Midway (5.5) at Castle Rock. It was one of the first technical climbs I did back in the 1960s and climbing with Rick again was wonderful.

On the same trip, Bob Odom and I climbed the Becky Route on Liberty Bell (four pitches, II, 5.6, swinging leads) in the North Cascades of Washington. It also was an enjoyable experience.

I returned to Yosemite in 2009 to climb Royal Arches with Chris Cover, a genuine Christian and nice fellow. Chris and I teamed up again in October 2010 to do Corrugation Corner at Lover's Leap.

In August 2011, Bruce Harrington, his son Kevin and I climbed Royal Arches. It had been 35 years since Bruce and I had climbed together and was another déjà vu experience. Afterward, Bruce and I took a quick swim in the Merced River at El Cap Meadows – a tradition we had established in the early 1970s. The next year, Bruce and I climbed some routes at Joshua Tree in Southern California which brought back many shared memories.

October 2011, VO Roberson and Peter Smeltzer, friends from North Carolina, met me in Yosemite to do some climbing. I led the first nine pitches of Royal Arches, but VO was running out of gas. We decided to retreat from the route half way up, right after the pendulum pitch. The first rappel was only anchored with an old runner on an old fixed pin. Yes, it was scary!

VO treated me to a fantastic dinner at the Ahwahnee Lodge after the climb. The next morning, we went up the Center route on the Grack (5.6 – really a neat route) before returning home.

Reminiscing

Over the years as I progressed to longer and harder routes, I developed a special relationship with Yosemite. In increments of days and weeks, I spent considerably more than a year in the valley pursuing the lofty faces of those fantastic granite walls.

We were all aware we had just missed the Golden Era in Yosemite Valley and the other California climbing areas – but it never bothered us. We had helped to usher in the clean climbing ethos, pushed many routes from aid to free and in general had a fantastic time doing it.

It was not the carefree hippie lifestyle of the real rock climbing pioneers – we all had jobs and lived relatively normal, productive lives. Also, by blending the alpine and rock climbing with other sports and family travel it was much more satisfying then a narrow focus on a single activity within a sport.

I do feel a oneness with Yosemite Valley after so many years of climbing there. If you drew an imaginary line between Leaning Tower and El Cap on the west end of the valley and another between Half Dome and Washington Column on the east end, I have climbed on all major formations within those boundaries. Personally, this has been a great accomplishment.

Training for these climbs and other expeditions required a great deal of time. I would often wake up well before dawn to stretch, lift weights, run and cycle to my real day job. During my lunch breaks while at Aerojet, I would walk to the climbing wall at Wilderness Sports and practice daily.

In the early 1980s I dislocated my left shoulder during a skiing accident and, as a result, had lost some range of motion in that shoulder. On one lunch break, while practicing at the climbing wall, I fell and was left dangling with my left hand wedged into a crack. Once the pain subsided, I discovered the adhesions had torn loose in my shoulder and full range of motion was miraculously restored. I still have some arthritis problems with the shoulder, but overall, it is in pretty good shape.

Rich Travis and I are talking about doing another climb together before too long – who knows for sure - at 68 years old, here we go again!

Lost Arrow Spire
Yosemite Valley

Doris and Wayne Klinger
The Womb, Joshua Tree

Bruce on Balance Rock
Joshua Tree 1975

Top right - Randy leading Thank God Ledge, Half Dome, Yosemite Valley

Top left - Willie Spencer and Randy after topping out on Half Dome

Upper left - Rich Travis following the Great Roof, The Nose, El Capitan

Lower left - Rich belaying below the summit overhang near the top of the Nose, El Capitan

Bottom left - Randy belaying on Leaning Tower

Bottom right - Rich leading, Zodiac route, El Capitan

Top left - Randy belaying from the bivy below the Mark of Zorro, Zodiac route, El Capitan

Top right - Topping out on Zodiac, El Capitan, Yosemite Valley

Right - Randy climbing near home in Northern California

Bottom right - Randy leading the interconnect pitch on the Triple Direct route, El Capitan

Bottom middle - Bob Odom leading on the East Buttress Middle Cathedral, Yosemite Valley

Bottom left - Randy after climbing Liberty Bell

8

Into the Void

It had been two years since I was first kicked out of Yosemite National Park on suspicion I had intended to BASE jump from El Capitan. I had two years to get it right. But that afternoon in 1991, I found myself sitting in a Yosemite jail wondering what else I could have done to avoid getting caught...

Jumping

Funny thing about jumping off stuff – it is one big rush of excitement fraught with danger.

I started jumping while living in Northern New Mexico and it sort of grew on me. I would jump a precipice into a creek pool and then challenge myself to go even higher. Next it was from the cliffs of the Grand Canyon into Havasu Creek and then, while in Idaho, my younger son Todd and I jumped from a bridge spanning the Middle Fork of the Salmon River while on a rafting trip.

After moving to California, Todd and I would jump from large rock formations along the American River near Folsom. It was during this time, a kayaking friend told me in no uncertain terms exactly how dangerous that activity really was.

This same friend ran a driving school where many of his clients had to learn how to drive as paraplegics. He said a large number of those in that condition resulted from jumping off objects into the water. That was a wakeup call so I completely phased out the activity.

Jumping Out of Perfectly Good Airplanes

First of all, let me assure you there are no perfectly good airplanes! I should know; I helped design them.

Skydiving entered the picture in the spring of 1988. The Explorer Post where I was the advisor wanted to try a skydive, so we made plans and researched the cost. All the youth committed to the activity, but as the planned date approached, the parents of all but one of those boys objected. So only one scout, Todd and I ended up doing the tandem skydives at a facility in Lodi, CA. The only problem I encountered during the two days following the jump was getting over the adrenaline rush and sore cheeks from two days of smiling.

After this experience, Todd and I were hooked. In July 1988, we took static line courses to become certified and then started doing free-fall jumps on our own. It was difficult watching Todd jump ahead of me and disappear from sight. That both scared and excited me, just before I was to jump.

Todd also had a number of malfunctions which didn't help either. However, Todd finished the course with flying colors; it took me a little longer because I couldn't achieve the control I needed near the end of my free-falls. I finally gained the confidence I needed after taking some accelerated free-fall jumps from an instructor in Davis, CA. I then returned to Lodi to finish my course and earn my license.

Bill Dause, who owns and operates the Parachute Center in Lodi, is still among my friends. To this day, he has the most free-fall time (more than 456 hours) of anyone in the world and had logged over 30,200 skydives as of November 2011. He has a unique sense of humor and on occasion has done some rather unorthodox things during free-fall.

For example, during Todd's solo graduation skydive, without his knowledge, Bill followed him out of the airplane, quietly flew up behind him and grabbed his ankles in mid air. Todd said he nearly had a cardiac arrest.

On another occasion, as we neared the end of our planned free-fall, he reached over and pulled my pilot chute without my knowing it. Imagine my surprise when my parachute suddenly opened. But make no mistake, I genuinely trust this man and even sent my wife, Doris, with him on a tandem jump.

On one flight, I watched an instructor give last minute instructions to a tandem student as we climbed to jump altitude. He carefully strapped the student to his harness and after reviewing the procedure said, "When we move to the door I will ask you if you are ready to go. It doesn't matter what you say – we're going anyway."

Although skydiving is something I no longer do, during that time it became a passion I really enjoyed. I completed more than 368 skydives for a total of four and a half hours of freefall over the eight years I was involved in the sport. Five jumps were BASE jumps and one was from a hot-air balloon. During a peak four year span I averaged greater than 80 jumps a year. I did quite a few jumps with Todd; and during that time, I earned several licenses and awards.[41]

A Really Big Rubber Band

By the early 1980s bungee jumping was becoming popular in America. My involvement with this activity was somewhat fortuitous, although probably not an example of my better judgment.

Steve "Kiwi" Wood and I kayaked on the Tuolumne River and had reached the Wards Ferry Bridge where we had parked our car. Kiwi was a professional skydiver who moved to the USA from New Zealand. We became good friends. He taught me how to skydive and I taught him how to kayak. As he and I crossed the bridge over the Tuolumne to return to our vehicle, there was a group bungee jumping from the bridge. They were also drinking heavily.

"Here are some brave kayakers – want to jump?" they called to us.

Perhaps curiosity trumped common sense in this case, but we both said yes.

Kiwi was the first to go. He jumped from a spot high above where the group was launching and went off without hesitation. Kiwi then challenged me to do it and sure enough, I did.

The jump went OK, but the car-pulley arrangement they were using to hoist their victims up to the bridge worried me. As I rapidly drew closer and closer to the pulley it appeared no one was paying attention to the situation. However, in spite of being drunk, they managed to safely pull me back up using the car.

It was fun, but I couldn't help but think of a cartoon I had seen concerning bungee jumping. It read, "Finally, a sport that makes professional wrestling look intelligent."

The Ultimate Adrenaline Rush

BASE jumping is free-fall parachuting from a fixed object. Legal issues are involved, but it's sort of allowed as long as the jumper doesn't do something too stupid. However, it is absolutely not tolerated in California's Yosemite National Park.

Perhaps the "outlaw" aspect of the endeavor holds some attraction, as I made up my mind to jump from Yosemite's El Capitan. El Cap is also one of the easiest since the top 500 feet are overhanging and this allows the jumper the time and speed necessary to track away from the wall before deploying the parachute.

I did 174 skydives in preparation for El Capitan, including stalled flight path exits and a balloon jump. It also required advanced planning with my friends Kiwi, Texas Tom and Willie to carry out the caper. Kiwi had introduced me to Texas Tom McCarthy, who was also a skydiver. Willie was a longtime climbing friend, who wasn't into skydiving, but was a willing partner in our intended "crime."

It was the summer of 1989. The four of us met in Yosemite the night before the planned jump. Texas Tom arrived ahead of us with his equipment and went to the site where we planned to hide our mountain bikes. Willie drove Kiwi and me up a dirt road and stopped near the base of El Capitan. I put my parachute on a log and Kiwi had his in a lightweight backpack which he left by the car.

We then bicycled about a mile farther up the dirt road where we met up with Tom who was ready to go. We chained our bikes to a tree and Kiwi and I headed back down the road to retrieve our parachutes.

The plan was that Willie would then drive the car down to the valley floor and casual camp while we walked back up the road to meet up with Tom. We would then hike to the top of El Capitan in the cover of darkness.

At dawn, we would jump and land in a small, more obscure meadow near where we had hidden our bikes. The plan was then to hide our parachutes, mount our bikes and ride out to the main road as if nothing had happened – at least, nothing we would have known anything about.

We knew of a larger meadow below El Capitan where previous BASE jumpers had landed, only to be apprehended by the rangers. Our plan was to avoid that obvious area completely to keep from being captured. Once the heat cooled off, we would return and retrieve our parachutes and gear.

All went well on the night of the caper until Kiwi and I made our way back through the darkness towards our parachutes. We saw car lights and assumed they were Willie's. Naturally, we hoped that oversight didn't attract any undue attention. It did - the lights were not his, but rather from a park ranger's patrol car.

As we approached, I noticed my parachute was no longer on the log, but Kiwi's was still in his backpack by the car. Once in earshot the ranger asked us if we knew Willie. We answered that we did.

"I thought you said you were here alone?" said the ranger turning to Willie.

Caper Lesson No. 1 – keep the story straight.

The ranger then got on his radio and called for backup. Shortly thereafter, a second ranger arrived. From that point on, it became a dumb ranger – smart ranger sideshow.

The second ranger was instructing the dumb one on how to interrogate us. Dutifully, the dumb one would start to ask us a question, stop mid-sentence and turn to the smart ranger to ask how to proceed.

Of no help to us was the chatter coming over the radio, "Airborne troops expected to jump El Cap tonight." It also included a heightened suspicion of our intentions because it was a full moon that night.

Caper Lesson No. 2 – don't BASE jump in Yosemite during a full moon.

Twice, the dumb ranger started to investigate Kiwi's backpack but stopped when we distracted him with our conversation. The second time, he actually had his hand on the pack's drawstring preparing to open it when our discussion took him down a different path. Luckily, my parachute was out of sight behind the log because Willie had the presence of mind to ditch it when he saw the ranger coming.

The rangers questioned us for about an hour and even accused Willie of being the driver of a potential getaway car. However, they were unable to come up with anything solid so they took our mug shots with a Polaroid camera. They also wrote down a description of our car. Toward midnight, they rudely escorted us outside the park gate located near El Portal.

We knew Tom had to be wondering what became of us, but there was little we could do other than roll out our sleeping bags. The rangers had left us on a dirt pullout and drove off. However, an hour later they returned and herded us a mile farther down the road claiming the pullout was still on park property. They also made it a point to inform us we were no longer welcome in the Yosemite.

Right before dawn and pretty certain the rangers had given up on us, we drove back to El Capitan Meadow and found Tom. He figured out that we had run into trouble. Willie lowered his tailgate to start breakfast while Kiwi and I went after our parachutes and bicycles.

As we finished packing up Kiwi's car to head back to Sacramento, we were surprised by the sudden appearance of two BASE jumpers who sailed over the top of us headed for the big meadow. We knew trouble would quickly follow so we said a hasty goodbye to Willie, jumped into Kiwi's vehicle and headed out.

Willie, unfortunately, was discovered and detained by park rangers before he could put his stove away. They were suspicious he was the getaway driver for the two aforementioned jumpers and began interrogating him all over again.

As we blew past the entrance station to the park, Kiwi and I began planning our next attempt to BASE jump El Cap.

Two weeks later, we returned with a similar strategy and before long found ourselves at the top of our destination via the falls trail.

At 3,000 feet up, I asked Steve how much time I would have before deploying my chute. Kiwi had done this before and I had complete trust in his judgment. He told me I had anywhere from three to 12 seconds, max. I was scared so I informed him I would like to pull at the three second mark.

Still, I knew from experience that I counted too fast when jumping. I knew El Cap Tower, about 2,000 feet down from the top, would be the maximum free-fall before deployment. It was also the safest point considering the gear we used.

One of the interesting things about jumping from a fixed object is the lack of noise and wind resistance, which is uniquely different then exiting a plane traveling at 80 miles per hour. That also means initially there are no aerodynamic forces in play so body position becomes critical.

I took three big steps and lunged from the precipice above Dawn Wall with my head held high. Holding your head high at exit is necessary in order to avoid tumbling and or hitting the wall during the initial part of the jump. As gravity took over and I rotated my body downward into a tracking position, I could hear Kiwi's shout of "congratulations" quickly trail off above me.

Flying next to a big wall gives one a real sensation of speed. I could see the wall a few feet behind my legs as I hurtled toward terminal velocity (120 mph). It was so cool that I quickly calmed down and knew I would take it all the way to El Cap Tower.

Meanwhile, Kiwi was up top counting down. He told me when he reached 13 seconds he had the horrible thought I had gone in, but that's when he heard the whoosh as my chute opened. He immediately took off after that. He carried his jump low, so we landed in the small meadow within seconds of each other. Once on the ground, we ran out of the meadow toward El Capitan and into the woods. We quickly found a spot to hide our parachutes, retrieved our bikes and pedaled off to have breakfast.

It was easy. Once we felt the heat was off, we returned to where we had left our gear, loaded it up along with our bikes and drove off. It was the most intense adrenaline rush I had ever experienced. I was terribly excited and completely hooked.

When I returned home, I registered my feat with the clandestine BASE Association and was told I was the 572nd person to have BASE jumped El Cap.

BASE jumping is the closest thing to pure thought I have ever experienced. I truly believe the mental concentration is similar to that of an Olympic athlete. You must completely focus, visualize the entire jump, exit properly and perform flawlessly.

On most BASE jumps, there is not enough time to deploy a reserve parachute so you have to get it right the first time.

Because of the concentration required it is actually very relaxing and therapeutic – a complete momentary break from all the hassles of the world – job, kids, finances, etc. As with many extreme sports, physical ability is only the entry card – the game is actually played in the head. Without the mental part you cannot be successful in these endeavors.

What's Next?

Over the next two years I completed 143 more skydives. In July 1991, I decided I would do one of each type of BASE jump to earn my BASE rating. Since I had already done El Capitan (i.e., earth), that would mean jumping from a building, an antenna and a span (or bridge) to complete the series.

I also wanted to BASE jump Half Dome; I was told it was exceptional. I had climbed both the face of it and El Cap, so BASE jumping both appealed to me as a significant goal.

Span

My first target was the Foresthill Bridge in Northern California, where I now live. It spans 730 feet above the North Fork of the American River. Kiwi agreed to help me. He had put together a new BASE rig with a Velcro closure and no reserve chute. He was happy I would be testing it and not him.

A little before dawn on the day of the jump, we parked my getaway car along the Old Foresthill Road just below the bridge. We then drove up to the new highway and parked in the parking area near the span. We walked out to the middle of the bridge where I laid down behind the pedestrian barrier separating the walkway from the road and slipped into my gear. At first light, Steve gave the all clear. I stood up, climbed over the guardrail, double-checked the pilot chute and launched into the open air. Steve videotaped the jump.

At three seconds, I deployed the sub-terminal pilot chute and rode under the canopy to the dirt road which ran parallel to the river. I stuck the landing perfectly, gathered up my chute, ran to the car and left the scene. I felt great!

I drove straight to work having completed my span requirement and wore a broad smile for two straight days.

Antenna

My next mission would be the Lodi Antennas. There is a Lodi, CA, but these antennas are not actually located there; they are in nearby Walnut Grove in the Delta. There are four of them, with the tallest rising an amazing 2,000 feet into the air. Kiwi and I chose the 1,800 foot antenna, assuming it would be the one least suspected of being the object of a BASE jump. That was only the beginning of our great plan.

We found a spot by a bridge one mile from the antenna. We put in a small raft at midnight and paddled our way to where the antenna was located. We hid our raft and hiked up to the chain-link fence topped with razor wire. We were surprised to see a truck parked in the compound and a light on in the small, maintenance building – no problem.

We scaled the fence, carefully climbed over the razor wire and dropped to the ground. We then crossed the yard and climbed the stairs leading to the antenna. Our biggest concern that night was the weather. It was drizzling rain and if it worsened we wouldn't be able to make the jump, but we persevered.

Climbing the metal ladders of an antenna this high is not only scary, but it turns one's forearms into mush. At the 1,000 foot mark, we were above the clouds in a steady 25 mph wind. It was truly amazing to see those clouds whizzing by a few feet below us.

We climbed another 200 feet and cleared the wind shear to enter a zone of complete calm. Now we could see millions of stars and the Milky Way. Shooting stars added to this incredible sight. As it turned out, we were in the middle of the Perseid meteor shower. That made the remaining 600 foot climb all the more worth it.

We reached the top about an hour before daybreak. As we sat waiting, we became concerned that the cloud cover might prevent us from being able to see the ground on our descent. We also couldn't tell if the truck was still parked in the compound. And, the microwave units on these towers can add a little intrigue as well. Some BASE jumpers have said they've had the fillings in their teeth heat up and start to vibrate. Fortunately, all that happened to us was my video camera died.

When dawn finally came, the clouds had dissipated and the jump was on. The relief of not having to climb down 1,800 feet was exhilarating in itself.

At 6:10 that morning, I was airborne and hit the silk six seconds later. Kiwi followed right behind and, in no time at all, we were back in our raft paddling toward our car. One more fantastic adventure down and off to work.

Kiwi told me sometime later a number of his friends got a key to the tower elevator and made several jumps in one night.

Building

Six days later, I was ready to meet my greatest challenge of all – jumping from a building. I decided on the Cal Plaza II building in downtown Los Angeles. It was still under construction at the time, but about 90 percent complete.

I was to meet up with Keith Jones in Palmdale. Jones was a well known BASE jumper in Southern California and agreed to let me go along on one of his night jumps. In Los Angeles, we planned to join David Nunn, a budding stuntman and several other movie-producer types who agreed to serve as ground crew.

We met at midnight in a café near L.A.'s Pershing Square. Nunn already had on his BASE rig under his windbreaker, making me think he wanted to get caught. The ground crew drove us to the site in a van and stood by to assist in our getaway. To avoid the guard, we climbed over a railing located on a freeway bridge near the construction site. We accessed the building through an open door, but the stairwell was locked. So, we went out through a window and scaled up to the third floor on the external scaffolding. From there we reentered the building through a window and gained access to the stairwell.

We came out on a balcony on the 51st floor and oriented ourselves to the separate landing sites we had chosen. From there, we made contact with the ground crew using two-way radios.

I was first to go and clearly remember standing on a ledge waiting for the traffic lights to change some 680 feet below us. When Keith gave me the "all clear," I exited with my head held high, delayed two and a half seconds and deployed my sub-terminal pilot chute. With a whoosh my canopy opened, I quickly checked it and made a hard left turn. What I saw nearly gave me a heart attack.

We were supposed to be on separate flight paths but there, not more than ten feet from me, was another jumper also doing 30 miles per hour. For an instant, I was gripped with terror fearing a potentially fatal collision – until I realized it was only my reflection in the building's mirrored glass – what a relief.

I cleared a large crane and made a nearly perfect descent onto Olive Avenue. I passed over traffic lights and signs and then maneuvered between several power lines and landed dead center in the middle of the street. I quickly gathered my gear and ran to the side of the street and hid in some bushes. The van picked me up first and then David. We returned to Pershing Square and watched Keith land. What an adventure. It was unbelievable!

After being dropped off at my car, I made the long drive back to Sacramento and was at work by 9 a.m. I dried my canopy on my desk and repacked my rig. I felt an inner glow that kept me smiling all day – what a satisfying and fantastic experience.

I called the BASE organization and registered my jumps. I was No. 310 in the world to register all four jumps. I also felt a sense of achievement and satisfaction knowing it took me only four jumps to complete building, antenna, span and earth.

Just One Last BASE Jump

A little over two weeks later, I was back at Half Dome. I promised myself it would be my last BASE jump. I felt excited and scared at the same time.

After arriving in Yosemite, I hiked the nine miles up to the cables that led to the top of Half Dome. There I was to meet Jonathon Bolin, who knew where the exit point was and the landing zones to avoid the ever-present park rangers.

It turned out that paraplegic Mark Wellman, a park ranger injured in a climbing accident, was climbing Half Dome's North Face. He and Mike Corbett were making their well-publicized way up Tis-sa-ack. They had been at it two weeks and planned to reach the top the day before I planned to jump.

Ironically, one of the reasons given for not allowing BASE jumping in Yosemite is to avoid a media circus that could spoil the park's tranquil environment. That seemed to me a double standard when it came to publicity for one of its own. Don't get me wrong, I'm all for the underdog and thought Mark's jumar to the top quite an achievement.

Much to my dismay, Wellman and Corbett didn't make it that day and would still be climbing the morning of my planned jump. When I reached the cable route up the side of Half Dome, I found a small village of press people camped there. They planned to climb to the top in the morning and await the duo's arrival estimated to be around 10 a.m. I asked and was told there was one guy already at the top looking after the camera equipment. I decided to go ahead and get some sleep and make my final ascent early in the morning ahead of the press.

At dawn, Jonathon had not yet arrived, so I went up alone at 7 a.m. I avoided being seen by the guy guarding the cameras and made my way to the edge of Half Dome to take a look. There, about 200 feet below me, were Wellman and Corbett. I put on my gear and started to go through the motions while waiting for Jonathon. I picked out an exit point based on descriptions I had heard from others and rehearsed the jump in my head. I knew I would have to fly up the valley away from Mirror Lake Meadow to avoid capture.

By 8 a.m. Jonathon still wasn't there. I thought about Wellman being a park ranger but also knew there was an unspoken alliance between climbers and BASE jumpers. After all, most BASE jumpers were climbers. I made up my mind that Wellman would take the high ground and not call me in if I jumped.

I was also pressed for time by the fact I planned to take Doris and the kids to the Giants game in San Francisco that evening. If I had to climb back down I'd never make it back in time. That's when things became sort of surreal.

I started to pretend I was going to jump and stepped back five paces as I would in an actual jump. Before I knew it, I was sailing over the edge exactly as I had rehearsed and couldn't believe I was doing it.

With head held high I started to rotate into a tracking position with Wellman and Corbett still below me. Half Dome's wall slopes out a little along a white streak called the "runway." The runway ends at a spot called "smiley face" and that's where I would deploy my chute. It's a full eight second ride, with the massive wall flashing by just a few feet behind my legs.

As I reached the smiley face, I extracted my pilot chute and heard the whoosh of my canopy opening overhead. As I looked up to determine its condition – holy shit – I realized my lines were twisted and I was flying straight back toward the wall!

The story was best told by Wellman himself in his book *Climbing Back.*

On the morning of our 13th day on Half Dome, I was stuffing my sleeping bag into the stuff sack when I saw a sight neither of us will ever forget. It was a body and it went plummeting right past our portaledge.

"Someone's fallen off the top," yelled Corbett. Maybe it's a reporter who got too close to the edge."

We were both gripped with horror as we watched the person dropping out of sight. Suddenly, we heard a "Woooof," and a big white parachute popped out of the persons back … He was too close to the rock face. His chute scraped the wall and he spun around away from the cliff. As his descent stabilized and he floated down towards the pine trees at Mirror Lake, I picked up the radio and called the ranger's patrol desk … The parachutist had broken the law and as a park ranger, it was my duty to report him. He landed safely and with the help of my radio call was later arrested.

Here are the problems with Wellman's account of the events that day: first, every serious, big wall climber has seen BASE jumpers before. A climber might be startled by the sudden appearance of a jumper, but BASE jumpers are immediately recognizable. The body position is unmistakable and I know Wellman looked right at me as I passed by about 100 feet from their portaledge. I know damn well Corbett knew I was a BASE jumper and not a "reporter." Second, my parachute wasn't white; it was multi colored. I did come close to the wall, but I steered away and was never "scraping the wall." And indeed, Wellman was responsible for my eventual arrest. I knew this even before his book came out, thanks to my friend Jonathon. He had reached the top just after I jumped and heard the entire conversation between Wellman and the park rangers on his radio.

Wellman acted as a spotter and immediately reported me. He gave the rangers my exact location as they arrived on the scene before I even landed. Jonathon watched the whole thing. My earlier assessment of Wellman had been wrong – he wasn't a climber, but rather an individual in great physical condition able to jug his way up a rock face thanks to the help of a strong climber. Shortly after the event, Wellman resigned from the park service.

After I landed at Mirror Lake Meadow, I saw two rangers headed my way. I crouched down behind a rock and quietly removed my parachute and buried it under some branches and leaves. I was able to sneak out of the meadow undetected and hid in the Indian Caves area. I stashed the rest of my gear there.

I waited about two hours before deciding the coast was clear - it wasn't. On my hike back to the stables, a ranger coming in the opposite direction stopped me and began to interrogate me. Dissatisfied with my answers, he insisted I take him to my vehicle parked at Curry Camp; from there he called in support.

After the other rangers arrived, they started the good cop/bad cop routine. The "bad cop" started yelling at me saying, because it was a national park he didn't need a warrant to search my vehicle, only probable cause. The probable cause was Wellman's description of me.

This troubled me, since I had a log book in my vehicle containing the names of many BASE jumpers. They certainly had a good description of me; especially a description coming from someone 100 feet away who caught a glimpse of me as I flew by. They also had found my parachute with my initials on the cut-away handle of my reserve chute.

After an hour or so, the "good cop" took over. His interrogation went like this:

This is no big deal. In fact, I wish I had the guts to do something like that. Just tell me the truth and you'll get off with a tax deductible donation of $1,000 and no criminal record. You won't even have to go to jail. I'll have you released on your own recognizance; you'll get your parachute back and be on your way.

Knowing my rig was worth about $2,700, I quickly did the math in my head and confessed – big mistake. Within minutes I was handcuffed and stuffed into the back of a patrol car. Next thing I knew, I was at the Yosemite jail where I was booked, photographed, given a disinfectant shower and clad in a yellow jumpsuit and slip-on shoes. I was told bail would be about $500, payable by a U.S. Postal money order.

Once in my cell, I was allowed my one telephone call. I immediately called Doris and told her to get the cash and head for Yosemite. I can still remember her reassuring words.

"I'm not driving to Yosemite; I told you not to do it - you figure it out." I told her to give the boys the Giants tickets and have them go to the game with some friends. I told her I would call again after my arraignment. I heard a click as she hung up.

As I sat in my cell, all I could think about was how I could have avoided getting caught. I decided I should have cut away my main chute and abandoned it. Had I done that, my most damning evidence would not have been found by the rangers. I could have then stashed the rest of my gear in the Indian Caves area.

I also shouldn't have been so willing to take them to my truck ... would have, could have and should have ... What was the point? Here I was in jail, so I decided to try and make the best of it.

I was eventually herded in with ten other inmates into a holding cell where we were introduced to the newly appointed public defender. It was there, I discovered I was in jail with none other than Warren Harding. No, not the former president; he was the Warren Harding who was the first to climb the Nose on El Capitan and complete a grade VI. As controversial as he was, it was no wonder he was in jail.

Harding's attitude was I'll do it my way and to hell with you and what you think.

Climbing magazines had depicted Harding as a devil holding a pitchfork when standing next to Royal Robins, climbing's version of Superman with RR on his chest. His book *Downward Bound: A Mad! Guide to Rock Climbing*, was indicative of his attitude and behavior. But, that aside, he was an amazing climber and I had done a number of his climbing routes. Many of them lacked good protection and required nerves of steel.

Harding befriended me and offered suggestions on how to deal with my arrest. He was in for his third DUI and had plenty of experience with Yosemite's "justice system."

We were shackled together in the holding cell and marched single file over to the courtroom where the public defender would handle our arraignment. We were introduced to Judge Pitts, the federal magistrate, who told me I had no rights in his court. Judge Pitts said I was charged with numerous violations of the Code of Federal Regulations. Those included powerless flight, conspiracy to commit powerless flight, public nuisance and more. I was then told those came with a five year sentence and up to $10,000 fine for each count.

Then he smiled sarcastically and said, "I suppose you could be innocent if you just happened to be walking along the top of Half Dome with a parachute on and fell off accidentally."

The whole arraignment can best be summarized by the bumper sticker on the judge's blue pickup which proclaimed, "Yosemite Law: It's the Pitts." My public defender then entered my plea as "not guilty," based on some Oregon state marijuana reform law. The court was like a circus and beyond belief.

When allowed, I covered the courtroom microphone and told the magistrate I wanted to be represented by my own attorney. The public defender managed to get me released on my own recognizance, so I returned to my cell, put on my own clothes, got in my car and drove home. Because of my security clearance and position at work, I went straight to my boss that next morning to explain what happened.

"Now what did you do?" he asked.

I told him I jumped off a rock with a parachute.

"Isn't that kind of stupid?" he again asked.

There wasn't much I could say to that, but my boss was totally cool about the entire incident. After that, I called the BASE Association and registered my jump. I was Half Dome No. 75.

However, the issue did not pass quietly into oblivion. I was later told that Wellman's ascent of Half Dome was announced over the information board at the Giants' baseball game. My boys figured the announcer would next say ... and Randy Peeters was arrested for BASE jumping.

On Harding's advice, I put in a call to the previous park public defender then living in Mariposa, CA. She was quite helpful and instructed me on how to deal with the situation. I then returned to Yosemite.

I first went to the Indian Caves to retrieve my gear. Once there, I was amazed at how alike all those caves looked. After searching for awhile with no success, I started marking each cave with a cairn, or pile of rocks, so as not to waste my time re-checking caves I had already looked in. It took me awhile to eventually find my stuff. With all those cairns, it looked like aliens had visited the place.

Once I had my gear, I went to the good cop and asked him to honor his promise if I confessed. I eventually convinced him to contact the district attorney and I ended up cutting a deal. I made a tax-deductible $1,000 donation to the Mountain Safety Fund, paid a $10 court fee and was promised

I'd get my gear back once I paid the money. I was also to serve one year probation and there would be no criminal record if I did so without incident. Judge Pitts was furious.

I offered to take him skydiving with me in Lodi, but the judge declined.

The former public defender later asked me if it was all worth it. What could I say? – Yes!

I learned a lot about the court system and quite a bit about myself. And it was a big deal for me BASE jumping two of the most recognizable natural monuments in the entire world – Half Dome and El Capitan.

As an example of how circumstances can keep things coming back, about this same time a female park ranger was murdered in Yosemite. Coincidentally, I bought a Ford Ranger truck shortly after the incident and received a call from the dealer asking how I liked the pickup.

My wife and I were on a business trip and my son Todd took the call.

The dealer said, "I would like to talk to Randy Peeters about the Ranger he bought."

Todd, still nervous about it all, thought he said, "I would like to talk to Randy Peeters about the ranger he shot."

Of course, Todd immediately stood up for me and acknowledged I was pissed about the matter, but most certainly wouldn't shoot a ranger over it.

My experience was also reinforced by none other than the *In Search of Excellence* author, Tom Peters. While attending one of his seminars he put up a slide that read, "I would not hire anyone who hasn't been to jail at least once."

I couldn't help but say out loud, "Check that box off!"

Fortunately, over the course of time, this all blew over at work.

What to do after BASE Jumping

I made 34 more skydives after my experience at Half Dome. When I turned 46, I was aware my reflexes were waning. BASE jumping is indeed dangerous – to date, more than 200 people have died doing the sport. That combined with the professional embarrassment of my arrest told me my BASE jumping days were behind me. I knew if I continued to skydive, I'd be tempted to BASE jump as well, so I sold my parachute in the fall of 1992. But, I would need one more reminder to give skydiving up completely.

The final straw came three and a half years later. A couple of friends and I were climbing El Capitan when the silence surrounding the Salathé Wall was interrupted by what sounded like a jet engine. Shortly after that, we heard the whoosh of a parachute and watched as a BASE jumper safely landed and ran from the meadows thousands of feet below us.

I mentioned to my fellow climbers from Austria, Christian Gabl and Rudy, that I had done that before. They immediately asked me to take them skydiving and, after the climb, I agreed.

I borrowed a rig from a friend and headed for Lodi. It had been well over three years since I'd made a jump and I really wasn't prepared for it in spite of my years of experience. Once over the target area, I attempted to chase one of the tandem pairs out of the aircraft but it didn't go well.

My form was off, so I attempted to do back loops in order to catch up to the pair below me. In the middle of one of my loops, my pilot chute dislodged and deployed. It tumbled me over onto my chest causing a hard opening when the main chute snapped open. In spite of landing safely, I did not feel very good after the experience.

Doris was away for the weekend, so when Christian and Rudy departed the following day, I decided to solo kayak the South Fork of the American River. Just a short drive from home, the water flows of the South Fork are controlled by a dam and not that treacherous, but every effort I made on the river that day seemed to hurt.

The following day, Doris was still out of town, so I returned with my kayak to make another run. When I reached the crux rapid called Trouble-maker, I hurt enough to portage it. I knew then, I had better see a doctor.

My visit to the clinic showed I had broken my sternum during my last skydive. The other bad news was the only cure for it was rest – three months worth. This injury cured my desire to skydive. I did entertain the thought of doing it again, but my risk-reward reasoning never justified it, so I officially closed that chapter of my life in May of 1996.

I revisited the Wellman incident while climbing Lurking Fear (5.10, A2, grade IV) on Yosemite's El Capitan. On this three and a half day trek, I was climbing with a gifted young climber named David Morrison. He had dropped out of the university to pursue his passion and was literally living in a cave a few hundred yards behind Camp IV.

When we reached Thanksgiving Ledge, David traversed over to the start of the next pitch while I hauled our gear up to the ledge. Shortly after his departure, David came scrambling back over to our position with his report.

"You're not going to believe this," he said. "Mike Corbett and his climbing partner are over there."

Corbett was the one climbing with Wellman when he reported me to the park rangers for BASE jumping from Half Dome.

I immediately jumped to my feet and rapidly traversed across the ledge.

"You're not going to do anything bad, are you?" David asked, as I moved away.

Corbett was already at the top of the pitch when I reached his partner, who was still on the ledge. I inquired of him if he was climbing with Corbett and he confirmed he was. I asked him if he would tell Corbett to "F--- himself" on behalf of Randy Peeters.

I was feeling pretty smug.

As I led the way up the pitch, I saw someone rapidly repelling toward me. I figured it was Corbett coming down to punch out my lights. He was younger than I and an excellent climber in terrific condition. It goes without saying, I was concerned when he stopped a foot from me as we both hung there about 2,000 feet above the valley floor.

He immediately looked into my eyes and began apologizing to me and included that he had tried to stop Wellman from making that call.

I ran into Mike Corbett several times after that and found him to be a great guy. Several years later, I met up with Wellman at a county fair, where he was doing a promotional presentation. I used the occasion to let Wellman know what I thought of him and his turning me in.

Those encounters really brought closure to that entire episode.

Todd jumping into the American River

Randy and Todd skydiving
Lodi, CA

Randy skydiving

Landing
Lodi, CA

Randy's hot air balloon jump in preparation for BASE jumps

BASE jump off the Foresthill Bridge - Kiwi Steve - 1987

BASE jump off Half Dome - Texas Tom watches as Tom
Scholz jumps - 1989

9

SEVENTY GOING ON NINETEEN

It was getting late as we drove our RV along a lonely stretch of Interstate 5 somewhere north of Bakersfield. We decided to pull off at a quiet, out-of-the-way location and casual camp for the night. At about midnight, something outside caught my attention. I peered out the window to see three men walking around our RV and tow vehicle trying to look inside. I was terrified.

I noticed their car was parked right in front of the RV, so driving off was not an option. Quietly, I retrieved my 12 gauge defender shotgun and carefully loaded the magazine with five rounds of double-ought buckshot. Just as I was getting ready to chamber a round with a familiar ka-chung and let out a yell, they got into their vehicle and drove away – what a relief.

Farewell to Parents

In the early 1990s, time began to take its toll and Doris and I started losing our parents. Doris' mother passed away in 1992 and my dad followed in 2000. I missed my dad terribly and constantly thought about him for more than ten years afterward.

Doris then lost her father in 2007 and my mother died in 2008. It isn't something you can mentally prepare for and one can never be ready for it. Fortunately, in 1996, I took the time to write my parents and tell them how much I appreciated their efforts in providing for me and instilling their values in me. It's something I still hold dear to this day.

The letter went like this:

> I love and appreciate you both. I know you know how I feel, but it
> is important to say it once in awhile. I have so many great memories
> about growing up – I often reflect back over my childhood and feel
> very good about it. And if you think about it for a minute, you two
> are at the central core of those years.

Learning from this experience, I also took the time to write a letter to Doris and the boys telling them how much I loved and respected them.

My letter to Doris said,

> We are over half way through our lives, we have been married thirty
> plus years, our kids are launched, we are grandparents and we are
> getting old. I really do love you very much. I still consider you my best
> friend and my lover. These things will never change. Another thing
> that gets in the way of expressing how I really feel is all the sports
> activities. As stupid as all these activities seem, they are important to
> my mental health. I am often happiest when we are not so busy, but at
> the same time I am torn by the desire to accomplish activity oriented
> goals. I would be lost without you. I want you in my life because I love
> you, not because I need you. It's not a dependence thing, but rather
> a choice based on love.

I feel Doris should be eligible for sainthood after I am gone because she put up with me for all these years. She is an amazing woman – an incredible mother, wife and lover – a true friend for life.

Will the World End?

Well, Y2K came and went without incident. In anticipation of the projected chaos, we stored up several months' worth of food, water, etc. and did not need it. Still, we continue to replenish our supplies from time-to-time never knowing when it might be needed. Big earthquakes, terrorist attacks and civil unrest are certainly possibilities and having extra supplies on hand is prudent planning. Who knows what the future holds?

Along these lines, in 2002, I rekindled my interest in amateur radio. I studied and obtained my Amateur Extra Class license. I felt having a ham radio available might be helpful in the event of some unforeseen disaster.

Pending my retirement at the end of March 2000, we purchased a lot in Foresthill, CA and started construction of our future home. Our house in Folsom sold sooner than we expected, so with completion of our new home more than three months away, we had to move all our belongings into storage and live in the RV.

We spent the first month in a mobile home park until my final day of work at Aerojet. We then set out in the RV on a planned vacation to Zion, Bryce Canyon, Las Vegas, Yosemite and up the coast to Seattle. From there, we took a cruise to Alaska and then met up with my sister, Joan and her husband, Ron.

We traveled around Alaska for a couple of weeks together. I was even able to get Doris to agree to camp overnight on the Kahiltna Glacier. We flew in on an air taxi, did two glacier landings and spent the night at the site that is used as Base Camp for those climbing Denali.

During our travels, we visited several remote Eskimo villages before beginning our trip back to Seattle. From there, we boarded our RV and headed back to California.

That year, after our home was finished, we spent a week SCUBA diving in Grand Cayman, took a trip on a houseboat with the kids, camped for a week at Anchor Bay with our church group, spent a long weekend at Capitola with the kids and did several weeks of camping and surfing at the beach.

The Retirement Home

Our new home in Foresthill turned out to be very nice and we really enjoy the location. There's a great view and the quiet is almost deafening. We can literally hear the train engines that pass through the foothills nearly five miles away. The elevation is such that we do get snow occasionally and the summers are very pleasant with clear blue skies.

Wildlife is another joy of the area. We enjoy feeding the deer, squirrels and birds. One day nine deer came to feed, including a five point buck. We also had a rafter of 13 wild turkeys with as many as three on the deck at any one time.

There are many colorful birds and a number of hummingbirds that visit as well. And speaking of visitors, we've even had black bears on our deck. The amazing thing is that the deck is more than 15 feet off the ground and there are no stairs! The bears literally climbed up a four by six beam to reach the bird feeders on the deck.

We added an enclosure where we store our RV and also a nice garden-potting shed. The back yard contains a 1933, 702 Aermotor Windmill and I built a super Tarzan swing. The swing is on a 30 foot chain hanging from a big oak in the yard, complete with a seat and launching platform. There's also a small tree house for the grandkids and a 185 foot zip line. The zip line is really scary and intimidates everyone who rides it because it feels like it's going at the speed of light.

We thoroughly enjoy living in the woods, but it does require us to do continuous landscape work. It truly never ends.

Damn, We're Getting Old

Doris threw a surprise party for my 50th birthday and really caught me off guard. However, I did the same for her 40th, 55th and 59th birthdays. Doris isn't easy to surprise, but with those three parties I managed to do exactly that. Planning one for her 59th birthday instead of the more obvious 60th was key for that one.

For our 40th wedding anniversary, we renewed our vows and threw a dinner party for our family and close friends. To make sure Doris would repeat her vows, I was tempted to try drugging her. The whole affair turned out great with the attendance of extended family and friends we'd known most our lives. It also offered some closure for our wedding, which was basically a fiasco.

We met during our senior year in high school and were married in 1965 after dating for three years. We have remained best friends and lovers since. Our sons, Todd and Shawn, have blessed us with five grandchildren and Jesus has richly blessed us as well.

When email came of age in the early 1990s, I started to communicate on a regular basis with Reid Parmerter, my PhD advisor. In one email he wrote:

> In some ways, we have a lot in common … neither of us ever really grew up … I'll probably still be kind of a naïve kid the day I die.

In my response I wrote:

> You are right, I never did grow up – luckily, Doris did and is willing to put up with me. As I have said many times, I sure am lucky to have her – I really love her and enjoy our time together – we are truly friends and lovers.

To have found my soul mate was a tremendous blessing; however, it does take work to keep a marriage in sync. Fortunately both Doris and I are willing to work at it. We have been together over 50 years now and, although there have been ups and downs, we have stuck it out and made a big difference in each other's lives.

Around Home

By the time our kids were old enough to benefit from the experience, we regularly attended church. I believe that salvation is a personal thing and comes with accepting on faith that Jesus Christ did indeed die for our sins. I don't think that church attendance really has much to do with salvation, but I do think hanging out with other believers is, in general, a good thing.

In Tehachapi, we started attending the Lutheran Church. After our moves to New Mexico, upstate New York and Northern California, we branched out and began going to nondenominational churches. Warehouse Ministries became our home church in Roseville for ten years and we later switched to Oak Hills Baptist Church in Folsom, where we spent more than five years. After our move to Foresthill, we settled on Canyon View Assembly of God Church, where I ultimately became an elder. Lately, we have been attending churches in Auburn nearby our home.

I love the Fourth of July. It is definitely one of my favorite holidays. To celebrate, I always keep a healthy supply of fireworks on hand and look for every opportunity to fire off a few. But such a practice hasn't been without incident.

To illustrate Doris' trust in me, she was watching one night as the boys and I put on our Independence Day fireworks celebration. We had purchased what we hoped would be a magnificent aerial display. Unfortunately, as soon as we lit the fuse the pyrotechnic device tipped over. The boys and I fled the scene as quickly as we could.

Doris, on the other hand, stood there emitting oohs and aahs while the exploding fireballs whizzed past her. She trusts me way too much!

Our friend Chuck John had a similar experience while we were watching a fireworks display at Cal Expo in Sacramento. One errant, unexploded report shot into the grandstand where we were sitting and literally passed between Chuck's legs.

I'm also big on Halloween and have accompanied our kids and grandkids when they went trick-or-treating for as long as I can remember. I still dress up and go "begging" for candy, even at my age – why not?

Christmas is also a terrific time for us. We loved watching our children and grandchildren open presents. We spent many Christmas Eve's at Shawn's house and later Todd's home just soaking up our grandkids' excitement. We enjoyed all of the holiday activities, culminating in the very special day of Christmas.

We often took family vacations together. For 20 great years, we rented a unit on the beach at Capitola, CA, only steps from the sand and ocean. We truly enjoy the water and also made ten trips in all to Shasta Lake, Trinity Lake and the Sacramento Delta to spend vacation time together on a houseboat.

Those times bring back some great memories, but ... there have also been some bad ones.

When Shawn's marriage began to deteriorate, we had very little contact with his family. For years after his divorce in 2004, we only occasionally saw his three children.

It was a very difficult time for Shawn and he made some bad decisions. His appearance went downhill and he became a "pharmaceutical horticulturist" in Northern California.

Then Todd's family began to exclude us at the holidays and that delivered yet another blow. I'm a sentimental person and very sensitive about family get-togethers, especially during the holidays.

After months of planning for a family trip to Yosemite, Todd decided to bail just days before we were to go. That started a chain reaction and eventually no one went. Things seemed to get worse with each passing day and family vacations became a thing of the past.

It seemed the harder I tried to keep traditions alive, the more stressful the situation became. I can be controlling and this was certainly a part of the problem.

Doris and I continued spending our holidays and vacations together, but apart from other family. We felt awful, but held fast to Proverbs 22:6 "Train up a child in the way he should go. And when he is old, he will not depart from it."

In 2008, at Shawn's request, we began counseling with him. It was a profound lesson for all of us and taught me that I'm not responsible for the decisions made by my adult children – good or bad.

In faith, we moved forward with our lives and continued to praise Jesus and pray for the situation to improve. Then, with a lot of prayer and patience, things turned around.

In 2011, we were able to re-establish good relationships with both sons and our grandchildren. Shawn became gainfully employed and became the dad he needed to be. He started on a path to figure out the rest of his life.

Todd went on to earn his MBA and sent me an email that I really liked.

> *Dad, I couldn't remember if I sent you a thank you email and I wanted to make sure I did. I really appreciate and value your willingness to help me further my education. I can't express in words how much this means to me. And in case I haven't told you lately: Thanks for putting me through college. Thanks for being so involved in Boy Scouts growing up. Thanks for always being there. P.S. I've got two A's going this semester. Only two classes left. Looks like I'll get a 4.0 GPA. I graduate in April. This went by fast. I love you and I hope you have a great day, Todd.*

Growing Old is Not for Sissies

In the summer 2000, Doris broke her left ankle and I had arthroscopic surgery on my right knee. The knee was "bone-on-bone" and would require a total replacement. My alternative was to "count my steps," and hope the knee would get better, since I could manage the pain without drugs.

I felt time was on my side, so started using a knee brace and planned to hold surgery at bay for as long as I could. I knew a replacement would limit my activities and I continued to defer recommendations to reconsider. Perhaps it was my sports medicine doctor that spurred me to keep refusing surgery when he said, "Don't even think about getting a replacement until you're willing to quit all this silly shit."

After being fooled by starvation routines during climbing expeditions, my body decided it was time to add a spare tire. It took me years to get back to my preferred weight. I have to constantly monitor my diet and stay hungry most of the time in order to keep my six foot one inch frame at 160 pounds. That was my target weight at 40 when we moved to upstate New York. By maintaining this weight, I feel better and I am able to do the sports I enjoy.

I also underwent Mohs surgery for skin cancer on my nose and Doris had major bladder surgery. Next, in 2007, Doris fell and broke her right ankle in Old Jerusalem while we were on vacation. After surfing in 2008, it was discovered I had a broken bone in my left foot and had an inguinal hernia (which required surgery). That year, Doris also fell and broke her elbow while picking up branches trimmed from our oak trees and in 2013 had major surgery to repair damage from her childbearing years.

For me, the worst was in 2011 when I fell and broke my right hip in the parking lot at Sugar Bowl after some extreme skiing. It never seems to end. In 2014 I broke my left thumb skiing and then, a few weeks later, preceded to crack several ribs kayaking.

How Many Times Will I Retire?

After retiring from Aerojet, I knew I would have to find consulting work in order to afford big-ticket type vacations. My retirement package would be enough to keep us comfortable, but wouldn't finance what I wanted to continue doing.

Two months after leaving Aerojet, I landed a full time consulting job with Ocean Power. Ocean Power was a start-up company developing Stirling engine technology to generate power for desalinating seawater in remote locations. Four months later, I was hired as the Chief Scientist at double my Aerojet salary and worked partly from home with two months leave of absence to pursue my activities.

Two years later, the company folded.

While with Ocean Power, I assembled a "dream team" made up of Aerojet scientists willing to work part time to do the design and manufacturing. We were working along with companies based in Norway and Sweden. I traveled to Europe on a regular basis and thoroughly enjoyed the experience while working with some incredible folks. It was a real challenge and a heck of a lot of fun.

I was able to hire my son Todd as a program manager and that allowed me time off to do some big climbing expeditions.

The long, overseas red eye flights I took for Ocean Power did present some problems: like the time I was given the middle seat in the last row that pressed against the toilet bulkhead. Not only would those seats not recline, but as soon as we were airborne all the seats in front of us reclined into our laps.

The flight was so uncomfortable that I began mentally reconstructing nights I had spent on rock walls. I could only recall twice out of more than 30 nights that were more uncomfortable than that flight.

Both of those were unplanned bivys on the Nose of El Cap. One was a night spent in slings in the Stove Legs crack system. The other was spent on a small, sloping ledge below camp IV. That meant, for every 15 nights I spent sleeping on rock walls, only one was more miserable than spending the night sitting upright on an airplane bound for Europe with some stranger asleep and nearly in my lap.

The demise of Ocean Power was unfortunate, but both Todd and I were able to move on successfully. Todd hired on at Aerojet as a manufacturing engineer. My take away was being the co-inventor on a patent resulting from that incredible project. We had combined rocket motor and Stirling engine technologies, thus enabling substantial gains in system performance.

Based on our patent, I was later able to convince Ocean Power's investors to reinvest in the project. That launched a new start-up company called Power Play Energy, LLC. We partnered with Stirling Technology Company in Pasco, WA and had a revolutionary breakthrough in technology within our grasp. We had the potential to develop a low-cost, maintenance-free, high-efficiency and low-pollution micro cogeneration device for use in distributed power generation applications. We developed and tested a prototype system and sold it to our partner.

I worked with some great folks who understood my motivation and I gave them my very best effort. I tripled my Aerojet salary and thrived in this truly professional environment. It was the most exciting and challenging project of my entire career.

Computers

Throughout my technical career, I had a unique opportunity to experience virtually the entire computational-computer evolution. In college, I used a slide rule and hand-crank calculators. At Boeing I worked with Wang desktops and a CDC 6400 computer. Programmable HP calculators began to phase in while I was at the Rocket Propulsion Lab. While at Los Alamos, the Cray IIs had just come online. At home, we went from primitive desktop computers to laptops, tablets and smart phones.

Our first home computer was a Commodore 64 and I eventually progressed to the laptop on which I developed amazing computational skills. I literally watched the evolution of networking and the Internet while at Xerox and now cannot imagine how we ever managed without such tools.

Some Unexpected Turns

In 2003, I served as jury foreman on a rape case. It was a very interesting five days and a completely new experience.

Later in the fall of 2003, I gave a pro-bono presentation to a group of key executives. The group was chaired by Dick Shorten, who was the father of one of the dealmakers for Power Play Energy. It had been suggested by his son, Rich, that this type of group would be a good source of clients for a Kilimanjaro expedition I was planning.

I had developed a seminar demonstrating how a personal vision could enhance one's life. I gave the presentation at the Mohonk Resort located in the Shawangunk Mountains of New York.

Shorten's group was part of an organization known as Vistage International. I was asked by Dick if I could put together a half day program to present to other Vistage groups. I was still buried doing start-ups and really didn't want to take the time to do that, but I had already been doing work on developing personal visions.

Following the start-ups, I was asked to be an expert witness in a lawsuit against a large aerospace company. The pay was incredibly good, but the work extremely difficult. It was the job of the opposing lawyers to make me, the expert witness, look like an idiot and they proved to be very good at doing so. During one deposition, the opposition's legal team really began to dig into me. That led me to ask them how many lawyer jokes they thought there were. They responded, "A lot." I then told them there really were only three such jokes … the rest were all true stories! Things really got nasty after that. After one session that lasted about eight hours, I was asked if I wanted to continue since we were close to finishing.

"At $500 per hour," I answered, "go on as long as you like."

Having learned not to take things personally, I probably would do the expert witness thing again given the opportunity.

Personal Vision Process

Early on, I determined what my priorities were and what direction I wanted my life to follow. I had already started the personal vision process at a young age and over time expanded my goals to include family, work, travel and athletics. However, it wasn't until the 1990s that I started to formalize the process.

I had been called upon to do a vision piece as a part of the Frontline Leadership program at Aerojet. Although my objective was to help employees understand the company's vision, I realized that many I spoke to did not have a personal vision of their own. With that, I turned my attention to helping people establish one. I also used the opportunity to fine tune my own.

I recognized that all the reasons for a company's vision would also apply to a personal vision. Since all the same principles applied, the transition was relatively seamless.

But it wasn't until the new millennium that I discovered a personal vision statement was the overarching criterion which is supported by prioritized goals. It not only had to be written down, but also shared with family, friends and all the important people in one's life.

In 2001 I had a very pleasant surprise when I received the Distinguished Alumni Award for the Department of Aeronautics and Astronautics at the University of Washington. And then in 2004, I was honored when asked to be the commencement speaker for the engineering department at California State Polytechnic University. My ten minute speech on "What is Your Vision?" not only proved to be an incredible experience, but also led to the finalization of the personal vision process – statement, goals/categories and associated tasks. After my address, the graduates and faculty welcomed me warmly and responded that they were inspired to incorporate my key points into the preparation of their own personal visions. In a subsequent presentation in 2012 to the Aerospace Engineering Department at Cal Poly, the department chairman said he planned to include setting a personal vision as part of the curriculum in one of their undergraduate courses.

The following from Lewis Carroll's *Alice in Wonderland* has become a cornerstone for my vision presentations.

Would you tell me, please, which way I ought to go from here? asked Alice.

That depends a good deal on where you want to get to, said the Cat.
I don't much care where ... said Alice.
Then it doesn't matter which way you go, said the Cat.
... so long as I get somewhere, Alice explained.
Oh, you're sure to do that, said the Cat, if you only walk long enough.

I believe that 98 percent of the population of the United States and perhaps the entire world go through life much like Alice and to me, that's scary. Many people want to "go with the flow," but that would be very frustrating for me. I don't want to go just anywhere; I have a desired outcome for my life. I often think about the things I want to accomplish, see and do; what I would want as a legacy.

Ironically, Doris is a little like Alice. She prefers not to use the personal vision process. In all fairness, from the beginning of our life together she has been an integral part of my vision.

One's vision could change, but I don't expect mine to change anytime soon. Things that do change over the years are prioritized goals or categories that support the vision.

Today my personal vision looks like this (my grade is in parentheses):

When it's Over – No Regrets ... *Love life and live it to the fullest and build great memories*

1) Solid Spiritual Life ... *walk the talk* – I have made some changes here – more community service (B)

2) Best Possible Husband, Father and Grandfather ... *loves his wife and family* – More travel with Doris (B)

3) Healthy Lifestyle ... *live to be greater than 90 years old in good mental and physical health* – Eat consciously, physical training (B)

4) Achieve Sports Goals – Climb another 8000 meter peak, Kayak Grand Canyon, Tow-in surfing, etc. (A-)

5) Successful Retirement Career – Resource and Inspirational Speaker, Expedition Leader (B)

6) Projects for Doris (A)

Under each goal (category) are prioritized tasks that specifically support the goal. The letter grade I give myself is subjective and based on my gut-level evaluation. I re-evaluate my vision annually to identify areas needing improvement. These grades are only relative indictors, a way to reach deep down inside to evaluate how I am doing.

I do this with Doris and she helps me grade myself and reset my priorities. We then set plans together for the coming year. This planning includes activities and projects important to Doris as well.

Where company visions differ from personal visions is in the flexibility. Most often, company visions are fixed with specific and measurable goals. Life is full of curve balls, so personal visions may need to be modified as circumstances change in our lives.

As to my own personalized goals – some I need to improve on and some I flat out blew. But, overall I haven't done all that bad.

Prior to formalizing the vision process, in 1988, I revised my goals and planned more tasks to help me accomplish my objectives.

Also that year, I added Athletic Goals to the list. The sports were rather incredible, with world-class goals in mountaineering, rock climbing, surfing, rafting, kayaking, skydiving, sail boarding, skiing, biking, hang gliding, running, hiking, etc.

On the travel list, I included the entire USA with emphasis on national parks. I also had the world on that list, especially emerging countries and areas still considered wild.

I backed up those goals with specific tasks and modifications as necessary. After 25 years, more than 90 percent of those goals have been reached.

Living the Vision

Four years after Dick Shorten's request, I began my vision quest, so to speak. There were more than 3,000 Vistage and TEC groups across the USA and in Canada. Not only would I have the opportunity to enrich the lives of others, but I would be able to spend valuable time with Doris traveling in our RV.

I took my half day "Setting a Personal Vision" program on the road and did 29 presentations the first year. It started on the East Coast and quickly increased to 40 sessions a year. As of the writing of this book, I've given the presentation to more than 4,000 CEOs and key executives throughout the United States and Canada. In seven years, Doris and I literally crisscrossed North America a dozen times in our RV. I have also presented to large groups of politicians, conventions, universities and elementary, middle and high schools.

The RV is used extensively for business purposes during the warmer months. In the winter, when I fly, I can take Doris along using my frequent-flyer miles.

RV Broker?

In 2003, we sold our 1995, 34 foot Bounder RV and bought a 2005, 21 foot Chinook Concourse on a 6L Ford diesel chassis. That first year alone, we spent 89 nights in it. Over a 39 month period, we totaled 403 nights in that rig and racked up 63,500 miles.

However, it had drive-train problems and proved to be too small for the amount of time we were spending in it. We sold it and bought a 27½ foot DynaQuest ST with a single slide out built on a Freightliner M2 Light Chassis with a Mercedes power plant.

Four years and 87,000 miles later, after spending 553 nights in the rig, we traded that unit in on an updated 30 foot dual slide version of the DynaQuest with a Cummins power plant. It has proven to be a fantastic RV. Doris calls it a "boy toy," but admits it offers the comforts of home and has plenty of space for our small zoo. In the past eight years, we've averaged 135 nights a year in our RVs. About one third of our time is spent traveling in our RV.

Travel Highlights

Highlights from these extensive travels in conjunction with the seminar business have been numerous.

A couple of memories include a really neat snowy December arrival in Chicago in 2008 where Doris and I decided to celebrate a "Christmassy" 43rd anniversary. Two years later, in similar conditions, we celebrated our 45th anniversary in Toronto, Canada.

On one trip in 2010, I attended President Barack Obama's "Get the Vote Out in 2010" rally thus satisfying my lifelong goal of seeing a sitting president in person. I was actually about 30 feet from him as he made his way from the podium after his speech.

Becoming a Gypsy

After retiring from Aerojet, travel became the central part of our lives. On business road trips and RV vacations I would present seminars, surf, ski, climb and snowboard. We even managed to take the grandkids on several RV trips.[42]

In 2002 we took the RV on a 45 day excursion from the Mexican Border up the coast of California to Anchor Bay, camping and surfing along the way.

I spent a total of 90 days surfing that year catching outstanding waves during storms. I also damaged two surfboards.

In another trip four years later we traveled for two months through the Southwest USA and mainland Mexico (including Copper Canyon) crossing by ferry to Baja. We managed to do some incredible beach camping as I surfed along the entire Baja peninsula. Finishing this dream surf trip was a major event in my life.

Other RV trips took us to virtually every out of the way place in the United States. Amish country is one of Doris' favorite areas. We have enjoyed many Amish areas by attending auctions, shopping at rural stores, staying on farms and at local gatherings as well as casual camping in literally dozens of these communities throughout the Midwest and Northeastern USA.

Our travels have taken us to every corner of the contiguous United States, including the Northern, Southern, Eastern and Western most points. We covered all but three (i.e., Northwest Territories, Nunavut and Newfoundland/Labrador) of the Canadian provinces.

In the winter of 2006 we traveled in the RV to Yosemite to attend the annual Bracebridge Dinner at the Ahwahnee Hotel. It was an awesome affair that recreated a Victorian Christmas dinner and had a hefty price tag of $690 for the two of us. Besides an elegant eight course dinner, it also included a history talk about this world class hotel.

Another of those dream trips took place in 2009 when we traveled through Western Canada up to Alaska and back doing seminars along the way. During that three and a half month journey, we also visited friends and saw amazing scenery and wildlife. We went hiking, soaked in hot springs and visited lots of museums and historic sites.

I fished for halibut and salmon and kayaked the glacier silt-filled Nenana River. We experienced indigenous cultures above the Arctic Circle, dug for fossils and I climbed the Becky route on Liberty Bell on the return trip through Washington.

Our itinerary was largely unplanned and we had Sarah and Kathmandu as traveling companions. We were able to pull off the road wherever we wanted and spend the night isolated in this vast wilderness of incredible scenery and diverse wildlife.

Over the years, the New Year's Day Rose Parade in Pasadena, CA has had a special hold on me. As kids, my grandparents would frequently take us to the parade and later in my teen years I attended on my own. We took our kids when they were very young and have attended with my brother's and sister's families several times. The RV adds a new dimension to this experience and I have taken full advantage of this by making mini-vacations to this spectacle. In 2010, by casual camping in Pasadena during the parade week (and yes it is allowed!), I've combined the parade with viewing the float building process, attending the Christmas Pageant at the Crystal Cathedral, roller skating at one of the original rinks from my childhood years and attending the Band Fest event. We are also able to get front row seats for the parade by knowing the system. I repeated this again in 2014 and surely this will continue in the future – at least a few more times.

Representative of literally hundreds of RV trips to the beach was one completed in the summer of 2013. Traveling through Tehachapi, visiting friends and checking out our old haunts, we arrived at Oceanside two days later. Casual camping on a back street, visiting with my sister, Joan and sneaking in a pre-dawn surfing session rounded out our visit in Oceanside. We then relocated to the state beach parks of San Elijo and San Mateo for two full weeks of camping and surfing. After 18 days, I delivered two half day seminars in Reno, NV before returning home.

Around the World

There were also numerous international trips. Arguably the best of all occurred in 2001 when I took on some big climbs. After climbing, Doris joined me in Kathmandu where we started a two month trip through Southeast Asia. It was spooky since it was right after the 9/11 terrorist attack on the World Trade Center, but we had planned and prepared for that vacation for a year so we pressed on. It turned out to be a fantastic journey through Nepal, India, Thailand, Malaysia, Indonesia, Singapore and Japan. We essentially traveled around the world from west to east on this trip.

The highlights included an elephant safari in Nepal, a boat trip at dawn on the Ganges River in Varanasi, India and the Grand Palace in Bangkok, Thailand. We also took in the Cameron Highlands of Malaysia and Kyoto, Japan.

While boating at dawn on the Ganges, we passed nearly 100 Ghats (a series of steps that lead down to a holy river) where people bathed and drank the water. This was right next to where cremations were performed. Doris asked about the sanitation of the water considering it contained the ashes from cremations and the bodies of dead cows.

The boat captain answered her with a matter-of-fact tone, "The water is perfectly safe to drink, since it is holy."

We decided not to try it.

Bali, Indonesia was so incredible that we spent nine days there and it was quite inexpensive. Bali had wonderful beaches, fantastic cultural experiences including dancing and shadow puppetry, as well as terrific surfing and SCUBA diving.

Down Under

In my quest to complete the Seven Summits, we headed for Australia in 2004 to hike up to the top of Kosciuszko, the highest point on the land down under. Since it was a hike, Doris made the climb with me.

Using the Seven Summits as our excuse, Doris and I extended the trip for a 29 day excursion including New Zealand, Australia and French Polynesia. In New Zealand, we rented a campervan for an 11 day tour of both the North and South Islands. I even managed to surf Reglan and Manu Bay in the Tasman Sea. In Australia, we visited Sydney, Manley Beach for more surfing, plus Alice Springs, Ayres Rock and Cairns. We also dove the Great Barrier Reef. On the way home, we took in Tahiti and Manahi, French Polynesia.

Here and There

While traveling in Tunisia, Doris and I had the pleasure of meeting a man named Tom. He and his wife divorced after 48 years of marriage and it wiped him out financially. He then rented his ex-wife some space in his post-divorce house. Tom was quite a character.

While visiting a temple in a Roman ruin, Tom asked the oracle if his wife would eventually take the rest of his assets. A voice from behind a rock wall gave him a resounding, "Yes!"

Tom and I visited a Turkish bath (Hammam) in a small, rural town in Tunisia. At these baths, one's entire body is vigorously scrubbed removing a lot of dead skin. As we prepared to leave later that evening, Tom was lagging behind. I asked him to hurry as I was leery of walking back in the dark to our remote camp at the oasis.

"Randy," he answered, "give me a minute ... so I can at least find my nipples before we leave."

Other international travels included virtually all the corners of the world and as often as possible, we preferred remote and less traveled areas.[43]

In 2008 we spent a couple weeks in Hawaii. The first week was on the Big Island with my sister Joan and her husband, Ron. Here I completed my quest of the highest points in the 50 United States by climbing Mauna Kea. On Oahu, I surfed in the double overhead waves along the North Shore fulfilling another lifelong goal.

Oh My!

In 2009 we took all five grandchildren camping in Coloma, CA. We stayed in the RV right on the bank of the South Fork of the American River. While there, I kayaked the Chili Bar run twice. The grandkids were well behaved and we knew we might not see them all together again for a long time as Todd and his family were relocating to Georgia.

One unfortunate part of the trip was our grandchild Chloe being bitten in the face by a pit bull mix. It was unprovoked and we asked Jesus to heal the face of that beautiful little girl and He did – not even a scar.

After a two year hiatus, I arranged for our granddaughters from Georgia to fly out for a week-long RV camping trip to Pismo Beach with our other three grandchildren from California. The kids were growing up fast and these visits with all the grandkids together were becoming less and less frequent. We planned to make the best of it.

Within the first ten minutes of arrival at the beach, Cameron's dog bit Olivia. Then, after running around in the sand dunes for an hour or so, the kids managed to stir up a hornet's nest near our campsite resulting in more than 30 painful stings spread among all of us, with the exception of Tyler. He managed to escape the ongoing melee. Emmy took the brunt of the stings. She was very brave. What a scene that was! The kids ripping off their clothes and screaming while Doris and I tried to calm them down and remove hornets from their hair and clothing. Somehow, everyone survived the hornets.

I ended up spending the first night sleeping on the picnic table. Tyler and Cameron spent the night in the tent with their dogs and Doris and the girls took over the RV. As if the picnic table wasn't punishment enough, I was awakened at two in the morning by raccoons getting into the dog food.

The trip was great after the initial rough start and we passed time with games of bocce ball and playing on the beach. Livy showed us some great form on the boogie board and Cameron really took to surfing. He caught some small waves and even stood up on his board. We then went dune riding on the Xtreme Hummer Tour and took in the nature programs at the campground. I even let Tyler and Cameron drive the Rav4 on the beach and that's where Tyler excelled.

Pismo Beach was a great place to spend time together. Tyler has now graduated from high school, is working and attending college, so trips with all five grandchildren together are becoming more difficult to plan.

I worked hard to build great memories with our grandchildren during these trips. Most recently, in 2014, we took a family camping vacation together at New Brighton State Beach near Capitola, CA. Having both boys and their families together with us for a week was very enjoyable. We have already started planning the next family vacation - a short cruise along the California/Mexico coast.

Are you Kidding - Burning Man!

My son Shawn and I took a four day trip to the Burning Man Black Rock City encampment near Gerlach, NV. In true burning man fashion, we took Shawn's $150 used camper on his beat up pickup truck along with a couple of cheap used bicycles.

After arrival at the remote site, while hunkered down during a sand storm, we had a very interesting conversation with our neighbors. One lady was explaining her experience at the "Orgasmatron," while her partner said he had a rather unique experience at the "Homo Depot." He said he "drew the line when his martini was stirred by the bartender using his penis." I then responded with, "I don't quite know what I am doing here – I draw the line at Reno."

Massive propane fires, explosions, pyrotechnics, nudity, drugs and alcohol – what a mix! Since I don't drink or do drugs anymore, from my perspective, it was like an acid trip without the LSD – totally surrealistic. It turned out to be a great father-son event. Honestly.

Losing Family and Friends

Time began to take its toll as we lost our dear Christian friends Blanche and Jim Caldwell. We had met them when we first moved to New Mexico more than 35 years before. They both spent their final months in a skilled nursing facility and died within months of each other. Blanche was the first to take the stairway to heaven and Jim followed shortly thereafter.

We last visited them in September 2012. At that time, Jim was nearly 93 and living with his daughter. Jim was the man who kept me grounded in my faith, simply by the way he lived and he was always there with a prayer when I needed it.

In June 2013, my older sister, Joan, was diagnosed with pancreatic cancer that had metastasized to her liver and spleen. Her prognosis was very grim with a three to twelve month life expectancy. We were praying along with a lot of our friends that she would be miraculously healed.

Sometimes good things happen as a result of a bad situation. When Joan's cancer started to take hold, both of our sons came out to see her while she was still relatively healthy. Todd flew in from Salt Lake City, UT and Shawn drove down from San Francisco, CA and they met up in Southern California where my sister lives. We were camping at the beach in our RV and both boys spent a long weekend with us after visiting with Joan. This was the first time in nearly 25 years that our immediate family was together: just Doris and me with our boys camping at the beach. That was a unique déjà vu experience that we all enjoyed very much.

Joan did pass away early in the morning in her home with Ron at her side in October 2013.

As we live through our "golden years," Doris and I are truly blessed. Life has been extremely good to us and we don't take that for granted.

With the Lord in our lives, we look forward to the future – 70 going on 19.

Top left - Mom and Dad's 50th Wedding Anniversary

Top right - Doris in Kathmandu Valley, Nepal

Upper Right - Ed Hohmann, dean of engineering, and Randy at Cal Poly

Lower right - Doris and Randy at Ngorongoro Crater, Tanzania, Africa

Bottom right - Doris and Mom

Bottom left - Camping in the Chinook at San Elijo State Beach

Doris on the Great Wall, China

Shawn Peeters at Burning Man

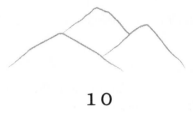

10

Gaining Experience One Mountain at a Time

Monsoon rains, loading and unloading all our equipment countless times as we portaged around numerous road closures; dealing with the Chinese Border Police to enter Tibet; staying in dirt-floor hovels en route: these were the norm for this expedition. Finally, after weeks of travel, we arrived at Advanced Base Camp. At last the drama was over ... or was it?

While carrying loads to Camp I on Cho Oyo, Marty ran up to me with an awful look on his face and said, "Randy ... You're not going to believe this. The World Trade Center has just been leveled and the death toll is over three thousand."

It was not clear if the Chinese would allow us to continue our climb or put us under house arrest. It would be a long agonizing two days before we would know our fate.

Alpine and expedition climbing is like a terminal disease – once you catch it – it is irreversible.

I became hooked at a young age and worked diligently to improve my skills during the early years. As I progressed, I would do harder and longer climbs that would ultimately lead to my climbing Mount Everest and the completion of the Adventure Grand Slam.

As mentioned earlier, I estimate I climbed over 100 alpine routes and rock climbs in the state of Washington and another 25 in other areas while living in the Northwest. Those climbs included an ascent of Mount Challenger via Rainy Pass in the Northern Pickets. It was only the thirteenth time in its history that it had been done.

High Sierra

After relocating to central California in the early 1970s, I picked up where I had left off in Washington.

While climbing in the Sierra Nevada Mountains with Nelson Walker, a longtime friend from the Seattle area, we bagged two alpine climbs: Darwin and Mendel in under 30 hours. Both are nearly 14,000 feet above sea level and this included traveling 12 miles round trip to and from our vehicles. We also experienced a few scares in the Sierra.

Disappointment Peak is nearly 14,000 feet above sea level but not considered that impressive. However, this is a rather dangerous, nearly vertical, rotten rock climb that Nelson, his friend Tim and I decided to negotiate. Going up wasn't that big a deal, but discovering we'd also have to descend the same way was.

I truly thought we were going to buy the farm. We would have to use anchorless belays followed by the one doing the belay, un-roping and free soloing down each pitch. Without good anchors, if the descending belayer was roped in and were to fall, we were certain the other two would be pulled down with him.

That meant when one's turn to belay came it required going down an ugly loose pitch un-roped. Fortunately, we made our descent without incident and had the satisfaction of climbing one of the more challenging and rarely climbed peaks in the Sierra.

Things began to wind down as I started moving about the country due to my career. Doris and I were raising two boys and our relocation to New Mexico and later to New York, put expedition climbing on the back burner. However, my vision of climbing Mount Everest remained.

I continued to do an occasional rock climb in Yosemite, but my alpine and expedition friends faded into the background. In spite of that, the notion of returning to snow and ice climbing never left my thoughts.

Alaska

In 1988, I planned to climb the West Buttress of Denali (Alaska's Mount McKinley). I began training 18 hours a week including carrying a heavy pack, wearing ankle and wrist weights while walking. I also ran and rode my bike.

I had always wanted to climb Denali but at this stage of my life I wasn't even sure how to put together such an expedition. I eventually decided to go on a guided trip with Genet Expeditions, a commercial outfitter.

In May 1988, I arrived in Anchorage, AK with 162 pounds on my six foot one inch frame and a resting pulse of 55 beats per minute. After meeting my climbing partners, we boarded a bush plane in Talkeetna and flew to Denali. We landed at Base Camp on the Kahiltna Glacier (7,100 feet elevation).

Our group dynamics were difficult. Several team members did not have the experience profile or ability for this type of expedition. As a result, we were never able to summit in spite of two attempts that took us within four hours of the top. To make matters worse, we were pinned down for over a week at the 17,200 foot High Camp because of extremely bad weather. Bottom line – it was miserable.

The atmosphere is different above the Arctic Circle. The air is actually thinner than at a level 3,000 feet higher in the Himalayas. This is because the air near the poles is colder and the spin of the earth molds it into an oblate spheroid shape. That thins the Arctic atmosphere and thickens it at the equator.

In fact, at High Camp the oxygen level was so low our bodies began to feed on our muscles. This happens because diminished oxygen suppresses appetite and results in muscle tissue being metabolized rather than fat.

The lost time also meant we would have to turn back when the weather cleared. Some members of the group were due back at work and simply wouldn't change their flight schedules.

The head guide and I led the descent, which the two of us made in a day. On our way down, we came across an all-women group who invited us to stop for tea. They were rather tough looking women and referred to themselves as the "Klondyke Expedition."

In spite of the disappointment of not making it to the top of Denali, I learned a lot about expedition climbing and became even more determined to return and conquer that amazing mountain. I returned home with frost-numbed toes, no taste sensation and 11 pounds lighter. I also came back smarter on how the Alaskan climbing system works and knew that I did not like guided expeditions.

One year later, I returned to Denali with two friends from the Sacramento area, Tom Long and Harlan Reese. I was the expedition leader so we called ourselves the "Frozen Peeters Expedition." And we put that moniker on every flag attached to bamboo wands we used to mark our caches.

I had upped my training to 25 hours a week and was confident we would be successful this trip. It turned out we were, except for Tom. He got frostbite on the sojourn and had to drop out at Windy Corner, short of 14,000 feet.

We used skis this trip and traveled light. It took us six days to reach High

Camp where we planned our final ascent. We departed High Camp at 9 a.m. and worked our way up to Denali Pass at an elevation of 18,200 feet. It was above here that Harlan and I decided to split up since he was starting to fall behind my pace.

I soloed to the top and Harlan hooked up with a British expedition. I reached the peak at 1:45 p.m. and immediately began my descent from the 20,320 foot summit. I passed Harlan on the way down and we stopped and chatted before I continued on my way. The weather was deteriorating fast and the winds had increased to more than 50 miles per hour. I got lost in the whiteout below Denali Pass but managed to work my way back to High Camp in spite of the conditions. I was exhilarated to have made it, but was also quite worried about Harlan as the storm continued into the night.

Harlan returned later that night and I spent the next few hours rehydrating him and feeding him. He had made it to the top as well and we were able to complete our venture in 12 days. We were very satisfied with what we had accomplished.

An unforeseen highlight came on our final descent. While retrieving a cache, three young women approached us and asked if we were the Frozen Peeters. When we answered in the affirmative, they told us they were the "Chicks on Pricks." The "pricks," of course, was a reference to the crampons they were wearing. So there we were at 11,000 feet, where the Frozen Peeters had met the Chicks on Pricks.

Denali is listed as one of the ten most dangerous mountains to climb. The success rate in climbing that mountain is 50 percent and more than 100 climbers have died trying to conquer it.

My conquest of Denali brought to mind Dick Bass's book, *Seven Summits*. He wrote of climbing the highest peaks on all seven continents and I began to wonder how many of them I could summit. Mount Everest had always been my ultimate goal, but the price tag was hefty and I couldn't afford to take three months away from work to complete the mission. Vincent Massif in Antarctica also required a huge cash outlay, so I narrowed my sights to five out of the seven mountains.

I had Denali behind me, so I concentrated on South America's Aconcagua, Africa's Kilimanjaro, Elbrus in Europe and Kosciusko in Australia. Bagging five of the seven wouldn't be that bad.

The Andes

Cerro Aconcagua is the highest mountain in the Southern and Western Hemispheres. It rises 23,000 feet above the border separating Argentina and Chile. I began working the weights, cycling and running. I again attached my ankle and wrist weights and went walking every day with a 50 pound pack on my back. I already had a vision of seeing myself at the top.

I partnered with Harlan and we took off for South America on Christmas Day 1991. It would involve spending the night in the Los Angeles Airport, taking a long flight on Aerolineas Argentinas and spending another night in Buenos Aires. From there, it was on to Mendoza, Argentina, where we purchased some last minute supplies including Benzeno Blanco (stove fuel).

Ricardo was my contact. He helped us through the permit process, took us by Jeep to Puente del Inca and arranged for mules to pack our gear up to Base Camp (14,340 feet). We had given ourselves 27 days to accomplish our goal, which allowed us a 16 day summit window at the 17,000 foot level, in case we were delayed by inclement weather.

Puente del Inca's elevation is 8,990 feet and that's where Ricardo was to meet us to complete our journey to the trailhead. He showed up an hour later than the agreed time, tapping his watch in an effort to pacify us. He then drove us to meet our mulas (gauchos who drive the mules and organize Base Camp – sort of). From there, it was a hike up to the Horcones Valley where we spent the night. The next day, we moved up to Base Camp. These stops were an important part of the acclimation process.

Keeping one's belongings safe from banditos while on the mountain is a necessity. Fortunately, our mulas fee included standing watch over our stuff in our absence. After two days at the 14,340 foot Base Camp, I ported some of our gear up another 2,200 feet to Camp I at Plaza Canada.

Back at Base Camp on New Year's Eve was quite an experience. It is a big celebration in South America and the Argentina Army camp near ours wasn't about to be left out. Shock waves rolled through Base Camp when the soldiers began detonating sticks of dynamite. I decided to get a closer look and was immediately invited to join in the festivities. I was leery since the U.S. had supported Britain during the 1982 war over the Falkland Islands, but it never became an issue, in what turned out to be a very memorable and explosive evening.

We had mixed weather after we left Puente del Inca, including five days of strong winds and snow. A number of climbing parties decided to call it quits and headed down. Harlan was suffering from altitude sickness, so I went on ahead while he spent an extra day at Base Camp. As I moved up by myself to Plaza Canada, the weather cleared and that evening at Camp I was wonderful. I sat in front of my tent at dusk completely alone and soaked up the beauty of my snow covered surroundings. It was New Year's Day and I reveled in the solitude: praying, reading scripture, playing solitaire and thinking about my family and the Rose Bowl game then underway.

It was another 1,700 feet up to Camp II, so I spent the next day carrying loads up to Nido de Cóndores, where the camp was located. Harlan made it up to Camp I and that evening asked me to check out his back. He said he had a small boil on his back and the pad on his pack was rubbing against it. I took a look and saw on top of his spine a sore about half the size of a tennis ball and it appeared infected – not good.

A doctor in Sacramento had checked the wound and given him the OK to proceed with the trip. But in this environment, the wound's rapid growth was serious enough to result in paralysis or even death. At extreme altitudes, there's not enough oxygen for the body to fight off infections as it would at sea level. But in spite of my warnings, Harlan insisted on helping me carry a load up to Camp II before retreating back to Base Camp.

After reaching Camp II, we said our goodbyes and Harlan's parting words were, "I'll be damned if I'll let some f … ing third world doctor operate on me on a dirt floor."

It was ironic that his words turned out to be prophetic.

From Base Camp, he was sent to a newly constructed trekking lodge where a local doctor lanced the boil and placed a wick in it to help it drain. For the procedure, Harlan had to lie on a dirty mattress illuminated by a single incandescent bulb swinging on the end of an electrical cord. The room was complete with dirt floor.

And for anesthesia, they had Harlan bite down on a stick!

Knowing there was a small three person A-frame refugio (hut) at Berlin located 19,490 feet above sea level, I decided to stash my food, abandon the tent and move up there in light of Harlan's worsening condition. When I reached Berlin, a four man Mexican team was occupying the small hut and insisted I join them. It was cozy, sort of like sardines in a can, but it beat sleeping out in the elements.

We rolled out at 7:30 a.m. and headed for the summit. It was brutal. I actually crawled on my hands and knees up the La Canaleta – a very steep couloir near the top. I reached the summit at 4 p.m. in shirt sleeve weather. Rouél and Carmen of the Mexican team were already there. I signed the register dedicating the climb to Doris, Harlan and Jesus. I then prayed, took photos, hugged the other climbers and 30 minutes later was making my way back down at full speed and arrived at Berlin three hours later.

Exhausted, I stumbled into the refugio knowing I should have spent two more days acclimating above 17,000 feet. But with the uncertainty of

Harlan's condition, I felt compelled to go as quickly as I could. The Mexican team fixed some food, which they shared with me and it was another cozy night in the refugio.

I began my descent early the next morning and by 11:30 I was at Camp II. I quickly broke camp, shouldered an incredibly heavy load to carry and arrived at Base Camp at 2 p.m. Harlan filled me in on the gory details and shared with me the note the doctor had written for him. The note indicated we had a medical emergency and to expedite our return to the states as soon as possible. Our hope was this note would help us get the airlines to change the return date on our tickets.

"My goal is to get the hell out of here as fast as possible," Harlan said.

By eight that next morning, we were on our way down the mountain and reached the trailhead six hours later. True to form, Ricardo showed up an hour and a half late tapping his watch. I had had enough.

I looked Ricardo straight in the eye and said, "Don't even try that s ... with me."

We had a great meal at Hosteria where we spent that night. Early the next morning, a car picked us up and took us to Santiago, Chile. From there it was straight to the airport and the "Airline Wars."

All flights to the U.S. were overbooked and even passengers with confirmed seats were being turned away. The doctor's medical emergency note did get us sympathy, but not much else. Harlan's attempt to look sicker than he really was didn't help much either. We did get our tickets changed so they would be good on any airline, but we were turned away by all of them.

That evening, we returned to Santiago and located the backpacker part of town where we found a place to stay for $10 a night. We had rented a room that could only be described as unbelievable.

We were led down a small hallway to a room in which big sheets of paint were peeling off the walls with messages scribbled everywhere. The sky was visible through the roof of the shower and the lock on the door was a spring catch, like that on a screen door.

For our listening pleasure, the desk clerk asked if we'd like "musica?" That consisted of twisting two wires together to connect a small speaker that squawked out the garbled sounds of a local radio station. I inquired as to food and was told the hotel was located in a "muy peligroso" part of town. In spite of the warning, Harlan and I ventured out and were treated to a rather nice, inexpensive indigenous dinner.

Upon our return, we signed the wall, pushed the broken-down couch against the door and climbed into bed.

Harlan's last words were, "There is no f ... ing way I am going to be able to sleep in this s ... hole." Seconds later, he was snoring away.

The next two days were spent negotiating with airlines, shopping and sightseeing. Eventually, I called American Airlines in Dallas and secured a connecting flight to Los Angeles. From there to Sacramento we would be on our own, but at least we'd be back in the good ol' U-S-of-A, or so one would think.

However, when we reached Miami, we were running late for our next flight and did our best to hurry through customs. We then frantically tried to find our departure gate, but couldn't get help speaking either Spanish or English. At least in South America we could get by on my attempt at broken Spanish – but not in Miami. It was unbelievable.

When we finally found our gate for the flight to L.A., we were relieved to see our plane was still there. However, we were informed the cabin door had already been closed and could not be reopened – Harlan lost it.

He threw down his backpack, carry-on luggage and anything else he could get his hands on and jumped up and down while swearing at the top of his lungs. I tried to calm him, but he was just too sick and tired to be consoled. Eventually, security arrived on the scene and they were able to help him get a grip on himself. They were extremely helpful and the gate agent arranged for a hotel, food vouchers and even a flight to Sacramento leaving that next morning.

In the end, it all turned out great and was a fantastic adventure. Harlan healed up fine and I had succeeded in climbing two of the Seven Summits, including the highest mountain outside the Himalaya.

California Climbing

While in California, I took several trips to the top of Mount Shasta – slightly over 14,000 feet. It's a peak I've never enjoyed climbing that much and most of my trips there have been less than satisfying. It's a rubble heap and deceptively dangerous.

While there, I've had to abort climbs, been lost in a whiteout, turned back in the winter on Casaval Ridge at 10,000 feet and subsequently reached the summit in terrible weather. However, I did have one nice climb in 1998 with my good friend Denny Swenson from the Sacramento area. While climbing to the top, we saw two passes of the Russian Space Station Mir and an Iridium flair from a satellite. We used skis that trip and made the round trip, car-to-car in less than 20 hours.

Europe

Mount Blanc is located in Chamonix, France. On previous trips I had been turned back twice by bad weather trying to reach its 15,772 foot summit. Then, in the summer of 1999, I made it.

I did the climb with Austrian Christian Gabl whom I had met in Yosemite Park years before. With his friends Peter and Reinhardt, we took the cable car to Aiguille du Midi station. From there it was a 45 minute climb to an abandoned hut situated on the mountain, where we spent the night.

The next day, we took the straightforward ice route traversing from Col du Midi over the summit. We made the 5,250 foot climb in 12 hours. From there, we dropped down to Refuge Vallot passing Grands Mulets and crossing the Glacier de Tacoma. That 8,530 foot descent brought us back to the cable car mid-station. We covered nine miles total that day.

We had some difficulty traversing the heavily-crevassed lower Glacier de Tacoma but otherwise it was a great climb.

Washington State

Inspired by the book *Fifty Classic Climbs of North America*, written by Steve Roper and Allen Steck, I climbed 20 of these fine routes described by them. For years, one of those routes I had wanted to tackle was the North Ridge of Mount Stuart in the Washington Cascades. Tom Dancs, a strong climber I had met in Yosemite and I first tried it in the spring of 2000, but encountered too much snow to accomplish it.

In May of 2000, Dancs and I put Mount Stuart on the back burner and set our sights on another classic 50, the ascetic Liberty Ridge on the north side of Mount Rainier. It is a steep, technical route rising more than a vertical mile from the Carbon Glacier and leads directly to the summit of Liberty Cap. I had tried it twice before as a graduate student, but without success.

Returning from an Alaskan vacation, Dancs picked up Doris and me at the airport and drove us to his home where we transferred our gear and our dog Sarah to our RV. We then drove to Rainier National Park.

Upon arrival, we climbed up to the col behind Thumb Rock and spent the night at 10,775 feet. From there, we reached the top that next day. We returned to the RV and enjoyed a bowl of Doris' awesome tomato soup.

Switzerland

I returned to climb the Matterhorn more than 25 years after Doris and I were turned back by too much snow on the mountain. I was lucky enough to secure a guide with the necessary permits and within 24 hours I was on the mountain.

The weather is notoriously bad on the Matterhorn and our forecast was mixed. Part of my lucky break was that someone had canceled due to the weather and I got that spot.

We took the Hornli Ridge and reached the 14,463 foot summit August 5, 2001.

Although I typically don't like using a guide, I was glad I had one this time. The route was much longer and more obscure than I thought. The Matterhorn has one of the highest fatality rates of any peak in the Alps. The problems range from technical rock climbing difficulties to overcrowding, not to mention rock falls and avalanches.

Acclimatization

The Himalayas have 14 peaks that rise over 8,000 meters (26,300 feet). Extreme altitudes of this magnitude are in what is known as the "death zone." That's because the atmospheric oxygen at these levels is too low to sustain life. Trying to survive at these elevations without proper preparation can result in the loss of vital functions or accidents caused by poor decision making, stress and physical weakening. The body slowly deteriorates, leading ultimately to death.

The method of preparation is called acclimatization. This is accomplished by spending weeks climbing to higher and higher elevations to work and then returning to lower elevations to rest. The adage is "climb high – sleep low."

Over time, the body generates more and more red blood cells capable of carrying adequate quantities of oxygen to the body despite the low levels being taken in by the lungs. The body literally ratchets up its ability to compensate for the extreme altitudes.

Mount Elbrus

At a time when Mount Everest was out of my reach, I decided to settle for Cho Oyo and began the trip by climbing Mount Elbrus in the Georgian Caucasus of Europe (18,510 feet). Marty Schmidt, a climber I had met in Yosemite a year before, would be my guide.

I met up with Marty in St. Petersburg, Russia. He added me to his expedition at little cost and I was still in pretty good shape having recently climbed the Matterhorn. On August 17, 2001 it took Marty and me eight hours to reach the top of the peak in cold, clear conditions and no wind. It was my third of the Seven Summits.

The rest of the trip we spent touring the area in a four wheel drive vehicle, before returning to St. Petersburg.

Tibet

Following Mount Elbrus, I continued on a roll that summer of 2001 and headed for Nepal via Thailand. There, I again met up with Marty at the end of the short monsoon season and we worked out our plans. It would be just the two of us. I traveled around Kathmandu in torrential rains buying last minute supplies while Marty, a fantastic climber, worked on the Base Camp arrangements.

We had to travel 60 miles on back roads to reach Kodari, Nepal. The monsoon rains had caused several road closures due to huge mud slides. The only way around them was to unload the vehicle we arrived in, hire porters to traverse the slide and then reload another vehicle on the other side. During those two days, we rode buses, trucks and four wheel drive units. We entered Tibet at Zhangmu and continued our acclimatization process as we traveled by truck to Tingri, Tibet.

A week later, we arrived at Chinese Base Camp at 16,000 feet and from there hiked to Advanced Base Camp near Nangpa La Pass a little over 2,500 feet higher up. The Advanced Base Camp was supported by Mountain Madness and there I met its owner Christine Boskoff and a fellow guide Charlie Fowler. Mountain Madness had about a half dozen climbers on its team, but two decided not to proceed up the world's sixth highest mountain which turned out to be a very poor decision.

On the way home, those two made a stop in Bangkok, Thailand, where one was later found dead in his room from an apparent drug overdose.

At nearly 21,000 feet, we established Camp I and then moved up another 1,000 feet to an intermediate camp at the top of an ice wall. Things were moving flawlessly when we got the news that terrorists had leveled the World Trade Center in New York.

We returned to Advanced Base Camp to wait and see if the Chinese government would allow us to continue. After an anxious two day wait, we got the go ahead. We immediately climbed back up to Camp I and then moved up to Camp II at 23,130 feet. After that, it was back to Advanced Base Camp for a three day rest.

On September 21, 2001 we began our summit attempt with overnight stops at Camps I and II before establishing High Camp at 25,000 feet. We left there shortly after midnight and reached the 26,906 foot summit at 7:30 a.m. on September 24, 2001. There Marty and I stayed for about 45 minutes. The view was fantastic with Mount Everest looking as if it was only an arms-length away.

The last 900 feet to the top, I used supplemental oxygen to help keep my body warm. The brain will actually try to conserve oxygen by shutting off the blood supply to the extremities in order to keep the core warm. I had no problem climbing upward, but I needed supplemental oxygen to avoid frostbite. My feet had begun to feel like solid wood and it wasn't worth losing my toes.

While at Base Camp, Charlie told us that toes were not that important and later showed us his toeless feet. He lost all of his toes to frostbite while climbing Shishapangma.

Although it was cold on top of Cho Oyo, my supplemental oxygen warmed my core and I had no problem with my toes.

While Marty went off to rescue a client on another expedition, I soloed down to Camp I. A day later we met at Advanced Base Camp to celebrate in a makeshift bar set up by two Sherpa women. It was a large Chinese military field tent heated by Yak dung, where they brewed a beer called Chang. Before long, Sherpas and climbers were drunk and making a spectacle that resembled the bar scene in "Star Wars." The shouting, cheering and singing went on well into the night. Although a teetotaler, I did drink up the ambiance – a truly surreal experience.

Technically, this was a guided trip, but Marty was more like a very experienced climbing partner; so experienced that he made a second speed ascent from Advanced Base Camp to the top setting a record of ten hours and 45 minutes. Through him, I learned the Himalayan climbing system and was satisfied I had made my last big climb. It was my first 8,000 meter summit and it took me one month to go from Kathmandu and back.

Top right -Randy on the traverse above the Col du Midi on Mt. Blanc, France

Top left - Harlan Reese approaching High Camp at 17,200 feet on Denali, AK

Upper left - Harlan Reese at Camp I in the Horcones Valley, Cerro Aconcagua

Lower left - Climbing Mt. Elbrus

Bottom left - Marty Schmidt and Randy on the summit of Mt. Elbrus, Caucasus, Russia

Bottom right - Randy climbing above Camp II on Cho Oyo, Tibet

Using supplemental oxygen above 26,000' on Cho Oyo

Randy on summit of Cho Oyo 26,906 feet

11

NEAR THE EDGE

What a miserable night it was. I had left my partner Peter Legate at Advanced Base Camp and proceeded up the 45 degree ice fields of Mount Everest's Lhotse Face with Mike Morris and Geoffrey Stanford.

We spent the night by ourselves at Camp III where the jet stream had us pinned down with winds of 100 miles per hour or more. Tents all around us were actually being ripped off the mountain.

The next morning things hadn't improved much. To make matters worse, I was suffering frostbite on my fingertips so we decided to retreat back to Base Camp. I met up with Peter at the base of the Lhotse Face as he was starting to make his way up.

"Be careful up there – it is really nasty," I said in passing.

"No problem," was his reply.

In less than 48 hours Peter was dead.

I didn't get the news until after I had reached Base Camp. I was devastated by it and didn't know what to do next. Since I had to descend even lower in order to heal the frostbite, I was torn between coming back up to finish the climb – or just giving up and going home.

I had over 40 years of climbing experience and even as a teenager I had seriously thought of climbing Mount Everest. But there's considerably more to it than being able to scale a rock wall covered with ice, especially when in the fifth decade of life.

Everest is located on the border between Nepal and Tibet. Nepal is a third world country that was rife with corruption and in the midst of a Maoist uprising. It wasn't as simple as rolling up an ice axe and crampons into a sleeping bag and heading off for the mountain. By 2002, there were 176 recorded deaths above the summit's Base Camp. There were a lot of hoops I was going to have to jump through, my family and my safety notwithstanding.

I had the winter of 2001/2002 to prepare and prayed for the Lord's guidance. I also had the arduous task of soliciting sponsors to help pay for my participation in the expedition. And, I was given a rather special package to carry out a promise made to one of my sponsors.

The permit alone to climb Mount Everest was $10,000 per person. Throw in airfare ($1,500), specialized mountaineering gear ($6,000), expedition provider/Base Camp/Sherpa support ($23,000) and my budget for the trip would be $40,000. Still, 40 grand was a far cry from the $75,000 and up required for some climbing packages. Fortunately, through sponsorships, my out-of-pocket expenses would total only $16,500. The final cog in the wheel was the support and encouragement given to me by my wife, Doris. With all other things in place, her blessing was the final step in fulfilling this dream of a lifetime.

My group would be led by Henry Todd of Edinburgh, Scotland. There would be nine of us in all: two teams of two each and a five man Hungarian National Team, plus the Sherpa we would have to hire. Our route would be via the South Col located on the Nepal side of Mount Everest.

I had met Henry during my fall 2001 ascent of Cho Oyo in Tibet. Henry and fellow climber Russell Brice were expedition providers and each invited me to join them on their upcoming assaults of Mount Everest. Brice was to go up Everest's North Ridge; Henry would approach from the south. I chose to go with Henry. Not only had his teams made several successful summits of Everest, but he had an excellent safety record as well. And, Henry offered to take me along at close to cost.

I left California, March 20, 2002 and flew to Japan. Twenty nine hours later I landed in Bangkok, Thailand. I had a little time to enjoy Bangkok before boarding an airplane for a four hour flight to Kathmandu, Nepal. And, in spite of the horror stories about the airlines losing luggage, all mine arrived intact.

On March 24, 2002 the Everest team came together to set strategy and make final arrangements. This is done even though scrambles up big mountains never go as planned. Kathmandu was where I first met Peter Legate, the man designated to be my climbing partner.

Peter was a rugby player from England. Typical of the British, his personality was reserved. Although we didn't hit it off right away, during the weeks we spent together we became good friends. He was a ruggedly handsome man who had had put his life on hold for two years in his determination to climb Everest. We gradually started to share openly about personal things such as faith, family and values.

He told me he had split up with his fiancé because of this climb, but that he planned to return to England afterward and propose marriage to her on the spot. As time went on, I began to have reservations as to Peter's ability to make this ascent. Even with my four decades of experience, I felt I was the weakest member of Henry's teams and Peter was less qualified than I.

My confidence was further shaken when Henry announced in Kathmandu that he wouldn't be going with us. Although he was cleared by the British Government to make the trip, the Nepalese Government said no. In fact, he was told to leave the country - immediately.

It turns out Henry was serving a two year suspension following an altercation he'd had with a journalist from television's Discovery Channel. This particular journalist was turning in some rather unfavorable reports concerning Henry and his methods. So, "The Toddfather," a sobriquet given the Scotsman because of his temper and checkered past, chased down the reporter and gave him a good shaking. Although it was said the reporter stumbled and hurt himself and no witness confirmed that Henry actually struck the fellow, Henry was still put on probation for this incident. He had also spent considerable time in prison in Great Britain for distribution of LSD during the 1970s.

I liked Henry a great deal, in spite of his past exploits. After informing us of his dilemma, he suggested we either change our plans and take the Tibetan route, or continue on without him. We were a pretty mature group, so we chose the latter and Henry bid us goodbye.

Geoffrey Stanford, from England, became our expedition leader. He partnered with Mike Morris, who was from the United States. The team was also made up of Peter and me and the Hungarian National Everest Team of Zoltan Ács, Zsolt Erőss, László "Mezo" Mezey, László "Laci" Mécs and László "Konyi" Várkonyi. We were later joined at Base Camp by another two man team climbing Lhotse.

The Hungarians were all professional climbers and guides. They were considered capable of climbing the world's tallest mountain without Sherpa support or supplemental oxygen. Their quest was to put the first Hungarian on top of Everest.

Safety is paramount on this type of trip. Even nationally recognized mountaineers have lost their lives on Everest. The dangers include falls, avalanches, crevasses, oxygen deprivation and most worrisome – exposure. Everest is high enough that it extends into the jet stream, which can shift without warning and hit climbers with 100 mile per hour plus winds.

The climbing season on Everest is narrow and severe weather can become a problem even in the best of conditions. Beside the winds, there are blinding blizzards and temperatures that can plummet to 75 degrees below zero Fahrenheit. I was well aware of these dangers and took every possible precaution to be prepared and ensure my safe return. In fact, I had made up my mind that if conditions were too bad, I would give up trying to make it to the top.

I completely agree with Ed Viesturs when he said, "Getting to the top is optional. Getting down is mandatory."

Knowing what lay ahead, I decided to treat myself to a haircut, beard trim, shampoo and upper body massage – all for a total of $5. The process took place in the order listed and left me puzzled as to why they didn't shampoo my hair before they cut it.

March 25th of 2002, Peter and I flew to Lukla, elevation 9,350 feet and began our trek to Everest Base Camp. We left some of our gear in Kathmandu, which would later be transferred to the Khumbu region and taken by porters and yaks to Base Camp. Thinking I would not need it until Base Camp, I left behind my sleeping bag.

It took us about three and a half hours to hike to the village of Tok Tok. We spent the night in the small Himalayan View Lodge that included food and boiled water – all for $3. We shared the kitchen with the owners of the place, which was fascinating. Snow was still on the ground in Tok Tok and it was quite cold – that's when I realized leaving behind my sleeping bag wasn't such a good idea.

I literally froze at night and had to borrow blankets from the teahouses where we stayed for most of the trek to Base Camp. Peter thought it hilarious that I had my pajamas, but no sleeping bag. Sponsored by the British Broadcasting Company, Peter made sure my bedtime dilemma was reported.

As we trekked along the banks of the Dudh Kosi River, we had to cross it many times on wild suspension bridges. They were laden with prayer flags. We entered Sagarmatha National Park at Jorsale and made a strenuous ascent to Namche Bazaar at 11,300 feet above sea level. Namche was a neat village with many interesting shops, vendors, good food and great views of the surrounding mountains.

It was there we met our Sherpa, Ang Tsering. Together we made plans to climb Island Peak. At over 20,000 feet elevation, the Island Peak climb would help us acclimatize and prepare us for the dangerous Khumbu Ice Fall located just above Base Camp on Mount Everest.

In 1953, during the first ascent of Everest, Edmund Hillary and Tenzing Norgay went up Island Peak for that same reason. Almost 50 years later, we would repeat the process.

The next morning, I took a short hike to an altitude of about 12,500 feet and visited the Sherpa Museum on my way down. I spent the rest of the afternoon checking out Namche and getting used to the higher elevations. The big news was the week-long strike planned by the Maoists. However, we were in the Khumbu region and it was too remote to be affected. Still, I did manage to catch a cold, but partially recovered before we were scheduled to climb Island Peak.

We left Namche Bazaar on March 30, 2002 to continue our trek along the Dudh Kosi River where the views are magnificent. When we reached the Thyangboche Monastery, we spent a fortuitous night there. National Geographic was filming a documentary commemorating the 50th anniversary of the first ascent up Everest and the locals were performing a full-blown prayer-scarf blessing ceremony. Typically, the monastery has a prayer service twice daily featuring the Lama and monks, but this one was special and included amazing hats and robes, horns, cymbals, chanting, milk tea and more. It was fantastic.

Peter Hillary and Jamling Norgay, sons of the first summit team, were there. Inside the monastery were incredible wall hangings and a 20 foot tall sculpture of Buddha. We remained in Thyangboche until Easter Sunday.

Spending Easter in Thyangboche made it that much harder for me that day with thoughts of home and family – bottom line, I was homesick the entire day.

From Thyangboche, we dropped down to Debuche. We crossed another wild bridge to the Imja Khola Valley and climbed to the village of Pangboche, where mani stones lined the path. It was also the home village of our Base Camp Sirdar and Sherpa team and there we spent the night.

We continued our acclimatization by moving up to Dingbouche, a village at a little over 14,000 feet with super views of Lhotse, Island Peak and Ama Dablam. We took a rest day at Dingbouche, so I did a stiff hike up to Nangkar Tshang at 16,728 feet. We left Dingbouche, April 2 of 2002 and climbed farther up the Imja Khola Valley to a small settlement called Chhukung for a two day stay.

I facilitated my acclimatization by going up Chhukung Ri at an altitude of 18,208 feet. Our next stop was Island Peak Base Camp, where Ang Tsering Sherpa would meet us with the porter carrying our gear (including my sleeping bag).

At 1:45 the morning of April 6, 2002, we set out to scale Island Peak. Both Peter and I were amazed at how difficult and exhilarating the climb was. It took five sets of fixed lines to get us over the rocks and ice before we finally topped out shortly before 9 a.m. We then descended back to Base Camp and returned to Chhukung.

The next morning, we traversed farmlands and meadows; then up the terminal moraine of the Khumbu Glacier to the village of Lobuche. We stayed at the new Eco Lodge paying $20 for bed and food – over twice what we'd been paying. From there, it was on to Mount Everest Base Camp.

We skirted the glacier's edge passing through Gorak Shep. The 17,600 foot Base Camp was on a jumbled moraine with glacial ice chunks as big as buildings. It was there, below the infamous Khumbu Icefall, that we were joined by most of our team with the rest due a few days later.

After a couple days of acclimatizing, we practiced on the ladders that would later assist us through the dreaded icefall. We would follow a precarious route of fixed ladders and ropes to assist us over those chaotic blocks of shifting ice. Our expedition was tasked with fixing the icefall and Henry Todd had arranged for the ladders and two Sherpa Ice Fall Doctors to prepare and maintain the route. Other expeditions were to establish other parts of the route up the mountain, including the Lhotse Face and the summit ridge of Everest.

It was cold and nasty at Base Camp, with nighttime temperatures dropping to 15 degrees below zero Fahrenheit and it snowed almost daily. It would snow up to six inches and then melt when the sun came out. The sounds of avalanches, rock falls and gnawing of the glacier as it continuously churned down the Khumbu Valley interrupted our otherwise silent surroundings.

Over time, the weather stabilized and the storms were less frequent. Other than a minor cough, I had recovered from my cold by the time I reached Base Camp. The Maoist strike had been postponed, so it would have no impact on our expedition. I had been able to send emails and use a satellite phone in Kathmandu and some of the other villages, but at Base Camp it was nearly impossible.

Because some of our communication equipment had not shown up, I had to use a large commercial expedition's communication center to send my first email from Base Camp to Doris and my sponsors. The bill was $51!

When I questioned the charge, the expedition leader bluntly said, "You don't suppose it cost that much since you are on a cheap expedition, do you?"

I was angered by the remark and, without Henry around, felt they were taking advantage of me. I think the leader used the opportunity to vent on me.

I resorted to asking other groups to help me with emails. I had to use a host account since I couldn't use mine and, therefore, couldn't receive emails, but only send them.

I later networked with a group of outcasts and loners at Base Camp to improve the situation. Particularly helpful was a group from Brown University there to do a research project. They were doing oxygen deprivation tests at that level and at higher elevations. Also helpful was Sean Swaner, a Christian double-cancer survivor. He was on a one man expedition for the Cancer Climber Association and had Base Camp support from his brother and a few others.

It turned out to be an excellent working relationship. We had movie nights that rotated among our camps and shared resources on a cost basis for emails, satellite phone calls and, in general, provided moral support for one another. We also volunteered as test subjects to help the Brown University folks complete their research.

It was April 10, 2002 when I climbed a quarter of the way up the Khumbu Icefall and first experienced those dreaded ladders. The scramble is on a very steep moving glacier with deep crevasses and towering seracs. The ladders were made of aluminum and were used to bridge the crevasses and climb steep faces – not an easy thing to climb when wearing crampons. Historically, this is where most deaths occur.

It was then back to Base Camp for two days rest, so I made the best of it by taking a bucket shower and doing my laundry. The third day was a six hour trip through the entire 2,000 vertical foot icefall to Camp I, where I dropped off a load of high-altitude gear and then worked my way back to Base Camp. The route through the icefall was altered daily in order to compensate for the constantly changing conditions that occur there.

I estimate there were more than 25 ladder crossings with one having three ladders tied together to span a crevasse over 200 feet deep. And if that wasn't bad enough, there was a four-ladder crossing over a gaping hole near Camp I right before the start of the Western Cwm.

Our Puja was scheduled for April 14, 2002, after which we would move farther up the mountain. A Lama from Pingboche came up to Base Camp to perform the ceremony and I brought out the special package I had carefully packed with my gear before leaving home.

The Puja is a Buddhist ceremony in which the Lama blesses the climb. My special package contained some of the ashes from Donald Barry's remains. Don had been co-owner of Monte Verde Inn in Foresthill, one of my sponsors. I asked the Lama to bless his ashes as well.

Donald died of cancer and his widow, Susan asked that I leave them in a country he loved so much. On April 16, 2002, after a short prayer, I deposited Donald's ashes in a crevasse at an elevation of 19,000 feet near the top of Khumbu Icefall.

I cannot explain how special that was, other than to say, "Thanks, Susan, for giving me that honor."

I then continued to climb another 700 feet to Camp I, where I spent the night. The next day, I carried a load through the Western Cwm to Camp II, our Advanced Base Camp 20,600 feet above sea level. I then returned to Camp I, where I spent a second night.

The Western Cwm is a "U" shaped valley carved out by the Khumbu Glacier. On the left is Everest (north) and straight ahead Lhotse. At 27,940 feet, Lhotse is the fourth tallest mountain in the world. Nuptse towers over the southern side of the cwm. The Western Cwm is straightforward, but not without danger. At 22,000 feet, the lightly filtered sun can reflect off the snow and ice-covered walls raising temperatures to 100 degrees Fahrenheit. Some of its huge crevasses have to be crossed on thin snow bridges in place of ladders. On the upper left end of the cwm lay Advanced Base Camp.

As mentioned before, for proper acclimatization, the adage is "climb high – sleep low." Although the percentage of oxygen in the air remains constant, at extreme altitudes there is simply less atmosphere. On Everest, it is necessary to spend weeks climbing to higher elevations to work and then descending to lower elevations to rest. This ratcheting up and down helps the body increase its oxygen carrying capacity by inducing the production of more red blood cells.

Early April 18, 2002, I descended the icefall and returned to Base Camp, my home away from home. There, I would spend several days resting before heading back up to Camp II and then on to Camp III for additional acclimatizing. The plan was to spend two or three nights at Advanced Base Camp before climbing half way up Lhotse Face to Camp III. After spending one or two nights there I would try heading up to the Yellow Band before returning to Camp II to spend the night. It would be my last acclimation before attempting to summit Everest.

One of the benefits of my return to Base Camp was the relatively excellent fare; it was not only tasty, but somewhat varied as well. There were many healthy, unprocessed foods, like dal bhat. Dal bhat was a mix of rice, lentil and goat meat or chicken. My appetite was good and I had absolutely no adverse effects from the altitude – not even headaches. However, I was often cold and frequently suffered from homesickness. Lending to my homesickness was an email I managed to receive from my wife:

> Please make it to the top of Everest safely and then race home to us. ... Boy oh boy do I miss you and need you. I send you my deepest love Randy and I am counting the days until I have you in my arms. Stay healthy and safe and I will write soon. ... Be careful and we love you. Doris Girl.

My partner Peter had a difficult time acclimatizing. He was slow in climbing and always seemed to have a bad headache. Even on Island Peak, he struggled to make the summit. I also observed him taking shortcuts while descending the fixed lines. He used a technique called "arm wrap" rappelling. It's a method of putting a spiral wrap around the forearm combined with a "cow tail" (a nylon webbing tether) hooked to the line with a locking carabiner.

On expeditions of this type, I've always rappelled using a figure 8 device hooked to my harness, as well as a cow tail for safety. I told Peter what he was doing was dangerous.

"Other people use this technique," he said.

"But it's dangerous, Peter," I repeated.

"But it's faster," he replied.

I again repeated the danger, knowing such a technique was risky for anyone cold and tired.

At changeovers (the place where the fixed line is anchored to the ice face) the climber using an arm wrap is anchored only by holding onto the line when the cow tail is moved to the next line, but with the figure 8, the climber is always anchored.

Critical here concerning the cow tail was a decision we made to switch from locking carabiners to those that didn't lock. This was done after our first trip through the Khumbu Icefall, where the heavy gloves we needed to wear made it difficult to handle the locking gates. This, of course, increases the dangers associated with arm wrap rappelling since non-locking carabiners can actually twist open against a rope and detach from the fixed lines.

My concerns for Peter started during our ascent of Island Peak. After observing his troubles there, I simply didn't feel he had the experience profile to take on Everest with a non-guided group. His background was Denali (Mount McKinley) and a failed attempt on Ama Dablam the year before. I kept my concerns to myself, thinking that telling him would only increase his determination to conquer Everest.

I left Base Camp on April 22 of 2002 and climbed directly to Advanced Base Camp (Camp II) in the Western Cwm, with a load I picked up at Camp I. I spent two nights there before deciding to head up the Lhotse Face with Geoffrey and Mike to Camp III. Peter chose to stay behind as he wasn't feeling well.

The Lhotse Face is a short distance from Advanced Base Camp and rises at a 45 degree angle. It is covered with hard-packed snow and ice, making it difficult to grip with crampons. It requires over 20 fixed lines to climb and one has to remain clipped at all times, even in camp. People have died on Lhotse Face and the Sherpa do not like to stay overnight at Camp III.

Mike, Geoffrey and I were avalanched twice from minor sloughing and we were hit by 80 plus mile per hour winds. The jet stream had shifted over the mountain and, on one occasion, struck me with enough force to knock me off my feet. Along with three Sherpa, we were the only ones to make it to Camp III that day. The Sherpa returned to Advanced Base Camp and Mike, Geoffrey and I spent the night in Camp III.

The strong winds continued all that night and I was grateful when Geoffrey came over to my tent to help me cook and rehydrate. Both Camps II and III were hit hard by the storm which destroyed more than 20 tents. Luckily, ours wasn't among them. The winds did keep the snow off Lhotse Face and the next morning we were able to rapidly descend to Camp II without danger of more avalanches.

At the base of the face, I ran into Peter who was starting up the fixed lines with Laci, a member of the Hungarian team.

"Peter, be careful up there," I said, "it is really dangerous."

"I'll be fine, Randy," he replied.

I spent the night at Advanced Base Camp and then made my way down to Base Camp. I was very glad to be back "home." In my 40 years of climbing, I had never experienced such a severe storm. In fact, it was reported that several climbers were trapped at Camps II and III, with no estimate of when they would get out.

Although I was away from the worst of it in Base Camp, I did suffer frostbite to five of my fingers. It would take two weeks to heal, but I had finished my acclimatization process. And depending on the weather and the other team's plans, the next ascent would be to the top.

In summary, my acclimatization above Base Camp involved two nights at Camp I, five nights at Camp II (or Advanced Base Camp) and one night at Camp III. I had climbed halfway up the Lhotse Face and made a total of three round trips through the Khumbu Icefall.

We were to rest in Base Camp for at least five days before making our final ascent to the top of Everest, weather and jet stream permitting. A part of our climbing fee included a forecast out of Britain as to the position of the jet stream. The airline industry also relies heavily on these forecasts. We could start back up the mountain in marginal weather and make it to Camp III. Beyond that, we would need a favorable window of conditions.

My frostbite had to heal before going back up the mountain and the air at Base Camp was too thin to facilitate that. Many of the climbers had decided to head down to Pheriche for a couple days of rest at a lower altitude. It had been reported that Maoists had attacked some mountaineers not far from where we were so I needed to make up my mind whether to tag along or stay put. I figured, freeze or be robbed – it's Nepal – Pheriche, here I come! I made plans to descend the next day.

A trekker had sent up a small guitar to Base Camp and after dinner that night, Mezo, a member of the Hungarian team, started playing some folk-rock songs. Some Sherpa showed up and added to the mix of music, with 14 of us huddled in a rock-walled room covered only by a tarp. It turned out to be a special night and I didn't hit the sack until 9 p.m. – the latest I stayed up the entire trip.

When I saw Peter on his way up to Camp III his pace was very slow. He began to fall well behind his partner as they ascended the fixed lines. The jet stream was on Lhotse Face again and the storm raged for another two days. Laci had stopped part way up the face to look for Peter and, when he didn't spot him, assumed Peter had returned to Advanced Base Camp.

After a radio check he realized Peter had to be at Camp III, which is where he found him the next morning lying in a tent and in pretty bad shape. Peter was dehydrated and he hadn't eaten. Laci spent the second day feeding him and forcing him to drink so they could start back down to Camp II.

On April 30, 2002 at 7 a.m., Peter fell out of the fixed lines and to his death. It happened shortly after leaving Camp III. Apparently he miss-clipped the fixed line and tumbled more than 1,000 feet down Lhotse Face. His battered and lifeless body was later found in a deep crevasse below a huge serac. It was decided to leave him there on the mountain.

I had no direct access to a radio, so it wasn't until the second day back at Base Camp that I learned of Peter's fate. It's the kind of thing that rocks a person to the core. I was devastated.

Peter was a true gentleman and I had a great respect for him. We had spent five weeks together, mostly one-on-one. Geoffrey communicated the tragedy to his family and his personal effects were collected and ultimately sent to England. At Base Camp we held a memorial service and farther down the mountain our Sherpa built a chorten for him; a chorten is a mound-like structure with a slate plaque attached.

Sean and I left Base Camp for Pheriche and then continued down another 1,500 feet to Deboche to give my frostbitten hands a better chance to heal in the oxygen-rich air. Deboche is located in the Rhododendron Forest and was a great relief from the cold and sterile environment of Base Camp. It turned out to be the right choice.

I discovered my frostbite was worse than I originally thought. It was determined the frostbite was third degree and I would need more aggressive therapy to get it to heal. Because I did that, it improved dramatically. I went on a three day course of ibuprofen combined with soaking my hands in warm, salty water. The tissue turned black and died, but eventually I regained feeling in my five fingers and both thumbs. I was warned of the serious consequence should those same digits become frostbitten again. Believe me, I was careful after that.

While in Deboche, I called Doris and broke down over the satellite phone. As I cried, she told me to "just come home." I explained I had equipment strung out from Base Camp to Camp III and would at least have to retrieve that. However, I returned to Base Camp on May 5 of 2002 feeling very good physically, with the moment of truth finally upon me.

The weather and jet stream had opened a window of opportunity. I was acclimatized, rested and ready to go. Mentally, I was able to put aside Peter's death and I left for the summit on May 12, 2002.

I soloed on fixed lines up to Advanced Base Camp and spent two days there. I then soloed up to Camp III and spent another night. The next day I continued solo up the Lhotse Face using supplemental oxygen and crossed the Yellow Bands and the Geneva Spur on my way to the South Col. The rock barriers, while not technically difficult, are quite a challenge when climbing at 25,000 feet.

I reached Camp IV on May 15 of 2002 where I met Ang Tsering Sherpa, who would be my climbing partner. I had great confidence in this man, who at age 26, had been to the top of Everest twice before.

The South Col is otherworldly. At 26,300 feet (8,000 meters) it is located between Lhotse and Everest. It is as desolate as Antarctica, with winds that can reach hurricane-like forces. From this point and above, we would be in the "Death Zone." Any mistakes here would likely be fatal. At this altitude, dropping a glove, losing an ice axe or crampon, any small miscalculation can mean – game over. Up here there is no margin for error.

Anatoli Boukreev put it best when he said, "Lingering above Camp IV has all the pleasurable possibilities of picnicking in a minefield."

At the South Col, Geoffrey again came to my aid by helping me cook and rehydrate. Six hours later, I donned my 8,000 meter down suit, put on my plastic boots and minus 40 degree over boots and climbed out of my tent. In this hypoxic environment, I carefully attached my crampons, turned on my headlamp and left for the summit at 10:30 p.m. on May 15, 2002. I had a self-imposed deadline to make it to the summit by noon, or turn around and go back down.

The weather was absolutely perfect and I had no trouble staying warm. The supplemental oxygen not only allowed me to keep climbing, but it also helped keep my extremities warm. I kept a steady pace as I slowly moved up the steep, south slopes and then turned west. We were delayed just above the 27,500 foot Balcony, where Mike, Geoffrey and others, including Sherpa, had to fix ropes over a difficult stretch of rock slabs and ice.

In spite of this area's neglect we made steady progress. I had been the last to leave Camp IV and moving at my slow pace, never really had to stop. I remember looking up in front of me in the predawn darkness and thought

I saw a curious string of boulders. As I got closer, I realized those "boulders" were climbers waiting for the lines to be fixed. Again, my pace played to my advantage. When I reached their location, they had moved on and I was able to continue up without stopping.

To avoid overheating, I removed my 8,000 meter parka at 28,700 feet as the sun had come up. We were right below the South Summit. As the sun rose, the views were truly amazing – just awesome. I thrive in this type of environment - it gives me great mental awareness. I become completely focused and very relaxed.

After reaching the South Summit, I got my first good look at the route to the top of the world and it was terrifying. Before me was the "Cornice-Traverse," a ridge that dropped down below me and looked like the edge of a serrated knife. I descended to the Nepalese side where I could look down 3,000 feet of the Southwest Face. The other side was a 5,000 foot drop over the heavily corniced Kangshung Face. This was the most exposed section of the Southeast Ridge approach. Still, I was completely focused as I moved the ascender along the fixed rope and knew exactly where I was going to place each foot.

When I reached the bottom of the infamous Hillary Step, things were busy that day. It was the first weather window that season and I estimated more than 40 people gathered to make their way to the top. It was a classic traffic jam, with climbers both ascending (one hour) and descending (half hour). Although it's only a 40 foot fixed section of rock climbing, at nearly 29,000 feet elevation, it can be a real challenge for most. It was the only spot where I had to stop and wait, which I did for almost an hour.

With 40 years of rock climbing under my belt it was only a jug up a short pitch for me. As I made my way up the summit ridge, I ran into Sean coming down. We hugged and spoke briefly as we passed.

At 11:15 a.m. on May 16, 2002, I stepped onto the summit of Mount Everest. I had 45 minutes to spend on the top of the world. I soaked in every minute of it. The temperature was comfortable; the visibility super and there was no wind. So good were the conditions that Geoffrey referred to it as a beach party in down jackets. Geoffrey was doing snow-depth measurements for Bradford Washburn when I arrived. Once finished, he and Mike started back down.

"Randy, you look pretty tired," said Willie Benegas, as he prepared to descend. "Don't stay up here too long."

In spite of Willie's words, I removed my mask and shut off my oxygen to conserve as much as I could. I was completely out of oomph, totally spent and, with continuous use of the oxygen I had left, it wouldn't get me back to the South Col. Yet, in spite of that and Ang Tsering's pleading to the contrary,

I made my way over to an exposed shelf about 29 feet from the summit and collected nine small rocks.

Following that, I spent the next 30 minutes taking photos with my cardboard, disposable Kodak camera. Ang Tsering and I were the only ones there – we had the top of the world to ourselves!

I took in the entire experience with no parka wearing only fleece on my upper body and a heavy balaclava over my head. This window of good weather was projected to last another two full days before it would shut down again for several weeks.

I was acutely aware that most climbing accidents happened during descent. As I prepared to go down, I again donned my oxygen mask, rappelled the Hillary Step and traversed back to the South Summit. It was there I formulated a plan with Ang Tsering to have him watch me closely. We cut a piece of old, fixed line and roped ourselves together. It turned out to be a good thing because I stumbled several times while making my way down the mountain.

We ran into Charlie Fowler trying to locate one of his clients. He inquired as to whether or not I had seen him, but unfortunately I had not. As we neared the Balcony, the jet stream again shifted and the weather deteriorated. It was here that I ran out of oxygen. In spite of adjusting the liter flow to conserve my supply, I went through two four liter bottles and one three liter bottle during my climb above Camp IV. I also hadn't put my parka back on and my upper body was dressed only in fleece.

I decided not to put on my jacket. I was following the fuzzy logic that if I took the time to remove my gloves and take the parka out of the pack, I might drop something and that would be far worse than not wearing a coat. It was a difficult descent, to say the least and it took me another couple of hours to reach High Camp. It was a six hour descent from the summit to Camp IV at the South Col.

Later, I learned that Zoltan from the Hungarian team nearly died from pulmonary edema during his ascent. He was climbing without supplemental oxygen and collapsed in an area below the Balcony. Mike Morris made a Herculean effort to climb back up and aid in his rescue. They literally had to drag Zoltan's limp body down the Lhotse Face.

History was made a few weeks later when Zsolt of the Hungarian team made a successful summit using supplemental oxygen. He later went on to climb 12 of the world's 14 highest peaks before perishing while descending from the summit of Kangchenjunga.

After arriving at Camp IV, Ang Tsering knocked off my crampons and I crawled into my tent and collapsed. When I awoke, I looked at my watch to discover I had been asleep for eight hours. Unfortunately, at that altitude without supplemental oxygen the body does not recuperate. I actually felt more tired than when I had arrived.

I found a partially-filled bottle of oxygen, strapped it on and began my solo descent to Camp III. The oxygen ran out above Camp III and I descended the rest of the Lhotse Face to Camp II, my destination for that day. With this being the place where Peter lost his life a few weeks before, I was truly anxious. It took me eight hours to reach Advanced Base Camp solo - I double clipped and rechecked each rappel setup.

I spent the night at Advanced Base Camp before making my final trip through the dreaded Khumbu Ice Fall to Base Camp. Mount Everest is a climb that is not over until one is safely in Base Camp. Dangerous terrain combined with extreme fatigue is a sure-fire formula for disaster. Once in Base Camp, I treated myself to a meal of fried eggs, Vienna sausages and French fries.

As a Christian, I gave Jesus all the credit for my accomplishment. In this case, the power of prayer was unmistakable. Not only was I continually praying during the entire ordeal, but my friends and family did the same. I even read the complete New Testament while waiting in Base Camp. There is something about the ongoing exposure to high anxiety that drives one in that direction.

Once I had learned the summit window would be open to climb Everest, I emailed Doris and had her put me on our church's prayer chain. She then notified all our Christian friends, who in turn notified others. There were literally thousands praying for me, as I prayed for good weather along with a safe and successful summit. So powerful was this experience that I could literally feel the power of prayer while on the summit ridge. The incredible inner peace I felt was an amazing spiritual experience for me.

I would later discover that friends of mine in the State of Washington, whom I hadn't seen in years, were praying for me during the time I was above Camp IV. Believe me, this was an on-the-edge, scary experience. I completely underestimated the difficulty of this journey and know I would not have made it without the inner peace given me through that prayer support.

Back in Base Camp, it was time to make good on some stupid deals made contingent upon my summit and safe return. I agreed to eat an entire jar of Vegemite before leaving Base Camp, which was not something one should agree to as part of a celebration. Vegemite is a dark brown, Australian food paste made from yeast extract. It proved to be the worst tasting stuff imaginable.

After that and once I was back home, I would have to fulfill another promise. I said I would wear my 8,000 meter suit during Foresthill's 2002

Fourth of July Parade. Come Independence Day, I did just that. Boy, did I sweat in that sucker.

Bottom line, I was pleased to have climbed Everest, but really looked forward to again seeing my family and friends. Would I do it again? No, it is just too dangerous; although I was exhilarated at having done it. On May 19, 2002, I sent out my last update from Base Camp – "NEWS FLASH – Old man summits Mount Everest and lives to tell the story! Praise Jesus – I have climbed that sucker and I am leaving Base Camp tomorrow."

I left Base Camp May 20, 2002 and began the 40 mile hike to Lukla which took me two days. Along the way I spent the night in a very small teahouse near Phunki Tenga and watched a monk do his prayer wheel. In spite of his frequent coughing the ceremony was quite interesting.

In Lukla, high winds prevented any flights back to Kathmandu, so I had to stay there an extra day. It turned out a nearby village was holding its annual Wonz Blessing complete with horns, cymbals and chanting. The ceremony also called for the monks to wear ornate hats and robes. The event involves a reincarnated Lama and was attended by many nearby villagers. Only two other Westerners and I were there to witness it. However, there were also hundreds of armed, uniformed soldiers milling about because of the Maoist uprising.

After flying back to Kathmandu the next morning, I met with Henry (who was now allowed back in Nepal) and a group of friends for a celebration dinner. The following day, I started my journey home flying first to Bangkok, then Osaka, next to Los Angeles and then on to Sacramento. However, shortly before I departed Kathmandu, I began to feel sick. I spent two days in the air suffering from a fever, chills, shortness-of-breath, chest pains and an unbelievable headache. It was the sickest I had ever been in my life.

When Doris picked me up at the Sacramento Airport, I was so debilitated I had to have her carry my duffel bag to the car. Once we reached Foresthill, I tried to tough it out, but when my condition worsened, I went to the hospital. It was there I was told I had bacterial pneumonia. I suspect I picked it up from that coughing monk during my stay at the teahouse in the Khumbu. I was still tired and exhausted when I reached Phunki Tenga and probably quite susceptible to catching something.

Although the drugs prescribed worked quite fast and allowed me to work the next day, I didn't reach full strength until months later.

Top left - Peter Legate at Base Camp in April 2002

Top right - Ladders in the Khumbu Ice Fall

Upper right - Randy at the top of the Khumbu Ice Fall

Lower right - Peter Legate on the four-ladder crossing just below Camp I

Bottom right - The Lhotse Face just above Camp II

Bottom left - Randy at Camp III on the Lhotse Face

Top left - Lower Western Cwm

Top right - In the Western Cwm with the Summit of Everest in the background

Upper right - Climbing above Camp III on the Lhotse Face

Lower right - Fourth of July, Foresthill, CA

Bottom right - Randy and Ang Tsering Sherpa on the Summit of Mount Everest

Bottom left - Randy back at Base Camp after summiting Everest

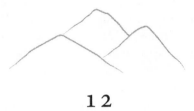

12

There's Still Adventure Out There

Boy, were we in trouble now. Our helicopter had not arrived to pluck us out of the isolated jungles of New Guinea which left us stranded and facing a five day march without food or support.

In a torrential downpour, we walked into a massive pit-mining operation where we were forced to surrender to the Indonesian Army. We were then placed in a large storage container and left there with six army regulars.

Communication was difficult since we did not speak Bahasa Indonesia nor they English. What happened next did not encourage us. The Indonesians began showing us videos on their cell phones of hostages being decapitated.

Africa

With Everest behind me, would it now be possible to complete the Seven Summits? What an amazing challenge, so why not go for it.

In August 2003, I had set my sights on Carstensz Pyramid, Irian Jaya (Papua New Guinea), Indonesia but circumstances prevented it. Technically, from a rock climbing perspective, it is considered the hardest of the Seven Summits, but even getting there is a challenge in itself.

First, the Indonesian Army would not issue me a permit at the time because a shooting had recently occurred in the region. And then, the day

I planned to fly there, the Marriott Hotel in Jakarta had been car-bombed.

After being turned away from Carstensz Pyramid, I immediately focused on Kilimanjaro. In November 2003, I organized an expedition to Africa, which I would lead. I chose the Machame Route. The route is approximately 30 miles long with exceptional beauty and superb views of Kilimanjaro's ice fields. It also had several steep sections and because the route traverses approximately half the mountain, one actually acclimatizes along the way. Kilimanjaro is a huge mountain with a diverse ecosystem including all five climate zones.

After nearly 30 hours of flying, we landed at Kilimanjaro International Airport late on the evening of November 29, 2003. Early the next morning, we departed for the Machame Gate (5,800 feet) to begin the climb.

I chose Zaria Tanzanian Adventures to provide for our eight day climb. I brought nine clients to help offset the cost of my climb and Zara added 20 porters, two cooks, a head guide and four assistant guides. As we trekked through the jungle with this large entourage and the porters carrying all of the equipment on their heads, we looked like a Victorian era expedition.

It took us six hours to reach Machame Hut at 10,000 feet, arriving late in the afternoon. On the second day, we traveled among giant heather, along steep forested hillsides and rocky ridges. We arrived at Shira Camp five hours later and another 2,000 feet higher up. Here we encountered snow and rain which resulted in wet gear. It took the entire night to get things partially dried out in our tents.

Day three we traversed up Kilimanjaro past Lava Tower to Barranco Camp at an elevation of 12,500 feet. There we dried our gear. Next we scrambled up the Great Barranco Wall and proceeded to traverse over scree and ridges to Karanga Valley Camp gaining another 500 feet of elevation. It was located beneath the icefalls of the Heim Kersten and Decken Glaciers. It took us about four hours and added to our acclimatization.

We then climbed up a ridge to Barafu Camp, reaching there about noon on day five. At 15,100 feet elevation, Barafu is the final camp before making the ascent to the top and is exposed with virtually no vegetation.

At midnight, we started the final climb up to and along the rim of the Kibo Crater between the Rebmann and Ratzel Glaciers. By 8 a.m. on December 5, 2003, the entire team reached Uhuru Peak (19,340 feet), Kilimanjaro's summit.

The views were spectacular. We could see Mount Meru to the west and the jagged peak of Mawenzi to the east. While on top, Ron Abram from Sacramento and I took time to honor Donald Barry, a friend lost to cancer, by distributing a portion of his ashes into the summit crater.

A half hour later, we dropped back down to Barafu Hut for lunch and a two hour rest. From there we descended to our camp near Mweka Hut located in a giant heater zone. The following day, we dropped down through the rain forest to Mweka Village arriving at 11 a.m. It took us one and a half days to make our descent from the summit to the check out station. From there we drove to our hotel in Moshi and a welcome shower.

While not technically difficult, Kilimanjaro is physically demanding and certainly no "piece of cake." It was an incredible experience and we were all pleased to have accomplished our mission.

On December 7, 2002, we set out on a five day safari through Northern Tanzania to include Lake Manyara National Park, Serengeti National Park, Olduvai Gorge and Ngorongo Crater Conservation Area. We traveled through some of the finest blends of landscapes, wildlife, people and archaeological sites I have ever seen. The accommodations were excellent and food exceptional. Our driver-guides were extremely knowledgeable as we passed elephants, rhinos, giraffes, lions, monkeys, birds and baboons – just to name a few of the animals we saw. We toured the Olduvai Gorge Museum learning about Leakey's "cradle of life" and visited Massai Tribes practicing centuries-old customs.

I repeated this adventure five more times in the next eight years and improved the expeditions with each successive trip. On one trip, I did manage to get ripped off of nearly $10,000 by a person in Africa whom I trusted. He said he had formed a new guiding business and I agreed to sign up with his company for my next expedition. After sending my deposit and partial payment, I discovered it was a total scam.

On the second trip, my wife, Doris, wanted to go so I jumped at the opportunity. I recruited 17 for the team ranging in age from 11 to 63. It would be the same as the first trip but I added the regional Massai market as part of our itinerary. Rarely do Westerners visit this market. There women are traded for goats and cows and this was culturally captivating to witness.

Subsequent trips added Tarangire National Park to the mix, with its fantastic Baobab trees and elephants. With each new trip I added something different for myself after the climb and safari: Kenya, Zanzibar, Zimbabwe, Zambia, South Africa, and Rwanda. Using local transportation and frequently traveling solo during these excursions, I did a variety of activities such as SCUBA diving, seeing mountain gorillas, chimpanzee trekking, surfing, river boarding and staying in bush camps.[44]

A truly unique trip took place in January 2011. It was my sixth time to climb Kilimanjaro and it was fantastic. After the climb and safari, we visited Lake Eyasi and spent the day with a hunter gatherer bushman community. We took a four wheel drive vehicle to a remote region of Tanzania and had a tracker and a guide take us to visit a nomadic Hadzabe tribe speaking

Khoisan, a nearly extinct click language.

While we were on a hunt with them, they killed a green monkey with a bow and arrow and then rubbed some sticks together to start a fire. They tossed the monkey on the fire and ate the animal on the spot – eyeballs, brains and testicles – every bit of it! All of this within ten minutes.

On one trip, I traveled alone to Ethiopia. I went to the Danakil Depression to visit the lowest point in Africa when a border conflict arose between Ethiopia and Eritrea. I had an armed guard and two army escorts with me when the fighting began.

The two army escorts drafted my guard as soon as the fighting started, and they participated in the skirmish. In spite of this, it was an amazing adventure to an extremely remote part of the world.

The large camel caravans hauling salt from the depression were incredible to watch. I also saw an Epiphany celebration in Lalibela and visited the rock hewn churches. The colorful and vibrant celebration involved hundreds of clergy dressed in robes and carrying umbrellas of many hues. Large crowds joined in the primitive dances and songs as they worked themselves into a frenzy both in and around the fantastic 13th-century monolithic cave churches.

Undisputed Seven Summits

The Seven Summits are composed of the highest peaks on each of the seven continents. However differing opinions exist as to which mountains make up those seven. Some see Mount Elbrus in the Caucasus as a part of Asia, not Europe. That would make Mount Blanc in the Alps the highest European peak. Debate remains over whether Mount Kosciuszko in Australia should be replaced by Indonesia's Puncak Jaya (Carstensz Pyramid). Dick Bass, the originator of the Seven Summits, says Kosciuszko. Reinhold Messner, considered by many to be the best climber alive, says Puncak Jaya. And neither includes Mount Blanc.

From a mountaineering point of view, Messner's list is the more challenging. Kosciuszko is little more than an easy hike; Carstensz Pyramid is an expedition. I think it should include all eight from both lists plus Mount Blanc. I call that the undisputed Seven Summits. By adding the North and South Poles, this becomes the explorer's or adventurer's grand slam.

Fundraising

I held a fundraising dinner-presentation at Monte Verde Inn near my home to help finance some of my climbing expeditions. More than 100 people attended, netting more than $4,000. I then held a similar event at Donner Ski Ranch and made a personal appearance for Townsend Bracing Solutions, picking up $4,000 at each. I had another 17 individual sponsors which brought my total fundraising to $16,000. This covered the total cost of my Everest expedition and cleared the way financially to climb in Antarctica.

Antarctica

By this time, I felt my goal of Seven Summits was coming into sight. I chose for my next conquest Vinson Massif in the Ellsworth Range of Antarctica. If time allowed, I planned to travel to the South Pole as well.

Private excursions to Antarctica are nearly impossible to arrange, so I decided to work with Alpine Ascents International in Seattle, WA. My expedition consisted of 17 climbers and four guides. These trips require carrying a heavy pack and pulling a sled equally as heavy. This requires being in excellent physical condition, with prior experience at high altitudes in cold temperatures.

I left Sacramento January 2, 2004 - summertime in Antarctica. The temperatures average approximately 18 degrees below zero Fahrenheit and can drop to minus 40 degrees on a cold day. Antarctica's strong winds contribute to the chill factor.

The lack of oxygen must also be considered because the South Pole is so far from the equator. Vinson Massif is slightly over 16,000 feet, but the oxygen pressure equates to 20,000 feet. Although not technically difficult, all the other extreme conditions rank it as the seventh most dangerous climb in the world. Fewer than 500 people have ever reached the top.

My predestination was Punta Arenas, Chile, for a final gear check and a four day wait to determine weather and ice conditions. Because of the expense of the flight and Antarctica's rapidly changing conditions, one has to be packed and ready to depart Punta Arenas within two hours. A flight that has to turn back after takeoff can cost the traveler a small fortune.

While there I enjoyed the sights made even more spectacular by the Christmas decorations still in place.

When the time came to leave, we boarded a dilapidated Russian IL-76TD Ilyushin airplane which resembled a mini C5A. It had a crew of four out of Kazakhstan and rested on a set of tires with the wire plies showing through. We had an exciting ride and landed on a three mile strip of blue ice at Patriot Hills Station. Patriot Hills is a seasonal camp of about 48 people located 1,800 miles from any city. We were given an introduction and orientation on the camp and the surrounding area.

The next afternoon, the weather cleared and we boarded a DHC6 Twin

Otter ski plane for a 90 minute trip to Vinson Base Camp 7,100 feet up on Branscomb Glacier. After a day there, we ferried loads to Camp I at 9,100 feet and then returned to Base Camp to spend the night. My pack weighed 40 pounds and the sled I pulled was 35 pounds. On the second day, we repeated the effort, but this time stayed at Camp I.

From there, we elected to bypass the traditional Camp II and carry loads directly to High Camp. High Camp is situated in the Vinson-Shinn Col at 12,300 feet. This decision saved us about two days, although we did make two trips up from Camp I, spending one more night there.

After only five days of climbing, we blew off a rest day and left for the summit. It was a tough day made even worse by a cold I caught from a fellow climber. My illness was at its worst the day we departed for the top, but the logistics and cost of this trip gave me no choice but to press on.

Misery can't begin to describe my journey, as mucous froze to the inner lining of my lungs and made it even more difficult for oxygen to enter my bloodstream. I hacked and coughed as each step became a huge chore. It took me nine and a half hours to reach Vinson Massif's summit and another two and a half hours to descend to High Camp. The views from the top of Ronne Ice Shelf of Mount Shinn and the surrounding area were incredible; that is, when I wasn't hallucinating and could see them. I threw up three times during our descent. It was the first time this had ever happened to me on a climb.

We took a rest day at High Camp and then loaded up 70 pound packs and headed back to Base Camp. I was still sick when I got there, but felt better by the time we arrived back at Patriot Hills. I took great pains to see to it no one caught my cold, as I felt no need to share the misery.

The trip was a success, but being sick didn't make it any easier. Nursing a cold in minus 40 degree temperatures made the climb much harder than expected.

Antarctica is roughly the size of the United States and Mexico combined with a permanent population of zero! The remoteness makes it otherworldly, but it is an amazing place. The interior is completely pristine and void of any life forms. We actually transported our feces back from the mountain leaving the area as we found it. I did suffer frost numbness in seven of my toes and lost my taste sensation. However, from experience, I knew my taste buds would eventually return and my toes would recover in three months.

It was truly an unrivaled and formidable challenge.

Following the climb, I arranged a flight to the South Pole to meet a team of five overland explorers. They had finished a 61 day, 600 mile trip from Hercules Inlet to the South Pole. One of the team members told me he became so bored during the trek he recited nursery rhymes to keep from going crazy. Some opt to do the "last degree," and hike the final 60 miles to the South Pole. Fortunately for me, I only had to go 600 feet to reach the South Pole from where the Twin Otter had landed – I felt no regrets doing it this way.

The South Pole experience is truly amazing. I did 31 clockwise laps around the geometrical pole and crossed the International Date Line each time, thus taking a full month off my age. I also toured the Amundsen-Scott South Pole Station and visited the ceremonial South Pole. I took some pictures and nearly froze off my rear.

The elevation at the South Pole is 9,300 feet above sea level and that day it was minus 40 degrees Fahrenheit. The skiing at the South Pole is great - two inches of powder on an 9,000 foot base.

After my trip to the South Pole, I had to wait several days at Patriot Hills for my flight back to Chile. I used the time to meet the staff and explored some abandoned stations. One under-ice storage area had an airplane inside. I also visited a repair site, where attempts were being made to restore a storm-damaged DC-3. Mechanics were working to fix it in time to fly back to Chile before winter set in.

Anxious to return home, I checked in so often with the station meteorologist that he finally took a cup containing chicken bones and tossed them on the floor. After studying them briefly, he announced my flight would be there the next day. To my amazement, the airplane arrived the following day.

It was the same Ilyushin that had dropped me off weeks before. I nicknamed it "The Illusion" since it never seemed to show up. But it came in, unloaded some fuel and supplies and wasted no time getting ready for the return trip to Punta Arenas.

There were only a few of us onboard for the trip to Chile. During the flight, I decided to look around and climbed up a ladder to the cockpit only to find the entire crew asleep, including the pilot. Of course, the aircraft flew on autopilot, but I did startle them when they awoke to find me standing there. In spite of my unexpected visit, the captain let me sit in his seat as we flew over the ocean, a very cool experience.

Upon my arrival in Chile, I rebooked my flights home and arrived in Foresthill less than a month after I had left. It was an exceptional experience, with all objectives accomplished.

Australia

In October 2004, while vacationing in Australia, Doris and I decided to go to the top of Kosciuszko (7,310 feet). It was near a ski hill where we planned to use the chair lift, but the journey still offered some unexpected challenges.

A storm was coming in and in our haste to get to Kosciuszko, I was stopped and given a speeding ticket. When we arrived, the chair lift was ready to close and would only take us up to the top, but not bring us back down. After hiking to the summit, we had to work our way down in the dark with the storm fast approaching. We had only one small flashlight between us, so I gave it to Doris as we stumbled our way back down the ski slope toward the small village below on a dark and stormy night.

I made better time than Doris and was 150 feet in front of her when, in the darkness, I spotted what I thought was a bear. Having lost sight of me, Doris called out for me to wait. I didn't want to answer for fear the bear might decide to attack, but that infuriated Doris more and she read me the riot act. However, the "bear" turned out to be a huge, harmless wombat, so we passed by without incident and reached our car just as the storm hit full force. We returned to the coast without further incident.

North Pole

Having reached the top of Kosciuszko on October 27, 2004, I completed the Bass version of Seven Summits. At 58 years, 321 days, I became the 91st to climb them and the second oldest American to have done it. With that behind me, I immediately started planning a trip to the North Pole to complete the Adventure Grand Slam.

It would be the final expedition of this daunting project and there were plenty of hurdles to overcome. I first made my arrangements through Curtis Lieber of Global Expedition Adventures. They planned to utilize a French organization to handle logistics and get our team to the Arctic ice flow. Historically, the Russians controlled logistics to the Arctic and five days before we were to depart, the French and Russians had come to an impasse. Our expedition was canceled.

The cancelation was bad enough, but I had already wired a considerable sum of money to the French company. Thanks to Curtis, I did get my money back several months later. He worked tirelessly to get me a refund and eventually took the money from his own resources after the French enterprise went belly up.

With the promise of a refund, I hooked up with Robert Russell of Eagles Cry Adventures to arrange an alternate expedition. Robert proved to be a miracle worker and a deal was made with the Russians two days before our scheduled departure. I would be part of a ten member team led by Victor Boyarsky. Boyarsky was a famous veteran of Arctic and Antarctic expeditions.

On April 6, 2005, I set out on the arduous 27 hour journey to Longyearbyen, Spitsbergen, Svalbard, an international group of islands under Norwegian sovereignty regulated by the Svalbard Treaty of 1920. Longyearbyen is located 78 degrees north and well above the Arctic Circle. It was quite cold, despite the fact the sun never sets at that time of year. It is a settlement of approximately 1,800 inhabitants and the major form of transportation is by snowmobile.

While there, I visited a church, the museum and took a couple of snowmobile trips to Temple Fjord and the Russian settlement of Barentsburg. I also entered into an ice cave where the ice was 3,000 years old, visited a working coal mine and mushed a dog sled.

A rifle must be carried at all times when outside the settlements or on the ice flow because of polar bears. I also sampled polar bear meat, as well as reindeer and raw whale. After paying the Russians for the expedition, I boarded an Antonov 74 (a high-wing, jet engine cargo plane) for a two and a half hour flight to Borneo Ice Base (89 degrees, 12 minutes north). The temperature there measured minus 30 degrees Fahrenheit with a 20 mph wind, which equates to minus 60. Exposed flesh freezes in about five minutes. There is no solar heating because the sun only gets a few degrees above the horizon in April, which is essentially the tail end of winter.

It is necessary to time the trip in early spring to avoid running into leads. Leads are long narrow areas of open water which increase as summer approaches. Unlike summer expeditions on glacial land masses in the Himalayas and Antarctica where the sun is higher in the sky offering warmer temperatures, the Arctic is cold beyond imagination in April. The temperature never rose above minus ten degrees Fahrenheit and with the constant wind the equivalent temperature never exceeded minus 35 degrees. The consensus among those in the know in our group was that it felt colder than usual in spite of there being a lot of open water. To avoid confusion, everyone remained on Norwegian Daylight Savings Time, which is two hours behind Coordinated Universal Time (UTC).

We decided to spend the night at Borneo Ice Base to allow a large lead north of us to freeze over. This also gave each of us a chance to check out our skis, sledges and personal equipment. To help pass the time, two talented members of the group played guitar and sang for us.

A helicopter rescue was mounted while we were in Borneo Ice Base to bring back a Swiss skier who attempted to solo the last 120 miles to the North Pole. He had lost his tent in a fire and was exposed to the extreme Arctic conditions. Four other Swiss members of our party dropped out of the expedition after spending an extremely cold night in the large unheated tent with us. They had come to the conclusion they were not equipped or prepared for what lay ahead.

Georges, the Swiss who had been rescued, decided to join us and complete the final degree to reach the North Pole. I ended up paired with Georges when my partner who was the only other American in our group decided one half mile out that he, too, couldn't make it. Our party now included two Russians, our leader Victory Boyarsky and Victor Serov, two Czechs, Jakeš Meroslav (the guitar player now on his seventh trip) and his client Vaclav (a 42 year old film maker), Georges and me.

At 40, Georges planned to solo from Siberia to the North Pole the following year. These five were strong and experienced Arctic explorers. At 59, I was the weakest of the bunch.

It was an amazing journey, both difficult and deeply moving. To begin with, we had to travel over a sheet of ice larger than the contiguous United States that varied in thickness from two inches to 30 feet and floated on a 13,000 foot deep body of water. The ice floe, being driven by the wind, was in constant motion so our position could change even when we camped.

This movement caused pressure ridges to form up to 15 feet high and leads spanning 100 yards in all directions to open and close daily. When climbing over pressure ridges, the shifting ice would make loud noises as the ridge would literally move beneath us. All together, it made progress slow, dangerous and extremely difficult.

Using GPS, we would travel for six to eight hours on skis with skins while wearing a heavy pack and pulling an even heavier sledge. We averaged a net distance of five to 12 miles a day. I say "net," because travel was rarely in a straight line and the drifting ice always seemed to be working against us. One day, we peaked at 12 miles only to have the ice move us back three miles over night.

We often crossed leads on thin layers of young sea ice. As the ice formed it would trap pockets of water and, in effect, squeeze the salty sea water out the bottom and leave the newer ice flexible and weak – the younger the ice the weaker it was. One could actually see the ice bend under our weight while skiing across it.

Vaclav, 15 feet in front of me, broke through the ice and was submerged chest deep in freezing water. He slithered out but within minutes literally turned into a cartoon-like human Popsicle. We had to immediately set up camp as Jakeš began the long process of drying him out.

Typically, it took an hour to set up camp and another hour to break it down and pack the sledges. Cooking and drying gear took three hours at night and another two in the morning. The nice part is that using the stove in the tent made it relatively warm inside. We rested ten hours a night and I slept amazingly sound. One expends a great deal of energy each day just keeping warm.

It is important to either keep moving or seek shelter because when standing still outside it doesn't take long to freeze. Going to the bathroom was a chore we had to time carefully.

While moving, it is necessary to be dressed on the verge of staying cold because sweat can freeze on the body and drop one's core temperature. Melting it with vigorous activity only makes the body wetter and the core temperature drops even faster.

The diet consists of lots of fluids and fats to generate the energy necessary to survive and work in such a hostile environment. I was warned the food supplied by the Russians would not be palatable, but I stuck with the program. This meant eating raw meat, munching on cubes of butter and lots of chocolate – I had no problem with the last one.

Another little annoyance occurred when we came across some fresh polar bear tracks – they measured 16 inches across! We immediately readied two rifles, just in case the bear should decide to continue tracking us and attack.

Besides the cold, perhaps the worst part of the trip turned out to be Georges. For whatever reason, Georges hated Americans. He had no respect for me and managed to make my life a living hell for seven of the eight days we spent together on the ice. He was extremely rude and condescending to me and arrogant to boot. He took the attitude he was always right and any problems which arose had been created by me. He made it abundantly clear he didn't want to engage in conversation unless he initiated it, which consisted of repeated attempts to belittle and taunt me. He ordered me around as if I were his servant instead of his expedition partner.

He was also physically intimidating, having placed third in European championship kick-fighting in the mid 1990s. He was a bodyguard by profession.

But his actions proved misleading. He was never physically abusive and was surprised when I confronted him to inquire whether he would try to beat me up if I pissed him off. In fairness to him, being as strong as he was, Georges carried more than his fair share of the total load on the trip.

He was used to going solo on outdoor excursions and did not want a tent partner, whether me or anyone else. His plans to solo to the North Pole had been thwarted by his tent burning down and he was as mad as hell. He occasionally did show moments of kindness and once loaned me his iridium phone so I could call home. What I found additionally frustrating, when we were together with the group, he was actually downright friendly to me.

But it was what it was: the single most outrageous and hostile experience I had ever encountered in my more than 45 years of adventure travel. And to top it off, when we reached the ice base at the end of our expedition, he told me I had earned his respect and actually engaged me in friendly conversation during our last night together in the tent.

Bottom line: it was a character-building experience. My deep faith in Jesus coupled with decades of outdoor experience helped me rise above the situation. I enjoyed the trip in spite of Georges and came to the conclusion that I was probably best suited to deal with him, as another might not have been able to cope with the added stress. In the end, it was just something that happened and I didn't feel a need to blame anyone.

Our fourth day out I did discuss the situation with Victor Serov, but knew I had limited options and prepared to complete the journey in spite of it. However, when it was over, I did give a detailed description of my ordeal to a couple of the others.

On the eighth day, we reached the North Pole at 2 p.m. UTC. I felt a real sense of accomplishment and didn't let my internal conflict spoil the experience. I knew Jesus had protected me and helped me to overcome all the physical and mental hurdles. It was an incredible journey. That same afternoon, a helicopter picked us up and took us back to the ice base.

Before leaving Borneo, I used the base shortwave equipment to make several ham radio contacts. I also visited with staff and those in other expeditions. I received a trophy commemorating my trip, along with the suggestion I deserved three: one for making it, another for doing it on Russian-supplied food and the last for putting up with Georges!

As for Georges, I sincerely prayed he would be richly blessed. In 2006, he did indeed attempt a solo Arctic crossing, but his trip was aborted.

Physically, I had some frostbite on my throat and on five of my fingers and some numbing to my ears and face. Over the next several weeks my tissue healed and nerve endings regenerated.

Perhaps Apsley Cherry-Garrard said it best in his book *The Worst Journey in the World*, "Polar exploration is at once the cleanest and most isolating way of having a bad time which has been devised."

It was April 20, 2005 when I flew back to Longyearbyen and my flight home left five days later.

New Guinea

Deep in my soul, I wanted to finish the undisputed version of the Seven Summits (Messner's list) and I was not willing to give up on Carstensz. At 16,023 feet, it is the highest peak of the Australian tectonic plate, often referred to as Oceania and is located in Irian Jaya (New Guinea).

It had great appeal, requiring a difficult expedition involving technical rock climbing in a very remote part of the world. The Indonesian government stopped issuing permits to any Western climbers and that made it all the more challenging. It must be pointed out that permits were being denied because of safety. The OPM rebel group was conducting guerilla activity in an attempt to gain independence for Papua.

The situation was further complicated by the presence of the enormous and not well publicized Grasberg Gold Mine, located between the mountain and Tembagapura. It was an area designated as strictly "off limits." The mine had become a flashpoint in the struggle for independence and was viewed as imperialist and a source of pollution.

The mine was owned by Freeport Mine, an American corporation. And to make matters worse, U.S. President George W. Bush had included Indonesia in the "Axis of Evil" for supporting terrorism. Permitting climbers to climb Carstensz was seen as adding to the bad press.

After three years, I finally got my breakthrough in 2005. Franky Kowaas of Manado, Indonesia obtained a permit and I was to be part of the first legal expedition granted since 2002. It would include Americans James Clarke and Pat Hickey. Clarke was a West Point graduate and former Army Ranger and special operations officer. He also had an MBA from Harvard. Hickey (DrPH) was a clinical assistant professor of nursing at the University of South Carolina.

There remained considerable apprehension regarding our safety in Indonesia. However, when we arrived in Manado on the north end of the Sulawesi Province, the people were helpful and friendly. It turned out to be one of the nicest places I had ever visited. Not only were we welcomed, but the natives went out of their way to assist us. We had contact with the police in Nabire, Enarotali and Timika and found them all to be professional, polite, thorough and extremely helpful.

Clarke proved invaluable in assessing helicopter capabilities, logistics, mission planning with the pilots and when interacting with the local military. He also had knowledge of the region and knew how to maintain the lines of communication. Hickey served as our health care professional, while I provided big wall climbing skills and expedition leadership. My ability to remain calm under stress also helped steady everyone's nerves.

This would be a trailblazing effort, working out the details as we progressed. Our particular skills and group dynamic gave us the patience necessary to pull off this risky adventure. Franky was a Christian and had the street smarts we needed, although the permits were only a part of what it would take to get us to the top of Carstensz. He earned the complete trust I placed in him.

Before leaving Manado to fly to Papua, Franky took us on a tour of the Minahasa Highlands, the local market at Tomohon where dogs, rats, bats and snakes could be bought for consumption. We also saw remote villages such as Rurukuna, rode in a Banndi (horse-drawn cart), had an incredible fish dinner at Lake Tondano and visited Sulfur Lake.

Franky secured our Surat Jalan (travel permits) in Jakarta and negotiated approvals from provincial and district police across Papua. We left Manado and flew to Biak, an island north of Papua. There we visited some caves used by the Japanese in World War II and also toured the MacArthur Museum. After our stay in Biak, we flew to Nabire and chartered a flight with Associated Mission Aviation to the highland village of Enarotali, where we planned to acclimatize. Enarotali is at 5,500 feet elevation and has approximately 4,000 residents.

After we exhausted every resource to try to go overland across the mine, we decided to charter a helicopter. That meant Franky and James would have to return to Nabire, while Pat and I held down the fort in Enarotali. We had packed malaria pills, but neither Pat nor I bothered taking them. Malaria is a real problem in the Papua Province. On a visit to a local medical facility, Pat discovered several patients had contracted malaria. Pat and I were beginning to wish we had taken the pills.

While in Enarotali, the province governor visited the area and we also witnessed a clan war. A dispute had arisen over the death of a tribal member. A dozen or so large clans formed warrior groups and converged with spears, bows and arrows. What took place became a thousand person strong day long "ritual war" consisting of war dancing with weapons in hand. They literally worked themselves into a frenzy. When it ended, one side paid the other side restitution of 20,000 kina, which is approximately $10,000 and everybody went home satisfied.

It was scary at first, because we didn't know what was going on as all hell broke loose around us. However, it turned out like something from a National Geographic special with men clad only with penis gourds and the village women dressed only in grass skirts. It proved both interesting and entertaining.

The delays we experienced became hurry-up-and-wait situations and Pat and Franky became discouraged. Pat was ready to abandon the expedition and go home. Franky's negotiations drove him to tears. I offered words of encouragement to help restore confidence while James made headway convincing the helicopter pilots the altitudes where they would be flying would not adversely affect them or their passengers. The pilots feared the oxygen pressure would not be enough to see us through.

Fortunately, James and I managed to keep our little adventure alive.

A Bell 212 helicopter arrived the morning of July 5, 2005 and by 9:20 a.m. we had the mountain in sight. A little over two hours later, we were hiking up to Base Camp carrying an incredible amount of equipment. Events finally turned our way as we met up with six indigenous natives near Zebra Wall. They were on a trek between villages and we managed to convince three of them to assist us with our gear. With their help, we reached the 13,800 foot elevation Lakes Valley Base Camp early in the afternoon of July 7, 2005.

We hoped for the arrival of a second chopper carrying a support team and more supplies. However, a storm moved in and the second helicopter never showed up.

Short on supplies and afraid we might never have this chance again, we pushed up the mountain right after midnight. Fortunately our acclimatization, cut short by the scheduling snafus, proved adequate to make the climb. It included our stay at Enarotali, a short stop at Zebra Wall (12,100 feet) and an afternoon and night in pounding rain at Base Camp.

Franky had reached the summit of Carstensz 22 times before and was well-versed on our planned route. Much to his credit, he let us climb as individuals. James and I had met in Yosemite National Park to plan for this trip and knew if we could get to the base of the mountain we would make it to the top. Franky's previous experience made it that much easier, but I was pleased he didn't try to guide us.

We were prepared to climb without fixed lines, but there were some lines in place from a previous Indonesian ascent. With the added precipitation of the storm, we were concerned we might run into ice and snow on the summit ridge.

Franky did give me an hour's head start and the go-ahead to tackle the route solo, but by the time I found it in the dark, the others had caught up. From Yellow Valley, it was nearly impossible to see the face of the mountain at night.

I jumared the first overhanging pitch and soloed up the first 1,500 feet, inspecting the fixed lines and their anchors en route. I then reached the halfway point a few hours later. The length and nature of some of the pitches made communication difficult, but before long we were together again to begin our ascent of the upper half of the route. We continued in pairs. James and I located the route above an area known as the terrace and made our way to the long summit ridge.

In the early light of dawn, we negotiated a series of airy pinnacles, notches and catwalks - rappelling and using the jumars when necessary. Although the rain held off, at times our visibility was limited by fog. Snow covered several pitches, but it did not present a problem. James and I made the summit before 9 a.m. and Franky and Pat arrived an hour later.

Upon our descent, the rains returned and pounded us once again. We arrived back at Base Camp cold and wet, but none the worse for wear. We were all elated to have climbed Carstensz Pyramid.

The next day, we returned to Zebra Wall to await pick up by helicopter. As time passed, while we stood in a downpour, it became painfully obvious our airlift back to civilization wasn't coming. It confirmed for us how essential satellite phones are for these types of expeditions and unfortunately we did not have one.

As we discussed our dilemma, we determined our only options were to go on a five day march through the jungles of New Guinea without food or support, or climb over the huge tailings of the Grasberg Mine. In spite of it being illegal, we chose to go over the tailings.

The sight of this pit-mining operation amazed us. Huge trucks, standing 24 feet tall on tires measuring 12 feet in diameter, hauled 400 tons of mineral-rich soil at speeds reaching 40 miles per hour – impressive.

Eventually, Franky flagged down one of these enormous vehicles and climbed the 15 stairs to reach the cab. After a brief conversation with the driver, Franky got in and the truck disappeared, while his three American companions remained standing in a deluge.

Realizing Franky was our only hope, we had little choice but to wait patiently for his return.

After an hour passed, a military vehicle pulled up and an Indonesian Army officer ordered us to get in. We were taken to a large storage container that doubled as barracks for the enlisted men. We remained there with six army regulars who spoke only Bahasa Indonesia, but at least we were out of the rain. Without Franky, we tried using sign language in order to communicate and eventually the soldiers showed us videos on their cell phones. Unfortunately, the videos were of hostages being decapitated – not too encouraging indeed.

After a few tense hours, Franky and the officer who drove us to our destination showed up. They brought with them box lunches and news we would be taken to the nearby town of Tamika – imagine the relief.

From Tamika, we arranged flights to Makassar and onto Manado. From there, it was on to Singapore, Seoul and San Francisco.   I reached Sacramento the afternoon of July 14, 2005.

After our complicated epic journey to the top of Carstensz, that mountain is now routinely climbed by Westerners booked through a variety of very expensive commercial expedition providers.

By far, Carstensz was the most exotic expedition I had ever experienced. At 8:51 a.m., July 8, 2005, I was the 46th and oldest person to complete the Messner version of the Seven Summits.

As for the undisputed Seven Summits (nine summits including Carstensz and Kosciuszko as well as Elbrus and Mount Blanc), I have no idea how many other souls, if any, have completed this daunting objective.

Adventure Grand Slam

I now have the distinction of being the eighth person in the world to complete the Adventure Grand Slam.[45] I was the oldest person to ever do it and only the second American. My quest began in May 1988 with Denali and over a 17 year period, I climbed the undisputed Seven Summits (highest peaks on the seven continents), plus Mount Blanc and Kosciuszko. I have been to both the North Pole and South Pole, including a 100 mile ski trip over the final degree to reach the North Pole. I've also climbed the elusive Carstensz Pyramid (16,023 foot elevation) in Papua Province, Indonesian New Guinea in 2005.

The majority of these expeditions I either led or they were facilitated (climbed independently with arrangements made by others).

Personally, I think I did this lifetime goal in the best possible manner I could which gave me tremendous satisfaction.

Leading Expeditions

During a 12 year period beginning in 2001, I began doing fundraisers and taking clients on expeditions to pay for my climbing sojourns. I was able to cover the expenses of previous outings and fully fund those I was planning. I liked that my excursions were not putting a drain on our retirement resources and I basically became a professional climber. I wasn't making a living at it, but no longer had any out-of-pocket expenses when traveling.

I was taking expeditions at least once a year and often twice a year. I also obtained sponsorship from technical instrument companies, event-type resorts, ski resorts, sporting-goods stores, radio stations and even a knee-brace company.

My fundraising expeditions were primarily aimed at introducing non climbers to lofty peaks and edgy situations they would not otherwise experience. I had been spearheading expeditions for as long as I could remember, but these were the first for newcomers. These group trips not only paid for my expenses, but also covered Doris' expenses when she came along. I worked through local guides and providers in the various countries to make sure things would go smoothly.

Russian Caucasus

In July 2006, I took six clients to the top of Mount Elbrus in the Russian

Caucasus with temperatures reaching 25 degrees below zero Fahrenheit. It was a virtual repeat of my first climb of the 18,510 foot peak five years earlier.

We also toured St. Petersburg and Moscow, including the capital city's 110 year old Sandunoff Bath House - it was like a sauna on steroids! We were told the banya was a favorite hangout for the Russian Mafia: everyone is naked (men's and women's facilities are separate) so conversations can't be recorded.

After a shower and ten minutes in the sauna wearing a felt-type beanie, we took turns beating each other with leaved branches called feniky to open our pores. Following this, we jumped into a pool of cold water to close those same pores. This process is repeated four times. Some do break this routine by having either some tea or beer and something light to eat while still in the nude.

After two cycles, I was cooked medium rare and ready for a break. I returned to the locker room and sat across from a Russian fellow who struck up a conversation. To my surprise, he told me he was a pirate!

After he laughed off my asking if he plundered seagoing vessels, he said he pirated illegal copies of American movies. He could pay off projectionists to get several thousand high-quality digital copies to sell on the streets within a day of the film's grand opening.

Third World Doctors

In January 2007, I organized an expedition to climb Cerro Aconcagua in Argentina. I had climbed that peak in 1991 and didn't expect the mess this turned out to be.

It started with flight delays in both Dallas and Santiago, putting my seven clients and me a day behind schedule. By picking up our pace, we made up the time and reached Mendoza, traveled overland to Puente del Inca and reached the first camp at Confluencia on the date originally planned. This happened before the blood-pressure debacle started.

Although I take medications for it, my blood pressure tends to read above normal. For that reason, I was held up at Confluencia for four days by a relatively inexperienced doctor authorized to turn back climbers at his discretion.

My frustration with the doctor was further exacerbated by comments from other staff employees speaking of his incompetence and bad attitude. His behavior told me he was nothing more than a government bureaucrat needing to turn back a certain quota of people in order to justify his position. Fortunately, my team was able to go on to Plaza de Mulas without me. In order to make good use of my time, I would sneak out of camp and acclimatize by taking difficult, high-altitude hikes.

I had thought having my blood pressure checked was a mandatory procedure. As it turned out, it was voluntary and I could have declined the "service" had I known. VO Roberson, a medical doctor and a member of our group, said a diastolic of less than 100 mm Hg would do fine at high altitudes and mine read less than 100. After sneaking out of camp for a seven and a half hour hike to Plaza Francia and back with a total elevation gain of nearly 3,000 feet, my BP reading an hour later in Confluencia was 150/80. An EKG was then performed which read within normal limits.

I was satisfied with that and with the fact I showed no symptoms of mountain sickness after my climb.

I radioed Al Albright, whom I had put in charge of the group in my absence and told him I would hike up to Plaza de Mulas "under the radar" and rejoin the expedition. Unbeknownst to me, my transmission was monitored and afterward I was summoned to the park ranger's camp. I was told I would have to leave the mountain the following morning or face arrest and a possible fine. What I did know was they had the authority to do it. I had no desire to see if the jails in Argentina were worse than the one in Yosemite!

In my absence, my clients climbed within four hours of Aconcagua's summit, only to be turned back by a storm which settled in at the 20,800 foot level. If I had been there with my leadership skills, the trip might have turned out differently – what a bummer.

After returning home, I had my blood pressure taken. It read 148/74, close to what it was at Confluencia. A week later, it measured about the same. My medical records showed a reading of 138/78 during a pre-climb physical in October, 2006.

Such readings are normal for me. I am convinced I was in no medical danger and should have been allowed to lead my expedition. Furthermore, I think my blood pressure was also affected by the stress brought on by the doctor in Confluencia. His incompetence was further demonstrated by his use of the oximeter readings as a screening tool to turn away climbers. High-altitude climbers know oximeter readings are only a relative indicator; low readings mean very little. As a matter of fact, my oxygen levels were quite high.

Déjà vu All Over Again

In April 2010, I arrived in Lhasa, Tibet three days ahead of some clients I agreed to lead to Everest Base Camp. With the extra time, I visited the Jolkhang Temple and Portola Place and they were mind blowing.

Lhasa is also a great place to do some people watching. Returning to Kathmandu, I met up with my clients.

We had a fantastic trek to the Base Camp. I wasn't under any pressure to climb and fully enjoyed the experience. We made many memorable stops and the food was excellent. There were 14 clients of which 11 had accompanied me on previous expeditions.

We climbed Kala Patthar on the way to Base Camp. Next we spent two nights at Base Camp during which time Al Albright suffered what appeared to be a trans-ischemic attack (TIA) and had to be taken out by helicopter. The ordeal frightened him.

In spite of this unfortunate episode, I visited with Henry Todd who had organized my Everest expedition eight years before and I enjoyed my time at Base Camp. After a brief lesson in ice climbing, I took the clients for a short unauthorized excursion into the Khumbu Ice Fall.

I was feeling a bit melancholy when we left. I kept looking back and thinking I may never see this again. On the way back, three clients and I climbed Island Peak, including a 1,000 foot ice face that angles about 70 degrees. It was in poor condition and the scamper was much more difficult than when I did it in 2002. Once back in Kathmandu, we took an extensive tour of the area before leaving for home.

In Search of Noah's Ark

My next expedition was to climb Mount Ararat (16,854') in Eastern Turkey in July 2012. This fantastic 16 day adventure included climbing the highest mountain in Turkey and the final resting place of Noah's Ark, as well as visits to Turkey's most exciting sights (e.g., Istanbul, Cappadocia, Ephesus, Pergamum, etc.). This area is rich in history and strife and for much of the 20th century was a militarized zone.

Only within the past few years has Mount Ararat been open for climbing by Westerners. I led a group of 17 folks plus Doris and me. This turned out to be one of the best expeditions I have ever experienced. For nearly a week we saw virtually no other Westerners and the places we visited were quite remote. Following this trip, Doris and I continued onto Uzbekistan and traveled along the "Silk Road."

Mexican Volcanoes

The next client-based expedition came in November 2013 to climb Orizaba (18,491 feet), a fantastic volcano deep in the heart of Mexico. Besides some great sightseeing we also rafted down the Rio Filobobos, did mountain biking, zip-lining, canyoneering and even some rock climbing. After the clients left, I stayed on in Mexico and spent a few days in Guanajuato and San Miguel de Allende, which are both fascinating World Heritage Sites.

One Last Big Mountain?

In July 2014, I finally made the journey to the mountains of Northern Pakistan. I had planned to climb Gasherbrum II solo and without supplemental oxygen. Having climbed Cho Oyo from Tibet and Everest from Nepal, I really felt this would be a fitting finish to my high altitude climbing by summiting a third 8000 meter peak in a different country.

The previous year, the Taliban had hiked into the Nanga Parbat Base Camp and proceeded to rob and murder 11 climbers. In fact, the US Department of State had warned Americans to defer all non-essential travel to Pakistan, stating that the presence of several foreign and indigenous terrorist groups throughout the country posed a significant threat. This made it impossible for me, as an American, to secure a climbing visa.

I settled instead for a trekking visa with the ultimate objective of hiking to the K2 Base Camp. To accomplish this, I hired a local outfitter to provide transportation, equipment, food and porters for my expedition. Next, I bought my airline ticket and amidst protests by virtually all my family and friends, I flew off to Islamabad.

My plans were to immediately fly to the small village of Skardu in Northern Pakistan, however this turned out to be a major fiasco. The airline canceled the flight at the last minute and this erupted into a big protest with all of the passengers refusing to leave the domestic airport terminal. After several hours of argumentative confrontations between locals and the airline officials, we were all promised compensation and re-booked for an early flight the next day. As soon as we left the terminal, the official reneged and we got nothing. They did, however, honor the re-booking and the next morning I arrived in Skardu.

Two days later after a mandatory meeting with government officials, I left in a four wheel drive vehicle for the remote Baltistan village of Askoli. Once again my plans were disrupted, this time by a suspension bridge that required repair before we could continue our journey. Two hours later after the "miraculous" repair and a bribe, we were again on our way.

After a night in Askoli, I began the long and difficult hike to the K2 Base Camp in the Karakorum mountain range. This 14 day trek was an order of magnitude more difficult then hiking into Nepal's Everest Base Camp. There are no facilities beyond Askoli and the trail system is non-existent in many places. Endless boulder hopping, difficult stream crossings, tricky route finding, and horribly hot weather characterize the travel along the 96 miles of glacial moraines one must traverse to reach the K2 Base Camp and return. Unfortunately while hiking alone, I made several route finding errors adding significantly to the overall difficulty.

The food was basic but healthy consisting of chapathi (flat bread), rice, dal (lentil), chicken and mutton (goat meat). The hygiene, however, was a problem resulting in having two separate multiday episodes of traveler's dysentery.

Concordia at an elevation of 15,255 feet is at the junction of several glaciers and is an area of exceptional beauty. To the left are K2 and Broad Peak and to the right are Gasherbrum I and Gasherbrum II. These four peaks are the world's second, 12th, 11th and 13th highest mountains respectively. Another beautiful peak, Gasherbrum IV, lies straight ahead. I spent a total of three days at this magnificent location.

After continuing onto K2 base camp (16,500 feet) for a visit with some climbing teams, then returning down the Godwin Austen Glacier to the Broad Peak Base Camp for an overnight stay, I encountered a serious problem. The two base camps are about three hours apart and while descending the glacier by myself from K2, I managed to fall into a glacial stream late in the day just as a storm approached. While being swept along the ice by the frigid water and becoming thoroughly soaked, I said out loud to myself, "You're really in trouble now Randy."

Racing against time to avoid becoming irreversibly hypothermic, it took me over an hour to reach the 16,000 foot elevation Broad Peak Base Camp. Once there, only after several hours in my sleeping bag was I able to control the shivering and re-warm my body. Did I mention that I had been suffering from a severe bout of traveler's dysentery for three days just prior to this incident?

By the time I returned to Concordia, I was actually relieved that I had not received permission to climb Gasherbrum II – I was just too sick and worn out to have climbed it.

The rewards of this trek were astounding – four of the world's biggest mountains are located in close proximity in this mountain range and the scenery is unparalleled. On one occasion, an army group stopped and asked me how old I was. When I responded that I was 68 years old they all clapped and cheered and then took a photo with me.

After returning to Askoli, I next traveled and hiked to Fairy Meadows located just below the Nanga Parbat Base Camp in the Western Himalaya. This was another fantastic experience and the views of the world's ninth highest mountain were a visual feast – just remarkable.

The plus side of all the negative reports regarding travel within Pakistan was that tourism was down by over 90 percent so it was not crowded and there were very few westerners in the country – I like it this way. I found the people to be very friendly and was frequently asked to pose for photos with local folks. Amazingly, a lot of people carried weapons and it was difficult to tell who was who since the army personnel didn't wear uniforms. The Taliban were indeed around, but I really did not feel threatened.

This was another journey to the edge – an amazing adventure.

Highpointing

Over the years, Doris and I gathered up the dog and cat, put them in our RV and went "Highpointing." It's a unique experience that involves reaching the highest point in each of the 50 states. We traveled to places we'd never been before, visiting sites where people typically don't go. Since I already had summited several hard peaks such as Denali, Rainier, Hood, etc., we decided to go for it.

Montana's Granite Peak (12,799 feet) and Gannett Peak in Wyoming (13,804) were more difficult, so I climbed these without Doris. They were also remote and the routes were not easy to find.

Adding to the difficulties of climbing Gannett was the prearranged transportation that did not show up. That meant, after hiking 45 miles, I had to walk another 13 miles to the highway and hitchhike my way back to our vehicle.

The transportation had been arranged with some Shoshone Indians, so I went to their home and refused to leave until they reimbursed me. As I sat in their living room, several big guys entered and glared at me. I started to wonder if standing my ground was worth the $100 I had prepaid. Fortunately, I eventually got my money back.

By bundling these climbs with Utah's Kings Peak (13,528 feet) into a nine day stretch, I hiked 103 miles and gained more than 29,000 feet of elevation. This included soloing 600 feet of fifth-class rock and 500 feet of a 50 degree snow couloir. After completing my quest going up Mauna Kea in Hawaii, April 2008, I became the 173rd to highpoint all 50 states and the third person in the world to ever complete the 750 – Seven Summits and all 50 States.

Fifty Crowded Climbs

In July 2007, while still working on the *Fifty Classic Climbs of North America*, I met up with Bob Odom and together we took care of some unfinished business by tackling the North Ridge of Stuart in Washington. It turned out not to be that easy, taking us 13 hours to go from glacier to summit. It involved two bivouacs: one on Goat Pass and one on the summit.

Bob started off in the lead and when he grew tired I took over. We had to climb some difficult pitches wearing mountain boots and carrying heavy packs - not my idea of fun. On top, where we spent the night, I had no food, water, shelter or sleeping bag and it was cold. What was to be a two day trip had turned into three, so the next morning we made our way back down and hiked out to the car.

Bob and I were trashed, but felt we had made a solid climb which resulted in a memorable experience. Being a day late getting back, Doris had expressed concern to other campers who advised her to call Search and Rescue. Knowing better, she wisely didn't make that call.

Odom and I met again to conquer the West Ridge of Forbidden, another Classic 50. We took turns in the lead and I took us up a crux pitch. We had great weather and good rock on the summit ridge, with only a few blowing clouds. However, it was a hard hike out leaving me quite stiff and sore afterward.

You've got to be Kidding!

Having climbed the highest point on each continent, I am now working on reaching their lowest points. Although the idea started as a joke, it has turned out to be rather difficult, if not nearly impossible. For instance, Antarctica's lowest point is 8,327 feet below sea level and is the lowest place on earth not covered by an ocean. It is however covered by ice and I took credit for at least standing on the ice covering it.

Also, I could only reach the minus 400 foot below sea level point of Ethiopia's Danakil Depression (512 feet below sea level) in Africa because of the acid pools. When I hiked to North America's lowest point of Badwater Basin (282 feet below sea level) in Death Valley National Park, no one could tell me exactly where that point was.

However, I did reach Asia's low point of 1,341 feet below sea level in Israel's Dead Sea. I now have Europe, South America and Australia to go. There is always a challenge out there somewhere!

Randy and Doris on Kilimanjaro

On Summit of Vinson Massif

Climbing Kilimanjaro once again!

Attempting amateur radio contacts at Patriot Hills

In the Pilot's Seat of the Russian IL-76TD Ilyushin airplane

Randy, Durk Gragg and Stacy Shaw, Sandun-off Bath House, Moscow, Russia

Top right - Leaving Borneo Ice Base in the Arctic

Top left - Mushing a dog sled near Long-yearbyen, Spitsbergen

Left - Near the North Pole

Bottom - On the summit of Carstensz Pyramid

Top left - Chief Yohanes Kudiai Mee Tribe

Top right - Franky Kowaas talking to Grasberg Mine truck driver while Pat Hickey looks on

Upper right - Randy, James Clarke and Pat Hickey in the storage container with the Indonesian Army Troops

Lower right - Local Resident, Enarotali, Irian Jaya

Bottom right - Randy and Doris in Turkey

Bottom left - K2 from Broad Peak Base Camp Karakoram Range, Pakistan

EPILOGUE

It would seem rocket science and extreme sports wouldn't have much in common – and in many ways that is very true. But one thing they do share is a need for acute mental focus.

In my profession, whenever I tackled a difficult technical issue I required a quiet environment to help concentrate my mind on solving the problem. The harder it was, the greater the concentration required.

I have often said that extreme sports are really played out in the mind. The physical requirements are only the entrance card; obviously, one must be physically prepared. But in reality, it is primarily a mental game – if your mind is not right there is no way to safely complete the task at hand.

Outside factors such as wind, loud noise, exposure, etc., have to be blocked out before one can proceed. It becomes a form of pure thought in visualizing and focusing on the activity before going for it. Well, I would argue that is a lot like rocket science.

The next step is how to accomplish all the things one wants to do in life in the time available. The key is to have a personal vision for your life – a sort of action plan that moves you forward in a desirable direction. Life here on earth is finite and thinking that through makes the desired outcome infinitely more likely if you make the effort and put a framework in place.

I developed mental goals early in life – things I wanted to do during the course of my life. I aimed very high. I was really fascinated by the idea of climbing big mountains and as a teenager dreamed of climbing Mount Everest. I had no doubt that I wanted to marry Doris. And as I grew older, my goals included earning a PhD, sorting out my spiritual life, surfing Hawaii, playing a significant role in the management and growth of a company and traveling extensively to see the world.

Dreaming big cannot be overstated. I truly believe having dreams is important as such dreams tend to become reality; especially if you make the effort to share them with important people in your life. You really have to think outside the box and if you do, nothing is impossible.

After reading this book it might appear that I am a risk taker. In truth, I am a risk manager. I realize some of these extreme sports are inherently dangerous and because of that I carefully weigh the risk versus reward for any activity. This includes all aspects of the risk, not just the possibility of dying.

I also evaluate the potential for injury and weigh the long term consequences of that injury against the reward associated with the activity. If it is consistent with my vision and remains something I want to pursue, I then carefully study the activity and determine how to mitigate the risk.

I have also put my estate in order so my family would be taken care of in the event something unexpected does happen.

There are many things I have rejected over the years and some activities I have ceased doing because the risk was no longer acceptable. For example, I gave up skydiving in 1996 although I do miss it and occasionally even dream about it. The death rate associated with sport jumping is very low and I honestly think the most dangerous part is driving to the drop zone. Still, the risk versus reward factor is no longer favorable for me.

One bad landing and I could easily destroy my already-damaged right knee. With that knee gone there would be no more skiing, climbing and surfing. Therefore, the risk outweighs the reward.

Everest is another classic example of risk management. Death or debilitating injury is a very real possibility in climbing Mount Everest. The historical death rate at the time of my climb was one death for every seven people who reach the top. In addition, frostbite and other injuries are sustained by a large percentage of those who attempt climbing it. From my perspective, when I did it the reward outweighed the risk. And as noted earlier, I did sustain some permanent injury to my lungs as a result of the pneumonia I suffered during the expedition. But I stand by my preliminary analysis – personally, for me it was definitely worth it.

When I look at mountaineering, I see the real prize as climbing K2. I would love to climb that sucker. But my skill level and age would make it an extremely risky endeavor, so I have chosen not to pursue that challenge.

The ultimate example of risk management is my approach to BASE jumping. The rewards are huge in this sport – absolute mental acuity and fear management, unbelievable adrenaline rushes and a tremendous feeling of accomplishment – everything about it is exciting to me. So why did I quit? The death rate, which is very high, increases with advancing age. As one's reflexes slow the risk accelerates exponentially.

At 45, I had done four jumps and earned my BASE number and that should have been enough. But I really wanted to jump off Half Dome. It was just one more jump.

Bingo! Getting busted by the park rangers solved that problem – I was definitely not willing to give up my job over the sport no matter how exciting it was. That was a case in which I violated one of my basic tenants - don't let desire sway judgment.

I have often been asked why I do these extreme sports. For me, the answer revolves around pure thought. When I am in the middle of an intense activity, I virtually never think about my job or my problems. Rather, I remain totally focused on the event at hand. The more extreme the activity, the more focused I become and BASE jumping is by far the most extreme of my activities. For the duration of each jump there is nothing else on my mind – it's just pure thought with maximum focus.

I suspect this is similar to what happens when a pole vaulter, gymnast or downhill racer competes in the Olympics. The athlete must visualize every aspect of the activity with total concentration. It is a very cleansing and therapeutic process.

I also like what Ed Viesturs had to say about climbing, "If you have to ask, you'll never know." Another quote that makes perfect sense to me is, "If you are not able to be scared, you either haven't been hurt or you're completely ignorant." That was from big-wave surfer Laird Hamilton.

Over the years, I've done numerous expeditions to remote regions of the world. I've stood at both the North and South Poles and the highest point on every continent. Looking back over my life, I realize the most important accomplishments have not been getting to those locations or reaching summits, but rather the journey itself – especially those related to family. Life is not measured by the number of breaths we take but by the moments that take our breath away and those times often have nothing to do with athletic endeavors.

Do I have some regrets? Yes, of course I do, but I routinely use my personal vision to make decisions and the payback for passing up traveling along some of those paths has outweighed the regrets. A classic example was my decision not to participate in the astronaut program. I would still like to go into space but I would have never given up the times we shared as a young family. The regrets that weigh heavy are the ones that came from making bad decisions and ignoring my vision. I move on in spite of having to carry those mistakes with me. In the end, I am who I am because of all the things I have been through – both good and bad.

I can honestly say I've been to the edge. It's a journey that takes place inside leading to the discovery of who you are and what is really important in life. It is learning to control fear while performing physically demanding tasks and the experience of pure thought, total concentration. These experiences combined with knowledge of a higher calling are an awesome formula for personal growth and self-discovery.

Last is some wisdom written on a toilet stall in a McDonalds located in Dawson Creek, British Columbia: "Success is getting what you want ... Happiness is wanting what you get!"

Best of all – I still have some time left. I cherish my wife and family and thoroughly enjoy life. Thank you, Jesus.

Carpe Diem.

APPENDIX A
GLOSSARY OF TERMS

Accelerated Freefall – Skydive training with one or two dedicated instructors per student. On the initial jumps, the instructor(s) hold on to the student until the student deploys their own parachute. There is no physical connection to the student other than the instructor's grip on the student, so once the student's parachute is deployed the instructors fly away and deploy their own canopies.

Acclimatization – The body's process of adjusting to high altitude. This is accomplished by spending time climbing to higher elevations and then returning to lower elevations to rest. Over time, the body generates more red blood cells and this increases the capability of oxygen transport to the body in spite of the low levels being taken in by the lungs.

Adventure Grand Slam – Consists of climbing the highest mountain on each continent, known as the Seven Summits and reaching both the North Pole and South Pole.

AFOSI – Acronym for Air Force Office of Special Investigation.

Aid Climbing or Direct Aid – Standing on or pulling oneself up on protective devices placed into the rock. Difficulty is indicated by A1-A5 (pitons, etc.) or C1-C5 (clean climbing protection).

Alpine Climb – Route that contains a combination of rock, snow and ice.

Arctic Circle – The southernmost latitude in the Northern Hemisphere at which the sun can remain continuously above or below the horizon for 24 hours (at the June solstice and December solstice, respectively).

Arm Wrap Rappel – A method of putting a spiral wrap of rope around the forearm to rappel down a fixed line.

ASPC – Aerojet Solid Propulsion Company, Rancho Cordova, CA.

Banya – Similar in some ways to a sauna; also known as a public bath. It is an institution in Russia used not only for cleaning, but also for socializing.

BASE Jumping – An activity where participants jump from fixed objects and use a parachute to break their fall. "BASE" is an acronym for the categories of fixed objects from which one can jump: buildings, antennas, spans (bridges) and earth (cliffs).

Bazaar – A marketplace or shopping quarter; found especially in the Middle East.

Belay – Protecting a climber by wrapping the rope around your body or running it through a belay device. Dynamic belay allows the rope to pay out during a fall to soften the impact while a static belay relies on the ropes dynamic stretch to soften the fall.

Belay Station or Station – Location on a climb where a belay is normally set up. On big walls (e.g., El Cap, etc.) this often means bolts have been placed to provide protection.

Bergschrund – A crevasse that forms where moving glacier ice separates from the stagnant ice.

Beta – Information about a climb, normally provided by someone who has done the route in question.

Bivouac or Bivy – An improvised camp site such as those used in mountain climbing. It may refer to sleeping in the open or on a ledge with a bivouac sack or utilizing a shelter constructed of natural materials.

Block Climbing – A single climber leads multiple sequential pitches (as opposed to switching leads each pitch) in an effort to speed up the ascent.

Boil Lines – The action of water rising quickly to the surface and creating the appearance of boiling water. Caused when too much water is being forced into one location. Boils often appear at the bottom of rapids and along walls. In both cases, the surging water has nowhere to go, so it gets pushed forcefully to the surface. Once it hits the surface, this water peaks and then runs off to the side to the lower-lying water around it. Where this shedding water hits the current around the boil, a seam line is created. These seam lines are one of the most unstable spots on the river.

Bolt – Permanent protection drilled into the rock. Often found at belay stations or on blank faces.

Boogie Board – A rectangular piece of hydrodynamic foam used by surfers to ride the face of a wave in the ocean. Swim fins are typically used for additional propulsion and control while riding a wave. This sport is known as body boarding.

Bowl – A wave that forms a concave, steep curved wall.

Brace – A technique using a paddle to keep a kayak from rolling upside down.

Bungee Jumping – Involves jumping from a tall structure while connected to a large elastic cord. The tall structure is usually a fixed object, such as a bridge or crane. The thrill comes from the free-falling and the rebound. When the person jumps, the cord stretches and the jumper flies upwards again as the cord recoils and continues to oscillate up and down until all the kinetic energy is dissipated.

Cairn – A man-made pile of rocks.

Camp 4 – Located in Yosemite National Park and listed on the National Register of Historic Places because of its nationally significant role in the development of rock climbing as a sport.

Canyoneering – Technical descent of a canyon using a variety of techniques that may include walking, scrambling, climbing, jumping, rappelling and/or swimming.

Carabiner – A metal loop with a spring loaded gate used to quickly and reversibly connect components in safety-critical systems.

Casual Camp – Laying out a sleeping bag outside of a campground or sleeping in your vehicle in a parking lot, for example, in Yosemite National Park, etc. Also, includes staying in an RV outside of campgrounds, for example, along a road, at WalMart parking lots, rest areas, truck stops, etc.

Cenote – A deep natural pit or sinkhole, characteristic of Mexico. It results from the collapse of limestone bedrock that exposes groundwater underneath.

CFS – Volumetric flow rate measured as cubic feet per second.

Chimney – A crack which is wide enough to wedge your body into.

Chock Stone – A boulder wedged in a crack in the rock face.

Chocks – A generic term for all passive protection that can be wedged into a crack or slot in the rock, i.e., hexes, stoppers, lo balls, tri cams, etc.

Chorten – A mound-like or semi-hemispherical structure used by Buddhists as a place of meditation.

Class of Climb – Climbing grades are inherently subjective and all climbing classifications used in this book were the ones used at the time the routes were climbed - many of these classifications have since been changed. Climbers give a grade to a route that describes the difficulty and danger of the route. The Yosemite System of grading is as follows: technical difficulty consists of five classes indicating the difficulty of the hardest section. Class 1 is the easiest and consists of walking on even terrain ... Class 3 involves the use of ropes for protection ... Class 5 is climbing on vertical or near vertical rock and requires technical skill, a rope and protective devices to proceed safely. Classes are subdivided decimally, so that a route graded 4.5 would be a scramble halfway between class 4 and 5 and 5.9 would be the hardest rock climb. Over time standards increased necessitating additional grades at the top of 5.10, 5.11, 5.12, etc. Letter grades were added for climbs at 5.10 and above, by adding a letter "a" (easiest), "b," "c" or "d" (hardest). Climbers also consider how sustained or strenuous a climb is, in addition to the difficulty of the single hardest move. Length of route is addressed with a Roman numeral grade that indicates the length and seriousness of the route. The grades range from grade I to VI spanning a one hour climb to a multiday climb respectively.

Class V River – All river classifications used in this book were the ones used at the time the rivers were run - many of these classifications have since been changed. Rivers are rated using Roman numerals I to VI to reflect the difficulty. Class VI is considered to be not runable. Note that a river's rating changes with fluctuations in water levels; a river rated Class IV at medium water levels might resemble a Class III river at lower water levels, while at higher levels, it might look more like a Class V. The rating system used in the Grand Canyon pre-dates the modern Class I-VI system and rates rapids 1 to 10. A "10" in the Grand Canyon is comparable to a Class V rapid elsewhere.

Classic Fifties – List of climbs from a book published in 1979 written by Steve Roper and Allen Steck entitled *Fifty Classic Climbs of North America*.

Clean Climbing – Using equipment for protection that does not have to be hammered into the rock (e.g., stoppers, hexes, nuts, spring loaded camming devices, etc.).

Climate Zones – Climate classification system consisting of five zones based on boundaries that have been selected with vegetation distribution in mind. It combines average annual and monthly temperatures, precipitation and the seasonality of precipitation.

Col – A dip in a ridge between two peaks. It is also know as a "saddle".

Coral Head – An outcropping of coral that extends above the reef forming a treacherous underwater obstacle for surfers.

Cornice – A ledge of snow which is formed by the prevailing wind and hangs over the edge of a ridge.

Couloir – A narrow gully with a steep gradient in a mountainous terrain.

Cow Tail – A nylon webbing tether attached to a harness and then clipped to fixed line with a carabiner.

Crampons – Traction devices used in snow and ice climbing. Forward angled points allow for a technique known as front pointing. Reduces the need for cutting steps.

Crux Pitch – The most demanding part of a climb up a mountain or rocks.

Cut-away Handle – Cut-away is a skydiving term referring to disconnecting the main parachute from the harness-container in case of a malfunction in preparation for opening the reserve parachute. The main parachute is released with the use of a cut-away handle.

Cwm – Pronounced "coom", it is a valley; the Western Cwm, often called the Valley of Silence, is a broad, flat, gently undulating glacial valley basin terminating at the foot of the Lhotse Face on Mount Everest.

Death Zone – In mountaineering refers to altitudes above 8,000 meters, where the amount of oxygen is not high enough to sustain human life.

DOE – Department of Energy.

Dory – A small, shallow-draft boat, about 20 feet long with high sides, a flat bottom and sharp bows.

Eddy – Current of water running contrary to the main river flow; a circular current similar to a whirlpool.

Eddy Fence – An eddy line forms between a river's faster current and the slower current of an eddy. In big white water the zone between a downstream current and the upstream spin of an eddy may turn the eddy line into an eddy fence. The two countercurrents rip along each other, separated by a discontinuity that can be several feet high. A boat on the eddy side of the fence may be looking "uphill" into the main flow of the river.

Endo or Ender – Using river hydraulics to cause a kayak to flip end over end.

Feniky – Leaved branches used to beat fellow banya users in Russia to open the pores.

FGBMFI – Full Gospel Businessmen's Fellowship International is a fellowship of lay businessmen. Its main purpose is to bring interest in the Christian gospel. Theologically, the organization has its roots in Pentecostalism.

Figure Eight Device – A descender used in rappelling made of aluminum in the shape of an 8.

Fixed Lines or Fix – Ropes attached to rock or ice faces with the use of anchoring devices and used later to regain a previous position on the route.

Flake – Slab of rock attached to a rock face. Sometimes these are loose and unnerving as they are passed or they expand when you place protection behind them.

Foredeck – Forward part of the deck of a sailboat.

Free Climb – Using placements for protection only and not standing or pulling on them.

Free Solo – Rock climbing without ropes or other safety gear.

Freefall – Falling through the atmosphere without a deployed parachute. After reaching terminal velocity, the aerodynamic drag forces produce the sensation of the body's weight being supported on a cushion of air.

French Free – Cheating by grabbing placements with your hands while still climbing with your feet; normally on difficult free sections.

Gendarme – An isolated pinnacle of rock on a mountain peak or ridge.

Ghost Run – Using a snow machine to transport skiers to the top of a run, then turning it around, locking the throttle partially open and allowing the machine to travel downhill by itself. One skis down behind it.

Glissade – Act of descending a steep snow slope via a controlled slide on one's feet or buttocks.

Goo – Energy food product in a small package.

Gooseneck – The fitting that connects the boom to the mast. The boom is the spar (pole) where the foot of the mainsail is attached and the mast is the large vertical spar (pole) for supporting the sail and boom.

Gun – Long narrow surfboard designed specifically for big, fast waves.

Ham Radio – Amateur radio is the use of designated radio frequency spectra for purposes of private recreation, non-commercial exchange of messages, wireless experimentation, self-training and emergency communication. A license is required.

Hang Glider – Non-motorized foot-launched aircraft using a Rogallo (i.e., delta) wing design. Made of aluminum tubing and nylon material.

Harness – A device made out of webbing which has a waist belt and two leg loops, connected in front and back. It is used to secure a rope to a climber.

Haul – Bringing your equipment, food and water up the face of a big wall by the use of a pulley system and haul bag.

Haul Bag – Heavy duty bag used in climbing which contains equipment, food and water.

High Siding – Throwing one's weight against a raft tube to try and keep the raft from flipping over.

Highpointing – Ascending to the highest point in each state.

Hollow Wave – A wave that has a pronounced hook cross section and results in a tubular or hollow internal section.

Hook – Specialized climbing equipment made of chromalloy and used for small flakes or ledges. Hook moves are scary because after moving off of it no protection remains.

Hybrid Aliens – Specialized spring loaded camming device with two different sized cam lobes that works particularly well in old piton scars or flaring cracks.

Hypoxia – Hypoxia is a condition in which the body is deprived of adequate oxygen supply and can occur at high altitudes. Total atmospheric pressure decreases as altitude increases, causing a lower partial pressure of oxygen. The oxygen remains at 20.9 percent of the gas mixture, but as the altitude increases the gas is less dense.

Ice Fall Doctor – Elite and highly experienced Nepalese Sherpa with specialized skills for setting ropes and ladders in the extremely dangerous Khumbu Icefall.

Impact Zone – Where the waves break most consistently and ferociously, i.e., where the falling lip of each wave usually meets the water.

International Date Line – An imaginary line on the surface of the earth from the North Pole to the South Pole that demarcates one calendar day from the next. It passes through the middle of the Pacific Ocean, roughly following the 180 degree longitude.

Iridium Flair – Bright light that emanates from a low earth orbit Iridium (telecommunications) satellite when its solar panels reflect sunlight.

Iridium Phone – A satellite phone that uses the Iridium constellation of satellites to provide voice and data coverage over earth's entire surface.

Jam Crack – Cracks into which hands and/or feet are placed in order to climb up the rock.

Jet Stream – Fast flowing, narrow air currents found in the atmosphere of the earth. Their paths typically have a meandering shape and flow west to east at altitudes between 23,000 feet and 52,000 feet. Speeds can exceed 100 miles per hour.

Jugging – Climbing up a fixed rope with jumars.

Jumar – A one-way ratchet device for ascending a fixed rope.

Layback – Using the edge of a vertical crack or flake for the hands in opposition with the feet on the face of the rock to climb upward.

Lead (Arctic) – Long narrow area of open water within sea ice expanses. Caused by an interaction between the ocean and the atmosphere.

Lead (Climbing) – Climbing first up the pitch (i.e., being in the lead) during roped climbing (normally involves placing protection for safety).

Mani Stones – Stone plates or rocks inscribed with the six-syllable mantra "Om mani padme hum" It is a form of prayer in Tibetan Buddhism.

Moraine – An accumulation of soil and rock formed by glaciers. The debris can range in size from silt to large boulders and may be on the glacier's surface or deposited in piles where the glacier has melted.

Mulas – Gauchos (cowboys) who drive the mules and organize Base Camp on Aconcagua.

Nail-up – A series of piton placements.

Oar Pin – A fixture on a raft frame that constrains an oar fitted with a matching clip to pivot in a fixed orientation allowing for no-miss powerful strokes.

On Site – Climbing a route one has never done before without practicing the moves beforehand.

Open Book – An inside corner on a right angle. The rock flares out from the corner looking like an open book.

OPM – The Free Papua Movement is a militant organization established in 1965 to cause the violent overthrow of the current government in the Papua province of Indonesia and to reject economic development and modernity.

Over the Falls – Being pulled over the top of the wave and landing in the impact zone. This is a very vulnerable situation and often results in being held underwater for a long time while being pummeled along the bottom.

Oximeter – A sensor that is placed on a fingertip to measure oxygenated blood.

Paddling Channel – A return route through the impact zone of the oncoming waves, often created by a rip current.

Pearl – When the nose of the surfboard dives under water, checking or completely stopping the board's forward motion.

Pendulum – Moving across a blank section of rock by swinging side to side on a rope anchored above until a crack system is reached.

Picket – Used as an anchor in mountaineering. It is driven into the snow.

Pilot Chute – A small auxiliary parachute used to deploy the main parachute.

Pitch – The length of a climbing rope. Typically 165 or 180 feet.

Piton – A spike-shaped piece of metal driven into cracks to support and/or protect a climber, e.g., lost arrows, angles, bongs, rurps, etc.

Placements – Protective equipment used for climbing that is placed into a crack (e.g., piton, chock, cam, etc.) or a runner around a tree, etc

Pogies – A neoprene type of mitt used in kayaking that attaches directly to the paddle and provides hand protection in cold water conditions.

Portaledge – A deployable hanging tent system designed for rock climbers who spend multiple days and nights on a big wall climb.

Pressure Ridge – Form in sea ice due to the interaction between floes as they collide with each other. In the Arctic the main driving force is wind. Composition is angular ice blocks of various sizes that pile up on the floes.

Puja – The act of showing reverence to a god, spirit, or other aspect of the divine through invocations, prayers, songs and rituals. During this ceremony Sherpa essentially ask the gods for permission to climb the mountain and bless the expedition with safety and success.

QED – Acronym for "quod erat demonstrandum", which translates as "which was to be demonstrated." It is a formal way of ending a proof. Its purpose is to alert the reader that the previous statement has been proved.

Rag Doll – When one is getting beat up so badly the entire body goes limp as it flops around.

Rappel – A technique of descending a steep face by sliding down a rope.

River Boarding – A sport in which the participant lies prone on a foam board with fins on the feet for propulsion and steering while navigating a white water river.

Roll Up – A kayak roll, often referred to as an Eskimo roll, is the act of righting a capsized kayak by use of body motion and/or a paddle.

Roof or Overhang – A section of rock that extends out over the face of a rock wall.

Rope Jumping – Jumping from a cliff, then being caught by a safety rope.

Scramble – Climbing over relatively easy terrain without the use of ropes.

Scree – A slope of loose rock debris at the base of a steep incline or cliff.

SCUBA – Acronym for self-contained underwater breathing apparatus and is a form of underwater diving in which a diver breathes compressed air.

Serac – A block or column of ice formed by intersecting crevasses on a glacier. Seracs are often found in large numbers within an icefall. They can be the size of a house or larger and are dangerous since they may topple without warning.

Seven Summits – The highest mountains of each of the seven continents. Summiting all of them is regarded as a mountaineering challenge. First postulated as such and achieved on April 30, 1985 by Richard Bass.

Sharp End of the Rope – Slang for leading.

Sheet – A line (rope) used to control the movable corner of a sail.

Shuttle Run – Using an automobile to transport skiers to the top of a run along a highway and then picking them up at the bottom.

Siege Climbing – Attacking a big wall or mountain by ascending and descending repeatedly to regain one's previous high point.

Sirdar – Leader of a group of Sherpa and in charge of Base Camp logistics.

Skins – Removable pieces of nylon fabric, whose nap runs at an oblique angle, allowing the ski to glide forward, but not back.

Sledge – A vehicle mounted on low runners drawn by animals or humans and used for transporting loads across ice and snow.

Sling – Loops of nylon webbing, cord or rope used for protection.

Slough – The snow that is set into motion when snowboarding or skiing in steep terrain. Due to the often loose cohesion of the powder layer, more snow can be accumulated by the already moving snow. One turn on top of a steep face can cause a slough that reaches avalanche-like proportions.

Spinnaker – Special type of sail that is designed specifically for sailing downwind. The spinnaker fills with wind and balloons out in front of the boat when it is deployed.

Sport Climbing – All protection and anchors are permanently installed prior to the climb.

Spring Loaded Camming Device (SLCD) or Cam – Protective climbing equipment. Consists of multiple cams in opposition that can be retracted by pulling a trigger and inserted into a crack. Releasing the trigger allows the SLCD to expand to fit in the crack. Typical types include: Friends, Camlots, Aliens, Tri Cams, etc.

Stalled Flight Path Exit – By flying a small airplane in an upward arc until it stalls, one is able to exit the craft at relatively slow speeds, which stimulates a BASE jump (i.e., little or no aerodynamic forces acting on the jumper).

Static Fixed Rope Belay – Tying a length of rope to an anchor and totally relying on the anchor and the stretch in the rope to hold a fall.

Static Line – In skydiving, a static line is a cord attached at one end to the aircraft and at the other end to the top of the jumper's parachute deployment bag. The jumper's fall from the aircraft causes the static line to become taut, which in turn pulls the deployment bag out of the container and allows the canopy to inflate.

Stem-Christie – A technique in skiing for turning. It is a refinement of the basic stem technique where, prior to the turn, the uphill ski is stemmed (tail skidded outward) from being parallel with the downhill ski to form a V shape.

Sub-terminal Pilot Chute – Oversized pilot chute specifically designed for deployment at slow speeds.

Surf (Whitewater) – In whitewater this term is used when a raft or kayak stays stationary in a rapid as the river continues to flow downstream.

Tandem Skydive – Refers to a type of skydiving, where a student skydiver is connected to a harness attached to a tandem instructor. The instructor guides the student through the whole jump from exit through freefall, piloting the canopy and landing. The student needs only minimal instruction before making a tandem jump with the instructor.

TDY – Acronym for temporary duty travel.

TEC – Member-based community of over 900 CEOs, entrepreneurs and business owners from across Canada. Each networking group has a chair and approximately 15 members. TEC is Canada's version of Vistage International.

Terminal Velocity – In skydiving, it is the velocity at which the wind resistance of the air equals the downward force of gravity on the body. In a belly-to-earth free-fall position it is 122 mph.

Top Rope – Climber is belayed from below by a rope running through an anchor at the top of the pitch.

Tow-in Surfing – Using a jet ski with a tow rope to pull a surfer into big, fast-moving waves that normally are too large to paddle into.

Trad – Short for traditional, which is a style of climbing where a climber places all gear required for protection against falls and he or another climber removes it when a pitch is complete.

Trans-Ischemic Attack (TIA) – Transient episode of neurologic dysfunction caused by loss of blood flow to the brain. TIAs have the same underlying cause as strokes and are frequently referred to as mini-strokes. TIAs and strokes cause the same symptoms, but unlike a stroke, the symptoms of a TIA can resolve within a few minutes to 24 hours.

Tree Well – A void or area of loose snow around the trunk of a tree enveloped in deep snow.

TSP – Trisodium Phosphate – an ingredient in Spic-n-Span.

Under Cling – Climbing by using the hands in a horizontal crack under a roof or flake in opposition with the feet on the face.

Undisputed Seven Summits – The highest mountains of each of the seven continents, including both Kosciuszko and Carstensz Pyramid, as well as both Elbrus and Mt Blanc.

Vistage International – Networking groups of approximately 15 members formed from CEOs, business owners and executives of small to mid-sized businesses. Each group has a chair. Founded in 1957, currently more than 17,000 members in 15 countries.

Whiteout – A condition of diffuse light when no shadows are cast, due to a continuous white cloud layer appearing to merge with the white snow surface. No surface irregularities of the snow are visible, but a dark object may be clearly seen. There is no visible horizon.

Wind Shear – A micro scale meteorological phenomenon occurring over a very short distance in the atmosphere resulting in drastic wind speed and direction changes.

Windward Mark – Upwind buoy which must be rounded in sailboat racing.

WX-3 – Weapons Group of the Los Alamos National Laboratory, NM.

Yellow Band – A distinctive feature on the Lhotse Face composed of sedimentary sandstone. It is the first rock one touches when climbing Mount Everest. The elevation at the top of the band is 25,000 feet.

Yosemite's Golden Era – The years of 1947 to 1971, during which the first ascents were made of the "big walls" of Yosemite Valley. The ending coincides with Harding's ascent of the Dawn Wall on El Cap.

Zippered – When protective climbing placements pull sequentially during a fall.

APPENDIX B
WHO'S WHO

Abram, Ron – Businessman, snowboarder and adventurer from Granite Bay, CA.

Ács, Zoltan – Climbing guide and member of the 2002 Hungarian National Everest Team.

Albright, Al – Met him during a Mountaineers training course in WA. He introduced me to the Explorer Post where I would later become the adult leader. Excellent climber, kayaker and a lifelong friend. Aeronautical engineer at the Boeing Company, Seattle, WA.

Anderson, Dave – Met through the Explorer Post in Seattle while a graduate student. Climbed together often in the early 1970s. Dave became a well known rock climber in Yosemite and the Southwest Desert.

Anderson, Pastor Marv – Pastor at Tehachapi Good Shepherd Lutheran Church during the 1970s.

Andrews, Ron – MBA (from Sloan School of Business at MIT) and PhD. My first boss at the Xerox Corporation, Webster, NY. He was great to work for.

Archuleta, Tony – Janitor at the Los Alamos National Laboratory. He lived in the small Hispanic village of El Rito, NM.

Baba Ram Dass – Born Richard Alpert, he is an American contemporary spiritual teacher and the author of the book *Be Here Now*. He is known for his personal and professional associations with Timothy Leary at Harvard University in the early 1960s and for his travels to India. Fired from Harvard University.

Baggett, Dave – Solid Christian man and occasional climbing partner in NM.

Baker, Bob – Engineering aide at the Boeing Company, Seattle, WA. Accomplished climber, ski mountaineer, outdoorsman and a lifelong friend.

Baker, Ralph and Dorothy – Neighbors in Upstate NY in early 1980s. Their daughter Effie had attended school in our converted school house home.

Baker, Sean – Climber I met through Willie Spencer.

Bakker, Jim – Co-Founder of the Trinity Broadcasting Network and former host of the PTL Club. A former Assemblies of God minister. A sex scandal led to his resignation from the ministry. Subsequent revelations of accounting fraud brought on his imprisonment and divorce.

Barry, Donald and Susan – Owners of Monte Verde Inn in Foresthill and one of my sponsors.

Bass, Dick – Owner of Snowbird Ski Resort in Utah and the first person to climb the Seven Summits. Co-author of *Seven Summits*.

Baxley, Bill – Free diver with the ability to go very deep for long periods of time.

Beasley, Joe – Friend I met while a graduate student who was an engineer at the Boeing Company, Seattle, WA. Later became a lawyer. Excellent skier.

Benegas, Willie – Climbing guide from Argentina. Summited Everest 2002.

Bill** – Ran the Grand Canyon with us in a 15 foot cataraft.

Bob** – Met Bob through kayaking with Tom Farren. Laid back individual. Strong athlete with successful history in motorcycle racing. Ran the Grand Canyon with us.

Bohemer, Tuck – Christian AF officer at the Rocket Propulsion Laboratory, Edwards AFB, CA.

Boland, Jonathon – Met him skydiving and climbed together in Northern California.

Boskoff, Christine – Owner of Mountain Madness. Expedition climber I met while climbing in Tibet and again in Antarctica.

Bostick, Don – Sport organizer for the ESPN X-Games and World Cup Skateboarding. Heli boarded and surfed together.

Boukreev, Anatoli – Russian mountaineer who made ascents of seven of the 8,000 meter peaks without supplemental oxygen. Boukreev was killed in an avalanche during a winter ascent of Annapurna in 1997.

Boyarsky, Victor – PhD in physics and mathematics. Well known Russian author and veteran of numerous Arctic and Antarctic expeditions.

Brice, Russell – A New Zealand mountaineer and the owner/manager of Himalayan Experience Ltd.

Briggs, Bill – Met him as an undergraduate at Cal Poly and our careers crossed paths many times in the ensuing years. Climbed together in Southern California and ski toured across the Sierra in winter.

Brown, Scott – Co-worker at Aerojet. Climbed and skied together in the 1980s.

Brubeck, Dave – An American jazz pianist and composer.

Bryant, Charlie – Surfer and good friends with Chuck John, Mike Weinberg and Bing Gleitsman.

Burwell, Dick – Fellow engineer at the Boeing Company, Seattle, WA. Climbed together from 1967 to 1973.

Bush, George W. – 43rd President of the United States.

Caldwell, Jim and Blanche – Met Jim in 1976 at Los Alamos National Laboratory, NM. Shared our lives in the Lord together.

Carey, Bob – Strong long time kayaker from Northern California. Ran the Grand Canyon together.

Carleone, Joe – My boss and Vice President of Operations at Aerojet.

Carlson, Kent – Pastor of Oak Hills Church, Folsom, CA.

Carson, Bruce – Gifted young climber from WA, who excelled at solo, big wall climbing. Shared a Yosemite trip together in 1972 and had several mutual friends.

Castaneda, Carlos – Controversial Peruvian-American author and student of anthropology. Wrote *The Teachings of Don Juan* that describes his alleged training in shamanism.

Cherry-Garrard, Apsley – An English explorer of Antarctica and author of *The Worst Journey in the World*.

Ching, Jeff – Donner regular and national champion in senior snowboard racing. Heli boarded together in Canada.

Chouinard, Yvon – Rock climbing pioneer, noted for his contributions to climbing, climbing equipment and the outdoor gear business. Chouinard is also a surfer and a kayaker.

Clarke, James – West Point graduate and former Army Ranger and Special Operations Officer. MBA from Harvard. Completed the Seven Summits.

Cogorno, George – Permit holder for the first Grand Canyon raft trip. Married to Mary.

Connors, Graham – Walnut farmer in the central valley of CA. Kayaker and skier. Ski toured together across the Sierra in winter.

Cooke, Charlie – Branch chief (i.e., my boss's, boss's, boss) at the Rocket Propulsion Laboratory, Edwards AFB, CA.

Cooke, Kathy – Branch chief's secretary at the Rocket Propulsion Laboratory, Edwards AFB, CA.

Corbett, Mike – Yosemite medical clinic janitor considered one of the most experienced rock climbers in Yosemite in the early 1990s.

Cordova, Hermanio and Gloria – Hermanio was a fellow employee of the Los Alamos National Laboratory, NM. Gloria, his wife, is a world renowned Santeria Wood Carver.

Cornea, Dick – Propellant chemist recruited from Thiokol, Brigham City, UT. Good friend – now deceased.

Cover, Chris – Solid Christian man. I climbed with him in CA.

Dancs, Tom – Excellent climber. BASE Jumper. Ran the Grand Canyon together.

Dause, Bill – Owns and operates the Parachute Center in Lodi, CA.

Decher, Reiner – Professor at University of Washington, Seattle, WA. Served on my PhD committee. Climbed together while I was a graduate student.

DeMarco, Mike – My nephew. Kayaker and surfer.

DeSilva, Frankie – Surfer I met at Turtles, San Elijo State Beach, CA. Ran into him at Makaha, Oahu, HI.

Donaldson, Marcus – Climber I met through Tom Dancs. Climbing partner in Zion, UT and Red Rocks, NV.

Doyle, Mike – UC Berkeley swim team and competitive at the Olympic level. Helped with the design and testing of the first self-bailing rafts. Owner of Beyond Limits Adventures. Ran the Grand Canyon together.

Duncan, Dave – Announcer for the 2002 Olympics snowboard half-pipe. Heli boarded together in Canada.

Duval, Jean Paul – PhD aeronautics and astronautics. Skied and climbed together as graduate students.

Edler, Peter and Christen – Met Peter through rafting with Wayne Klinger. Peter is extremely intelligent and a fine athlete. Has developed into a great oarsman. Married to Christen. Ran the Grand Canyon together several times.

Ellberg, Steve – UC Berkeley swim team. Helped with the design and testing of the first self-bailing rafts. Co-founder of Beyond Limits Adventures. Ran the Grand Canyon together.

Embry, Mark – SCUBA Dive Master and Instructor in Northern California.

Erőss, Zsolt – Climbing guide and member of the 2002 Hungarian National Everest Team. First Hungarian to reach the summit of Everest.

Farren, Tom – Intelligent. Very strong kayaker. Ran the Grand Canyon together several times.

Fisher, Carl – My boss's boss and president of Aerojet.

Flewelling, Peter – Member of the Explorer Post, Seattle, WA. Climber and a lifelong friend.

Fowler, Charlie – Well known Yosemite climber I met while climbing in Tibet and again on Everest.

Fox, Charlie – Climber, skier, surfer and bicyclist. Owned Wilderness Sports and was a sponsor.

Gabl, Christian – Climber and certified guide from Austria. Climbed El Cap and Mount Blanc together.

Garmager, Curt – Fellow engineer at the Boeing Company, Seattle, WA. Skier, climber and a lifelong friend.

Geisler, Bob – My boss's boss at the Rocket Propulsion Laboratory, Edwards AFB, CA. A solid Christian and member of our carpool – now deceased.

George** – My second manager at the Xerox Corporation, Webster, NY.

Georges** – Swiss adventurer. My partner for the North Pole trip.

Gleitsman, George "Bing" – Well known potter. Surfer and good friends with Chuck John, Mike Weinberg and Charlie Bryant.

Gustafson, Gary – My boss at Eastman Kodak in the research and engineering department of the Kodak Apparatus Division.

Hamilton, Laird – An American big-wave surfer, co-inventor of tow-in surfing and an occasional fashion and action-sports model.

Hansen, Darrin – Engineering technology degree from USC. I hired him after meeting him skydiving and he worked in my group at Aerojet.

Harding, Warren – Was one of the most accomplished and influential American rock climbers of the 1950s to 1970s. He was the leader of the first team to climb El Capitan, Yosemite Valley, in 1958. Many first ascents of big wall routes in Yosemite.

Harlan, Dave – Member of the Explorer Post in Northern California.

Harrington, Bruce – Son of a co-worker at the Rocket Propulsion Laboratory, CA. Was my primary climbing partner during the mid 1970s.

Harris, Bob – My boss (a very good one) and vice president of operations at Aerojet.

Hart, Brad – Friend and climbing partner from Sacramento area in CA.

Hawking, Stephen – English theoretical physicist, cosmologist, author and Director of Research at the Centre for Theoretical Cosmology within the University of Cambridge.

Hickey, Pat – DrPH. A clinical assistant professor of nursing at the University of South Carolina. Completed the Seven Summits.

Hillary, Peter – Son of the late Sir Edmund Hillary. Peter has climbed Everest twice.

Hillary, Sir Edmund – A New Zealand mountaineer, explorer and philanthropist. On 29 May 1953, Hillary and Nepalese Sherpa mountaineer Tenzing Norgay became the first climbers confirmed as having reached the summit of Mount Everest.

Holbek, Lars – Met Lars through Chuck Stanley and kayaked together in Northern California. Co-author of *A Guide to the Best Whitewater in the State of California*.

Hoskin, Tom – Kayaker from Canada who ran the Grand Canyon with our group.

Houlding, Leo – Strong young climber from Britain who climbs big routes throughout the world. I met him while climbing on El Cap.

Jakeš, Meroslav – Czech guide I met on his seventh trip to the North Pole.

John, Chuck – Met Chuck camping at South Carlsbad State Beach, CA in 1973. Excellent surfer, skateboarder, skier, all around athlete and a lifelong friend. Somehow I always refer to him as Chuck John, rarely using just his first name. Good friends with Mike Weinberg, Bing Gleitsman and Charlie Bryant.

Jones, Doug – Good friend of Al Albright and an excellent kayaker.

Jones, Keith – Well known BASE jumper in Southern California.

Katen, Randy – One of California's best snowboarders. Heli-boarded together in Canada and Alaska.

Keith, Joan – My sister, who passed away October 7, 2013. She was three years older than I.

Keith, Ron – My brother-in-law, who was married to Joan.

King, Marshal – Donner regular and an incredible rider. Heli boarded together in Canada.

Klinger, Wayne – Long time friend, river rafter and climber. Lives in the Sierra foothills near Yosemite, CA.

Knight, Rick – Member of the Explorer Post in Seattle, WA. Climbing partner and lifelong friend. Hang glider pilot.

Kowaas, Frankie – Owner of Manado Adventure and guide for Carstensz Pyramid, Indonesia.

Larson, Glenn – Good friend of Willie Spencer. They grew up together in Los Alamos, NM. Ran the Grand Canyon with us.

Leary, Timothy – An American psychologist and writer, known for his advocacy of psychedelic drugs. Leary conducted experiments at Harvard University when drugs such as LSD and psilocybin were legal. Leary and his associate Richard Alpert were fired from the university because of the public controversy surrounding their research.

Lefine, Robert – Met him when he lived in the University District, Seattle, WA. From France, he was a gifted climber and backcountry skier.

Legate, Peter – From England and my climbing partner on Everest.

Leo** – Skied and snowmobiled together in Alaska.

Lieber, Curtis – Owner of Global Expedition Adventures and organizes trips to the North Pole.

Long, Tom – Excellent kayaker. Climbed on Denali together.

Lorts, Ernie – High school friend and member of the Explorer Post in Rialto, CA. Now deceased.

Lou, Dick – Vice president of chemical research and development and my first boss at Aerojet Strategic Propulsion Company.

Magill, Connie – Secretary in Chemical Research and Development at Aerojet.

Manser, Gerry – Propellant Chemist recruited from Thiokol, Brigham City, UT. Good friend.

Martwick, Andy – Met him skiing at Heavenly Valley and did the Sierra High Route together.

Mary Ann** – My boss's secretary at the Xerox Corporation, Webster, NY.

McCamey, Dick – Employee at Aerojet. Went on several raft trips with me.

McCann, Elvis and Melissa – Adult leader in Boys Scouts and good friend. Married to Melissa.

McCarthy, Bob and Diane – Long time friends who live in Roseville, CA. Worked together as adult leaders in Boy Scouts.

McCarthy, "Texas" Tom – Skydiver and BASE Jumper.

McCauley, Tom – Excellent snowboarder from Montana. Heli boarded together in Alaska.

McMurray, Jeff – DJ at the Eagle in Sacramento, CA. Creator of the "Ask the Rocket Scientist" show.

Mécs, László "Laci" – Climbing guide and member of the 2002 Hungarian National Everest Team.

Messner, Reinhold – Mountaineer, adventurer and explorer from South Tyrol. He is renowned for making the first solo ascent of Mount Everest without supplemental oxygen and for being the first climber to ascend all 14 of the 8,000 meter peaks. Considered by many to be the best climber alive.

Mettee, Joe and Becky – Owners of VG Bakery and Donuts located across the street from San Elijo State Beach, CA. We have become good friends and Joe is a particularly strong surfer. Vacationed together several times.

Mezey, László "Mezo" – Climbing guide and member of the 2002 Hungarian National Everest Team.

Michael** – A friend I met skiing. Did the 34 mile, two day ski trip from Echo Summit to Rubicon with Denny Swenson and me.

Milne, Rob – Professor in Scotland. Became friends as we shared an expedition in Antarctica in 2004.

Money, Tim – Met through the Boy Scouts and climbed together for several years in CA.

Monk, John – Owned and competitively raced a 26 foot Thunderbird three quarter mast rigged one-design class sailboat. MS in aeronautical engineering and an employee of the Boeing Company, Seattle, WA.

Monsen, Monrad – Dedicated adult Boy Scout leader and friend.

Morris, Mike – Ski Patrol Supervisor at Snowbird UT. Guides Grand Canyon raft trips and Himalayan climbs.

Morrison, David – Gifted young climber from Seattle. Partner on several big wall climbs.

Morrison, Ross – Engineering aide and later an engineer at the Boeing Company, Seattle, WA. Also an engineering student at the University of WA. Climber and a lifelong friend.

Norgay, Jamling – Son of Tenzing Norgay who, along with Sir Edmund Hillary, completed the first ascent of Mount Everest. Jamling has summited Everest twice.

Norgay, Tenzing – Nepalese Indian Sherpa mountaineer. On 29 May 1953, Norgay and New Zealand mountaineer Edmund Hillary became the first climbers confirmed as having reached the summit of Mount Everest.

Nunn, David – Hollywood stuntman. BASE jumped together in Los Angeles. In May 2005, David was seriously injured during a BASE jump in Tonto National Forest. His parachute opened incorrectly and he slammed against the rock wall above the Salt River near Saguaro Lake, AZ.

Oates, Gordon – Professor at University of Washington, Seattle, WA. Served on my PhD committee. Climbed together while I was a graduate student.

Oberth, Mike – Co-worker at Aerojet. Kayaked together several times.

Odom, Bob – Member and adult leader of the Explorer Post, Seattle, WA. PhD in Physics. Climbing partner during and after graduate school and a lifelong friend.

Osmond, Dan – Met during an outlaw run at Heavenly Valley and later climbed together in Yosemite. World class sponsored climber, well known for onsite (never climbed this route before) free soloing (no ropes or protection) of extremely difficult routes.

Parmerter, Reid – Professor in the Aeronautics and Astronautics Department at the University of Washington, Seattle, WA. Committee chairman for my PhD and a lifelong friend.

Payne, Bill – Fellow employee at the Rocket Propulsion Laboratory, Edwards AFB, CA.

Payne, Charles – Major in the USAF when I worked for him at the Rocket Propulsion Laboratory, Edwards AFB, CA. Later became a full bird Colonel. I count him as one of my best friends.

Peeters, Cameron – Shawn's son and youngest grandson. DOB November 19, 1997.

Peeters, Chloe – Shawn's daughter and our granddaughter. DOB February 19, 2001.

Peeters, Doris (nee Berry) – Wife, lover and best friend. Married 49 years at time of publication.

Peeters, Emily "Emmy" – Todd's daughter and our oldest granddaughter. DOB September 19, 2000.

Peeters, Grant – My nephew. Ran the Grand Canyon with us.

Peeters, Olivia "Livy" – Todd's daughter and our youngest granddaughter. DOB June 8, 2003

Peeters, Randall Louis – Born December 9, 1945 in San Bernardino, CA. Student, husband, father, grandfather, climber, surfer, skier, snowboarder, skydiver, BASE Jumper, SCUBA diver, free diver, rafter and kayaker. This book is an autobiography/anthology about Randy Peeters.

Peeters, Ryan – My nephew. Climbed together occasionally.

Peeters, Shawn – Our first son, born September 11, 1968.

Peeters, Todd – Our second son, born February 12, 1971.

Peeters, Tyler – Shawn's son and our oldest grandson. DOB June 13, 1995.

Petefish, Andy – Owner of Tower Guides, Devils Tower, WY.

Peter** – Friend of Christian Gabl. Climbed Mount Blanc together.

Peters, Tom – Author of *In Search of Excellence* who speaks about personal and business empowerment and problem-solving methodologies.

Pitts, Donald – Magistrate, Yosemite National Park, CA.

Potter, Dean – Famous climber with many accomplishments in Yosemite.

Quinlan, Mike – Professor at University College, Cork, Ireland. I had been his advisor when he held a post doctoral position at the Rocket Propulsion Laboratory, Edwards AFB, CA. Terrific powder skier and good friend.

Rabin** – Senior technical specialist, Fusing Engineering Section, Xerox Corporation.

Redfern, Earl – Met him skydiving in Lodi, CA and spent time together there and in Yosemite.

Reese, Harlan – Chemist and fellow employee at Aerojet. Climbed Denali and Aconcagua together.

Reinhardt** – Friend of Christian Gabl. Climbed Mount Blanc together.

Rhinehart, Ed – Friend of Doug Williscroft. Fisherman in Alaska and investor. Ran the Grand Canyon together.

Ricardo** – Local contact in Argentina who helped with arrangements and transportation while climbing Aconcagua.

Rislove, Mark – Skier and climber from NM. Helped carry load to base of Half Dome.

Roberson, VO – MD, Anesthesiology. Client on several of my expeditions.

Roberts, Oral – American Methodist-Pentecostal televangelist and a Christian charismatic. He founded the Oral Roberts Evangelistic Association and Oral Roberts University. One of the most well-known and controversial American religious leaders of the 20th century.

Robertson, Pat – American media mogul, executive chairman and a former Southern Baptist minister, who generally supports conservative Christian ideals.

Robins, Royal – One of the pioneers of American rock climbing. Made many first ascents of big wall routes in Yosemite. An early proponent of clean climbing (i.e., no pitons or bolts). Instrumental in changing the climbing culture of the late 1960s and early 1970s. He also became an excellent kayaker.

Roper, Steve – Co-author of *Fifty Classic Climbs of North America*, 1979, Sierra Club Books, San Francisco, CA.

Rudy** – Climber and certified guide from Austria. Climbed El Cap together.

Ruminer, John – My immediate supervisor at WX-3, Los Alamos National Laboratory, NM. A very decent man and a great boss.

Russell, Robert – Owner of Eagles Cry Adventures and organizes trips to the North Pole.

Sanford, Alan – Professor at Cal Poly, Pomona, CA. While an undergraduate student we did several difficult hiking excursions together in the mid 1960s.

Sawyer, Tom – Title character of the Mark Twain novel *The Adventures of Tom Sawyer*.

Schmidt, Marty – Climbing guide I met in Yosemite. Climbed Elbrus and Cho Oyo together.

Scholz, Tom – Skydiver and BASE Jumper.

Sears, Nate – Climber and surfer from Bay Area, CA. Partner on Triple Direct on El Cap.

Serov, Victor – PhD. Russian veteran of numerous Arctic and Antarctic expeditions.

Sherpa, Ang Tsering – Pingboche Sherpa and my climbing partner for the summit of Everest.

Shorten, Dick – Chair for several Vistage groups in NJ.

Shorten, Rich – Deal maker for Power Play Energy start up. Son of Dick Shorten.

Simonsen, Richard "Dick" – Executive vice president of operations, Aerojet Corporation. My mentor at Aerojet.

Sitkin, Bill – Owned a climbing shop in Truckee, CA. Partner for Salathé Wall on El Cap in the 1990s.

Smelzer, Peter – VO Roberson's son-in-law and a client on several expeditions.

Smith, Chuck – Senior pastor of Calvary Chapel Costa Mesa, CA and the founder of the Calvary Chapel movement. Smith's influence now extends to thousands of congregations worldwide.

Smith, Jason "Singer" – Strong young climber who was held hostage in Kyrgyzstan for six days by Islamic rebels. I met him while climbing on El Cap.

Spencer, Bill "Willie" – Long time friend and gifted climber. Excellent river rafter and outdoorsman.

Spencer, Kevin – Willie Spencer's younger brother.

Spencer, Ron – Engineer and fellow employee at Aerojet. Ski toured and did the Sierra High Route together.

Stamentz, Lee – Co-worker at the Rocket Propulsion Laboratory, CA.

Stanford, Geoffrey – British Army officer in the Grenadier Guards, management consultant and Everest expedition leader. Geoffrey has a degree in Classics from Oxford and an MBA. He is currently head of Economics and Business Studies at Pangbourne College, UK.

Stanley, Chuck – Met while running the Stanislaus River; helped hire him at Aerojet and kayaked together many times in the late 1980s. 1980 National Salmon Kayaking Champion and co-author of *A Guide to the Best Whitewater in the State of California*.

Stroud, Eric – Peter Edler's Cousin.

Steck, Allen – Co-author of *Fifty Classic Climbs of North America*.

Stetler, Ruth – Employee at Aerojet. Dick Lou's secretary and later my secretary.

Stoffel, John – Kayaked together in Northern California during big water runoff on local rivers at flood stage.

Stronge, Bill – Climber from China Lake, CA. Did several routes together in NM and CA.

Stroud, Eric – Related to Peter Edler. Rafted the Grand Canyon with our group.

Sullivan, Greg – From Fresno, CA. Climbing partner for several big walls.

Sup, John – Climbing partner in climbing gyms at lunch for several years in the 1990s.

Swaner, Sean – Christian climber and double cancer survivor. Summited Everest in 2002.

Swenson, Denny – Chiropractor, climber, skier, outdoorsman, Abalone diver, SCUBA diver and a good longtime Christian friend.

Tepe, Les – Fellow employee at the Rocket Propulsion Laboratory, Edwards AFB, CA. A solid Christian and friend. Married to Barb (since deceased).

Terry** – Youth leader at Capitol Christian Church, Santa Fe, NM.

Tim** – A friend of Nelson Walker. Climbed together on Disappointment Peak in the Sierra Nevada.

Todd, Henry – Controversial expedition organizer from Scotland.

Torpey, Gene – Neighbor and friend in Victor, NY. Married to Harriet. Jim's dad.

Torpey, Jim – Neighbor and friend in Victor, NY.

Townsend, Jim – Co-worker at the Air Force Rocket Propulsion Laboratory, CA. We both lived in Tehachapi and car pooled, hunted, cut fire wood and shared family events together. Good friend.

Trainer, John – Previously was the manager of the Fusing Technology Area, Xerox Corporation, Webster, NY.

Trasher, Durwood – Fellow employee at the Rocket Propulsion Laboratory, Edwards AFB, CA.

Travis, Rich – Solid Christian from the Bay Area, CA. Long time climbing partner. Did numerous big walls and remote climbs together from the 1990s onward.

Trout, Jim – Friend and co-worker at the Rocket Propulsion Laboratory, CA.

Trump, Donald – American business magnate, television personality, author and presidential candidate.

Vaclav** – Czech film maker and Jakeš' client on the North Pole trip.

Varin, Jeff – Neighbor in Roseville, CA and friend of my sons. Raft guide. Ran the Grand Canyon together.

Várkonyi, László "Konyi" – Climbing guide and member of the 2002 Hungarian National Everest Team.

Viesturs, Ed – A high-altitude mountaineer. He is the first American to have climbed all 14 of the world's 8,000 meter peaks and the fifth person to do so without using supplemental oxygen.

Walker, Nelson and Linda – Engineer and lawyer. Climbed and skied together off and on from 1968 to 1976. Married to Linda.

Wally and Papillon** – Friends of Willie Spencer, who rafted the Grand Canyon with us in 1983.

Washburn, Bradford – American explorer, mountaineer, photographer and cartographer. He established the Boston Museum of Science.

Weinberg, Dick and Libby – Couple we met while camping in Southern California and introduced us to their son, Mike and his friends. Instrumental in getting me to learn how to surf.

Weinberg, Mike – Well known potter, son of Dick and Libby. Surfer and good friends with Chuck John, Charlie Bryant and Bing Gleitsman.

Wellman, Mark – Former paraplegic park ranger who had been injured in a climbing accident.

White, Dan – A San Francisco supervisor who assassinated San Francisco Mayor George Moscone and Supervisor Harvey Milk at City Hall in November, 1978.

Wiegele, Mike – Owner of a heli skiing, heli-boarding and snowcat skiing operation often referred to as "Wiegele World" located near Blue River, BC in the Monashee and Cariboo mountains.

Williscroft, Doug – Doug's father, our landlord, owned an old train depot located in the University District of Seattle, WA which had been converted into a duplex. Doug later joined the Explorer Post. Excellent skier and a lifelong friend.

Williscroft, Stuart – Doug Williscroft's son. Ran the Grand Canyon with us.

Wood, "Kiwi" Steve – Professional skydiver who moved to the USA from New Zealand. At the top of his game he was considered one of the best BASE jumpers in the world. Became an excellent kayaker.

Wood, Matt – Kiwi's Steve's Brother.

Zac, Heinz – Famous Austrian photographer and climber.

**** Indicates last name unknown or left out intentionally.**

Memorial

Alan Sanford – Backcountry hiker who died in 1970 during an ice axe self-arrest course.

Bruce Carson – Climber who fell through a cornice in the Indian Himalaya, September 1975.

Gordon Oates – Mountaineer who died of a heart attack while cycling, November 1986.

Ralph and Dorothy Baker – Farmers who died of old age. Ralph in April 1992 and Dorothy in December 1989.

Darrin Hansen – Skydiver who died after a collision under canopy while landing, November 1990.

Jonathon Boland – Skydiver/BASE jumper/climber who lost his life making a BASE jump near the Grand Canyon, January 1993.

Dave Anderson – Climber who died in a helicopter crash during a medi-vac attempt after being caught in an avalanche, January 1998.

Dan Osmond – Climber/free soloist was killed attempting a 1,100 foot rope jump off Leaning Tower, Yosemite, November 1998.

John Stoffel – Kayaker who died of a heart attack while kayaking the Sierra City run – North Fork of the Yuba River, June 1999.

Earl Redfern – Skydiver/BASE jumper/climber who died in an airplane crash, July 2000.

Dick Burwell – Climber who succumbed to amyotrophic lateral sclerosis (ALS, Lou Gehrig's disease), July 2000.

Peter Legate – Climber killed falling from Lhotse Face, Mount Everest, April 2002.

Rob Miline – Climber who died of a heart attack on the Summit Ridge, Mount Everest, June 2005.

Jim Townsend – Lifelong friend who died of cancer, July 2006.

Charlie Fowler and Christine Boskoff – Climbers who lost their lives in an avalanche in Tibet, December 2006.

Lars Holbek – Extreme kayaker/rock climber who died of a rare form of liver cancer, March 2009.

Bill Briggs – Climber who succumbed to multiple myeloma, September 2009.

László "Konyi" Várkonyi – High altitude expedition climber and member of the 2002 Hungarian National Everest Team. He died in an avalanche on Everest April 2010.

Mike Oberth – Extreme sportsman who died of injuries after a fall while skiing a steep couloir in the Sierra Nevada, May 2010.

Jim and Blanche Caldwell – Solid Christian friends who greatly influenced my life for more than 36 years. Both died of old age in 2013.

Zsolt Erőss – High altitude expedition climber and member of the 2002 Hungarian National Everest Team. Died descending from the summit of Kangchenjunga, May 2013

Marty Schmidt – High altitude expedition climber, who died in an avalanche at Camp 3 on K2, July 2013.

END NOTES

CHAPTER 1

1. Six Majors – Consists of the major glaciated peaks of WA including Mount Adams, Mount St. Helens, Mount Rainier, Glacier Peak, Mount Baker and Mount Olympus. This award is no longer available due to the eruption of Mount St. Helens in 1980.

CHAPTER 2

2. Local New York areas were Bristol and Swain. Other Northeast areas skied included Sugar Bush, Mad River Glen, Killington, Lake Placid, Gore, Stowe, etc.

3. Tahoe areas skied: Kirkwood, Heavenly Valley, Sierra Ski Ranch, Sugar Bowl, Donner Ski Ranch, Squaw Valley, Alpine Meadows, Homewood, North Star, Mount Rose, etc.

4. Double-diamond, diamond and intermediate terrain refers to the difficulty of the run with double-diamond being the most difficult. Extreme skiing is a step above double-diamond in difficulty.

5. The terms "backcountry skiing", "randonnée", "ski touring" and "off-piste skiing" are often used interchangeably; however, "backcountry skiing", "off-piste skiing" and "extreme skiing" specify where the skiing occurs, while "alpine", "telemark", "ski touring", "ski mountaineering" and "randonnée" describe the type of skiing.

6. Underground or outlaw runs at Heavenly: OB, Firebreak, Perimeter, Palisades (Vista and Easy Street) and the Gardnerville Run.

7. Alaska Heli board summary 2010: 1,000 foot shuttle run; helicopter runs of 4000 feet, 4500 feet, 3800 feet, 4000 feet and 4000 feet; ghost run of 1200 feet. Total in four days of 22,500 vertical feet.

8. Injuries sustained skiing: cuts requiring stitches in leg and eyelid; two surgeries on right knee; sprained both thumbs and wrists; severely winded and broke a rib hitting trees; dislocated left shoulder; partially dislocated right shoulder; broken hip; broken thumb.

CHAPTER 3

9. Promoted to a GS-13 step 3 earning $25,928 per year. Selected for the Director of Science and Technology Civilian Career Development Program in Washington DC, received several letters of appreciation, wrote and presented several technical papers and gave a seminar at Portland State University. Also served as an advisor for a postdoctoral candidate, chaired several committees and received an Outstanding Performance Award.

10. Local rafting in Northern NM included the Rio Grande from White Rock Gorge to Bandelier National Monument, The Lower Box and the Rio Chama.

11. Technical meetings attended while at Los Alamos National Laboratory, NM included the following locations: Maryland, California, Pennsylvania, Ohio, Georgia, Texas and Massachusetts.

12. Moving from Los Alamos, MN to Victor, NY, we visited Scotts Bluff, Wind Cave National Park, Mount Rushmore National Memorial, Badlands National Park, Wisconsin Dells, Greenfield Village/Ford Museum and Niagara Falls.

13. Extended family trips in the Dog Trailer included Upstate New York, Vermont, New Hampshire, Maine, Nova Scotia, Prince Edward Island and New Brunswick.

CHAPTER 4

14. North Shore of Oahu: I started at Chuns Reef (three times with overhead plus surf – some great rides), then moved to Rubber Ducky at Three Tables (chest high and OK). Pidley's was next (small and fast lefts), followed by Left Over's (inside with several overhead rides) and, finally, culminating in a great session at Sunset Beach with overhead plus surf.

15. Included in these surf sessions were some truly epic days at Nine Palms (Baja), Scorpion Bay (Baja), Sunset Cliffs (CA), Turtles (CA), Salt Creek (CA), Rincon (CA), Tarantula's (Central California), San Dollar (Central California), Asilomar (Central California), Steamers Lane (Central California), Black Point (Northern California), Threes (Oahu, HI), Durbin (South Africa), Kunta Reef (Bali) and Witch's Rock (Costa Rica).

16. SCUBA Dive Trips: numerous trips along the entire California coastline and destination dive trips to Catalina, Anacapa and Santa Rosa Islands (CA); Roatán (Honduras); Coronado Islands, Cozumel and Aukamal (Mexico); Watamu (Kenya); Zanzibar (Tanzania); Great Barrier Reef (Australia); Grand Cayman (British West Indies); Phuket (Thailand); Manado and Bali (Indonesia); Jupiter Reef and Ginnie Springs (FL); Manahi (French Polynesia); Galapagos Islands (Ecuador); and the Big Island (HI). From cruise ships we also dove: San Juan (Puerto Rico), Dominica (West Indies), Grenada (Eastern Caribbean), Aruba (Dutch Antilles) and Saint Thomas (US Virgin Islands).

17. Live aboard dive boat trips included the Cayman Aggressor IV in the Cayman Islands for one week. I made 27 dives and earned Nitrox Diver Certification and Doris completed 12 dives. We also took the Pro Dive III on the Great Barrier Reef off the coast of Australia.

CHAPTER 5

18. Other business/vacation trips during this period included: Los Alamos, NM (skied Pajarito with friends) and several in San Diego (surfed, visited friends and family and had several surf trips up the California coast to San Francisco). Also in California I spent time working at the Naval Weapons Center (China Lake), Rocket Propulsion Lab (Edwards Air Force Base) and Air Force Space Division and Aerospace Corp. (Redondo Beach). I also visited colleagues in Texas (University of Texas, Texas A&M), Georgia (Georgia Tech) and Massachusetts (University of Massachusetts, Amherst and MIT). Collaborative efforts included those at Aberdeen Proving Grounds (Baltimore, MD), NASA (Huntsville, AL) and locations in both Cleveland and Akron, OH. Technical meetings were attended in New Orleans, LA, Reno, NV, Ogden, UT and Miami, FL.

19. During a 12 month period of 1988 to 1989, with over 182 activity days, I completed the following: climbed Denali (aka Mt McKinley) in May 1989. At 43 years old, I trained (more than 27 hours per week) for the California International Marathon and ran it in 3:18:56; top on third of all men. Cycled the El Dorado Century (101.94 mi in 8:28:41 with over 6,000 feet of elevation gain) on a mountain bike. Competed in the Widow Maker Mountain Bike Race (fourth place, first time racers). Completed numerous Class V kayaking and rafting trips, surfed nine new spots, 126 skydives, BASE jumped El Cap and cycled more than 1,500 miles. Completed the Mammoth Mountain to Yosemite Valley Trans-Sierra (55 miles in three and a half days).

20. Sports Classic was a 34 hour event covering a total of 44 miles: Day 1: Hike in and surf for 75 minutes at Four Mile near Santa Cruz (three foot sets); complete two skydives at Lodi (two-way and three-way resulting in over two minutes of freefall); lead two pitches (5.7 and 5.4) and follow one (5.8-plus) at Bucks Bar; kayak the class 3 Chili Bar run for five miles; run three miles, cycle ten miles, do one hour of weight lifting and stretch for 15 minutes. Day 2: Ski five hours at Sierra Ski Ranch (22 runs) and then work out for a half hour on my ski machine at home.

21. Other work/vacation combination trips included CA (Monterey Peninsula, Newport Beach, Los Angeles, San Diego, etc.), NV, LA, FL, WA, OH, WI, NM, NH, MA, Washington, DC, AZ, Russia, Belgium, Holland, Luxembourg, Northern Germany, Great Britain, etc.

22. Typical Christmas week vacation – December 1993
• Attend Christmas Eve candlelight service followed by driving through a huge display of luminaries and Christmas lights in an upscale housing development.
• Christmas day celebrated at our home with our entire family.
• Camping and surfing at South Carlsbad State Beach for six days.
• Climbing one day at Joshua Tree National Park with my nephews.
• New Year's Eve party with my sister and her friends.

- New Year's Day at my brother's home.
- On the way home, work a day each at Aerojet, Azusa and the Phillips Laboratory at Edwards Air Force Base.

23. Telescopes and associated items owned: Edmund three and one quarter inch reflector, Essential Optics eight inch reflector, Celestron 11 inch Ultima II Schmidt Cassegrain, Celestron C-5, Televue 70 mm Pronto refractor, Nikon 10x42 Superior E binoculars, Obsession 25 inch Dobsonian reflector, Meade eight inch LX-90 Schmidt Cassegrain, Celestron 11 inch NexStar Schmidt Cassegrain, Discovery 17½ inch Dobsonian reflector, Oberwerk 22x100 Binoculars, Coronado 40 mm H-Alpha SolarMax telescope and numerous tripods, mounts, eyepieces, books, charts, etc.

24. 1997 Europe – Paris (Air Show), Germany (technical meeting at Karlsruhe), Czech Republic (Prague), Poland (Krakow), Slovakia, Hungary, Austria, Liechtenstein and Switzerland. Traveled by train and rental car across much of Europe.

25. 1998 Great Britain - traveled more than 2,100 miles by car (often on small narrow roads with hedgerows) all over England, Scotland and Wales. Sights included Stonehenge, Dartmoor National Park, London, Bath, Oxford, York, Edinburgh and Snowdonia National Park. One week in London – Attended the Farnborough Air Show and visited most of the sights in the area. Other highlights were punting on Cherwell River, overnight and dinner with the Baroness at Kilravock Castle (dates back to 1460), touring the Isle of Skye and a one day excursion to Belfast, Northern Ireland.

26. July 1999 – 19 day trip - Drove a total of 2,675 miles in the rental car plus another 600 miles with Christian Gabl to climb and we rode on ferries (four and a half hours total). Visited Munich and Fussen, Germany, then on to Christian's home in Schönwies, Austria. We also visited Saltzburg, then Vienna for five days and the Unispace III Conference and saw the local sights of Bratislava (Slovak Republic), Fertod and Sopron (Hungry), Telc and Prague (Czech Republic), Dresden, Berlin and Hamburg (Germany), Odense and Copenhagen, Hillerod and Helsingor (Denmark), Moss and Oslo (Norway), Goteborg, Fjallbacka, Lund and Malmo (Sweden) and Berlin. Highlights included a visit and climb with the Gabl's, Austrian scenery, overnight in Veltrusy in the Czech Republic, Berlin, Tivoli and Pension Bondehuset in Denmark and Sweden's West Coast.

27. During a routine one-on-one with my boss Joe Carleone in the fall 1999, he asked me if I would consider my previous proposal regarding a separation package. I was truly surprised – I expected this eventually, but not that soon. I immediately started negotiating the details and ultimately accepted a separation package. After an embarrassing and sparsely attended farewell get-together organized by my successor, my last day at Aerojet was March 31, 2000.

CHAPTER 6

28. Grand Canyon hikes and attractions - Silver Grotto, Red Wall Cavern, Nankoweap Granaries, Little Colorado River, Elves Chasm, Tapeats Creek, Deer Creek Falls, Havasu Creek, etc.

29. First Rafting Descents - Hayfork Creek (Lower Gorge, class V-plus with two and a half portages), upper North Fork of the North Fork Stanislaus River (Sour Grass Ravine to Calaveras, class V), North Fork Kings (Balch Camp to Kings River, class V with two portages), Fresno River (below Gold Hill, class IV), Dry Meadow Creek Falls on the Forks of the Kern (class V-plus).

30. Rivers rafted included runs on the Trinity, Cal Salmon, Upper Klamath, Scott, North Fork Yuba, North Fork American (Giant Gap – Ponderosa), Middle Fork American (Oxbow - Hwy 49), South Fork American, Lower American, Carson, North Fork Stanislaus (above Sour Grass to below Calaveras), Stanislaus (Stan Can), Tuolumne (Cherry Creek - Lake), Merced (El Portal – Bagby), North Fork Kings, Kern (Forks), Rogue River (Hogs Creek to Agness), Yampa, Green (Desolation and Gray Canyons), Salmon (Middle and Main), Colorado (West Water, Cataract Canyon and Grand Canyon). Many of these runs were done more than once (e.g., South Fork American more than 100 times) and at extreme flows.

31. Kayaks owned – River Chaser, Perception Eclipse, T-Slalom, Dancer XT, Corsica Matrix, Infinity, Mongoose, Dagger Vortex and a Fluid Solo.

32. Kayak Runs included the Russian River, Eel, South Fork Eel, Trinity, Cal Salmon, Klamath, North Fork Smith, Cache Creek, North Fork Yuba (Sierra City – Reservoir), South Fork Yuba (Washington – Purdon's), Fordyce Creek, North Fork American (Giant Gap –Lake Clementine), Middle Fork American (Oxbow - Hwy 49), South Fork American (Kyburz – Folsom Dam except for the Slab Creek section), Webber Creek, Lower American, Truckee (River Ranch – Floriston), Cosumnes, North Fork Mokelumne (Tiger Creek Dam), Mokelumne, North Fork Stanislaus (above Sour Grass to two miles below Calaveras), Stanislaus (Camp 9), Tuolumne (Cherry Creek - Lake), Merced (El Portal – Bagby), Lower Kern, Kern, Rogue, Illinois, Stillaguamish, South Fork Stillaguamish (Robe Canyon), Skykomish, Colorado (Grand Canyon), Mulberry, Warrior, Nantahala, Ocoee, Middle Fork Salmon, North Fork Payette (Cabarton Bridge), Payette (Banks to Beehive), etc.

33. Difficult Kayak Runs included Cherry Creek (V), Robe Canyon (V), Giant Gap (V), Fordyce Creek (V), Illinois (V-minus), Webber Creek (IV-plus), Tiger Creek Dam (IV), Sunset Falls on the Skykomish (IV), Smith (IV-minis), etc.

CHAPTER 7

34. Castle Rock, Peshastin Pinnacles, Index Town Wall, Snow Creek Wall and many others.

35. Royal Arches, Direct Route on Washington Column, Overhang Bypass on Lower Cathedral Rock, Lost Arrow Spire, etc.

36. Joshua Tree, Tahquitz, Suicide, Owens Pinnacles, Devil's Punch Bowl, Yosemite and the Sierra Nevada.

37. In the process of training for the Nose of El Cap, I was able to climb some of Yosemite's truly great routes: the Braille Book (III, 5.8-plus), Central Pillar of Frenzy (II, 5.9-plus), Higher Cathedral Spire (II, 5.9), linking Munginella (II, 5.6) and Selaginella Wall (II, 5.7), NE Buttress of Higher Cathedral Rock (IV, 5.10-plus), Lower Cathedral Spire (II, 5.9) and Reed Pinnacle Direct (II, 5.10). Other routes and areas included leading the Line (II, 5.9) on sight at Lover's Leap, several routes at Sugar Loaf, Hogs Back, Phantom Spires, sport climbing in Owens River Gorge, many routes at Pinnacles National Monument and even a quick trip to Joshua Tree National Park.

38. *Fifty Classic Climbs of North America* located in California: in Yosemite Valley - Royal Arches (III, 5.7, A1), Lost Arrow Spire (III, 5.5, A3), East Buttress of Middle Cathedral (IV, 5.9, A1), Steck-Salathé (V, 5.10b), Northwest Face of Half Dome (Grade VI, 5.8, A3), Nose of El Cap (VI, 5.8, A3) and Salathé (VI, 5.8, A3). Tuolumne Meadows (Yosemite) - Fairview Dome (IV, 5.9). Sierra Nevada Range - East Face of Mount Whitney (III, 5.6), South Face of Charlotte Dome (III, 5.7) and Clyde Minaret (IV, 5.8). Lover's Leap - Travelers Buttress (II, 5.9).

39. Sugar Loaf, Phantom Spires, Lover's Leap and Yosemite.

40. Yosemite Valley - Munginella, Overhang Bypass, Jam Crack and Maxine's Wall. Sierra Nevada climbing areas - Sugar Loaf, Lover's Leap, Phantom Spires and Donner Summit.

CHAPTER 8

41. Licenses and awards - A, B, Advanced C-19395 and Master D-12492 licenses. I was also awarded the Muff Brother No. 153, Falcon, Double Falcon, Eagle, Double Eagle, Star Crest, Star Crest Soloist, Four Stack Canopy Relative Work (CRW) and Canopy Crest Eight Stack CRW.

CHAPTER 9

42. Some of the Major RV Trips:
- 2002 – California coast from visiting beaches at the Mexican Border to Anchor Bay. 45 days.
- 2006 – Southwest USA, mainland Mexico and Baja. 60 days.
- 2006 - Northwest USA - visiting national parks. Saw the attractions at the Buffalo Bill Historical Center in Cody, WY and attended the Fort Bridger Rendezvous. Also visited friends along the way. 30 days.
- 2007 – Southeastern and Northeastern USA. Five weeks.
- 2008 - NASCAR 400 in Las Vegas. One week.

- 2008 – Canada and Northeastern USA – We visited relatives in Bonduel/Hayes area and De Pere, WI. Seven weeks.
- 2009 – Western Canada up to Alaska and back. Three and a half months.
- 2010 –Rose Parade, Pasadena, CA, Quartzsite, AZ and San Elijo State Beach. One month.
- 2010 – Southern USA - Kathmandu became ill and died. Six weeks.
- 2010 - Northeast USA in the fall. We visited family, friends, did some sightseeing and visited some Amish areas. Five weeks
- 2011 – Northeast USA. We lost our Cocker Spaniel Sarah while on tour. Two months.
- 2012 – Eastern USA and Canada. Two months.
- 2013 – USA loop. Six weeks.
- 2013 – Southern CA loop trips. Two weeks and three weeks.
- 2014 –Rose Parade, Pasadena, CA and San Elijo State Beach. One half month.

43. International Vacation Trips:

- 2001 - Southeast Asia - Nepal, Tibet (climbing Cho Oyo), India, Thailand, Malaysia, Indonesia, Singapore and Japan – Around the world. 90 days.
- 2004 - New Zealand, Australia and French Polynesia. 29 days.
- 2006 – China and river cruise on the Yangtze, Vietnam and Cambodia. Hiked part of the Great Wall of China. 30 days
- 2006 - Czech Republic, cruise down the Danube River from Hungary to the Black Sea and Transylvania. Traveled with Bob and Diane McCarthy and visited dozens of World Heritage sites. Three weeks.
- 2007 – Visited Egypt, Israel and Jordan. Doris fell in Old Jerusalem and broke her ankle. Some high school boys helped me get her out of the narrow streets and into a taxi cab which took us to the hospital. It all turned out fine and was an interesting experience. 28 days.
- 2008 – Visited Peru and Ecuador. Traveled with Joe and Becky Mettee. Visited the Amazon Basin and Machu Picchu. Took a cruise through the Galapagos Islands. 23 days.
- 2009 – Morocco, Tunisia, Turkey, Greece, Albania, Montenegro, Croatia and Slovenia. Cruised up the Dalmatian Coast and stayed at a remote oasis in Southern Tunisia. 45 days.
- 2010 – Visited Iceland and Greenland for two and a half weeks in August. We did a lot of soaking in hot springs and took a couple of helicopter rides. 18 days.
- 2013 – Mongolia, Myanmar, Bhutan and Laos. 36 days.
- 2014- Pakistan - Hiked to K2 Base Camp and to Fairy Meadows below Nanga Parbot. 28 days.

Chapter 12

44. Mombasa, Kenya and the fabulous beach areas of Malindi and Watamu (SCUBA diving) and returning to Nairobi, Kenya by overnight train. The next year, Zanzibar (SCUBA diving) using local buses and ferries; Zimbabwe (Victoria Falls), Zambia (river boarding the Zambezi River) and South Africa (surfing Durban and Kruger National Park bush camp and safari). In 2009, I traveled to Rwanda to see the Mountain Gorillas and do a Chimpanzee Trekking excursion.

45. Adventure Grand Slam: I reached the North Pole on skis at 1345 UTC, April 19th, 2005. At 59 years and 131 days, I was the eighth person in the world, the oldest ever and only the second American to complete this project. Beginning in May 1988 with Denali, it took 17 years to complete Bass's Seven Summits plus reaching both the North and South Poles.

Enjoy other Sastrugi Press adventure titles

Antarctic Tears by Aaron Linsdau

What would make a man give up his engineering career to ski across Antarctica alone? And what drove him to be the second only American to make the solo trip, something only a handful of people in history have ever accomplished? This inspirational true story will make you alternately cheer and then have your heart sink. Fighting skin-freezing temperatures, biological infections, and utter breakdown, Aaron Linsdau makes the experience real and shares his message of pursuing dreams, never giving up, and accepting change. Discover what the journey through the world's largest wilderness was like and learn what being truly alone is.

These Canyons Are Full of Ghosts by Emmett Harder

Driven to find his fortune in the most desolate and forbidding landscapes on earth, one prospector learns there is more to finding gold than just using a shovel and pick axe. These riveting tales of modern Death Valley prospecting will give you insight into what drives a person to keep looking for the next big strike. During his explorations through the massive national park, Emmett Harder discovers a famous lost gold mine, loses another one, and crosses paths with Death Valley's most notorious resident: Charles Manson.

The Blind Man's Story by J.W. Linsdau

Imagine one's surprise to be hiking in the great Northwest and coming across someone who spends his summers living high on a bluff – and that someone is blind, with a fascinating story to tell.

That's what happened to journalist Beau Larson, while on vacation near a mountain town called Fools Gold. He returns to work, but his chance meeting leads to intrigue when his newspaper sends him back to Fools Gold to cover a dispute between local timber workers and environmentalists.

Beau finishes his report, but soon discovers one of the key environmentalists interviewed has been murdered. He again finds himself in Fools Gold only to learn there is more to "The Blind Man's Story" than he thought.

Visit Sastrugi Press on the web at:
www.sastrugipress.com
to purchase the above books directly from the publisher. These titles are also available at your favorite bookstore or online retailer.

SASTRUGI PRESS

www.sastrugipress.com

CPSIA information can be obtained
at www.ICGtesting.com
Printed in the USA
FSHW010950170220
67129FS